THE EMPIRE OF LIES

Korsgaard Publishing
www.korsgaardpublishing.com
© Paul Craig Roberts 2023
ISBN 978-87-93987-49-4

TABLE OF CONTENTS

ABOUT THE AUTHOR

FOREWORD

CHAPTER 1
THE MINISTRY OF TRUTH

CHAPTER 2
ECONOMIC DECEPTION

CHAPTER 3
THE UKRAINE DECEPTION

CHAPTER 4
THE LIES OF HISTORY

CHAPTER 5
"THE BIG LIE"

About Paul Craig Roberts

Career

Paul Craig Roberts has had careers in scholarship and academia, journalism, public service, and business. He is chairman of The Institute for Political Economy, the website of which is www.paulcraigroberts.org.

Scholarship & Academia

Dr. Roberts has held academic appointments at Virginia Tech, Tulane University, University of New Mexico, Stanford University where he was Senior Research Fellow in the Hoover Institution, George Mason University where he had a joint appointment as professor of economics and professor of business administration, and Georgetown University where he held the William E. Simon Chair in Political Economy in the Center for Strategic and International Studies.

He has contributed chapters to numerous books and has published many articles in journals of scholarship, including the Journal of Political Economy, Oxford Economic Papers, Journal of Law and Economics, Studies in Banking and Finance, Journal of Monetary Economics, Public Choice, Classica et Mediaevalia, Ethics, Slavic Review, Soviet Studies, Cardoza Law Review, Rivista de Political Economica, and Zeitschrift fur Wirtschafspolitik. He has entries in the McGraw-Hill Encyclopedia of Economics and the New Palgrave Dictionary of Money and Finance.

He has contributed to Commentary, The Public Interest, The National Interest, Policy Review, National Review, The Independent Review, Harper's, the New York Times, The Washington Post, The Los Angeles Times, Fortune, London Times, The Financial Times, TLS, The Spectator, The International Economy, Il Sole 24 Ore, Le Figaro, Liberation, and the Nihon Keizai Shimbun. He has testified before committees of Congress on 30 occasions.

Books

He has written 12 books and has translations into German, French,

Spanish, Czech, Turkish, Russian, Chinese, Korean, and Japanese languages:

Alienation and the Soviet Economy; Marx's Theory of Exchange, Alienation, and Crisis; The Supply-Side Revolution; Meltdown Inside the Soviet Economy; The Capitalist Revolution in Latin America; Chile: Dos Visiones, La Era Allende-Pinochet; The Tyranny of Good Intentions; The New Color Line; The Failure of Laissez Faire Capitalism; How the Economy Was Lost; The Neoconservative Threat to World Order; How America Was Lost.

Journalism

Dr. Roberts was associate editor and columnist for The Wall Street Journal and columnist for Business Week and the Scripps Howard News Service. He was a nationally syndicated columnist for Creators Syndicate in Los Angeles. In 1992 he received the Warren Brookes Award for Excellence in Journalism. In 1993 the Forbes Media Guide ranked him as one of the top seven journalists in the United States. In 2015 he was awarded the Press Club of Mexico's International Journalism Award.

Public Service

President Reagan appointed Dr. Roberts Assistant Secretary of the Treasury for Economic Policy and he was confirmed in office by the U.S. Senate. From 1975 to 1978, Dr. Roberts served on the congressional staff where he drafted the Kemp-Roth bill and played a leading role in developing bipartisan support for a supply-side economic policy. After leaving the Treasury, he served as a consultant to the U.S. Department of Defense and the U.S. Department of Commerce.

Business

Dr. Roberts was president of the Inlet Beach Water Company, president of Economic & Communication Services, advisor to J.P. Morgan asset management, advisor to Tiedemann-Goodnow, advisor to Lazard Freres Asset Management, and a member of corporate and financial boards.

Honors

Dr. Roberts was awarded the Treasury Department's Meritorious Service Award for "his outstanding contributions to the formulation of United States economic policy."

In 1987 the French government recognized him as "the artisan of a renewal in economic science and policy after half a century of state interventionism" and inducted him into the Legion of Honor.

He is listed in Who's Who in America and Who's Who in the World. In 2017 Dr. Roberts was awarded Marquis Who's Who Lifetime Achievement Award.

Decoding the Future

There is no question that mankind faces grave challenges in the months and years ahead. These are not limited to governments mandating dangerous medical products, the possibility of nuclear escalation between Russia and the United States, global economic chaos, growing concentration of income and wealth, systematic censorship, false flag operations, totalitarianism, political correctness, self-censorship, and the agendas of the World Economic Forum.

To act appropriately to any crisis – whether it be a manufactured or an organic one – it is paramount that we have access to objective and trustworthy information. Governments and industry – which often act in collusion with each other – frequently exploit or create crises to implement their agendas, such as mass surveillance and mandatory vaccinations.

To do so, they use the corporate media to broadcast deception and employ a multitude of selected "experts" who agree with the official agenda. Even online, it is exceedingly difficult finding quality information. Having successfully concentrated the majority of internet activity to just a few sites, such as the Google search engine which handles over 90% of all search queries worldwide, the establishment is able to conduct censorship on an unprecedented scale by means of artificial intelligence, machine learning, and other advanced technologies.

Unfortunately, there is every reason to believe that large-scale censorship will only gain pace from this point on. In other words, it is becoming extremely difficult to find information outside the perimeters of official narratives. Without well-balanced information, the establishment is much more likely to be successful with all its aims.

The goal with this book is that readers can use it as a springboard for decoding future deceptions and "crises." If, as current trends indicate, the spreading of government-declared "disinformation" becomes illegal, we must be aware of past deceptions and know how to recognize future ones as it will be too costly for those who are knowledgeable to point out the lies. These essays by Paul Craig Roberts will help you to develop the ability to see through official narratives.

Søren Roest Korsgaard
www.korsgaardpublishing.com
February 2023.

CHAPTER 1
THE MINISTRY
OF TRUTH

Why Disinformation Works

Have you ever wondered how the government's misinformation gains traction?

What I have noticed is that whenever a stunning episode occurs, such as 9/11 or the Boston Marathon bombing, most everyone whether on the right or left goes along with the government's explanation, because they can hook their agenda to the government's account.

The leftwing likes the official stories of Muslims creating terrorist mayhem in America, because it proves their blowback theory and satisfies them that the dispossessed and oppressed can fight back against imperialism.

The patriotic rightwing likes the official story, because it proves America is attacked for its goodness or because terrorists were allowed in by immigration authorities and nurtured by welfare, or because the government, which can't do anything right, ignored plentiful warnings.

Whatever the government says, no matter how problematical, the official story gets its traction from its compatibility with existing predispositions and agendas.

In such a country, truth has no relevance. Only agendas are important.

A person can see this everywhere. I could write volumes illustrating how agenda-driven writers across the spectrum will support the most improbable government stories despite the absence of any evidence simply because the government's line can be used to support their agendas.

For example, a conservative writer in the June issue of Chronicles uses the government's story about the alleged Boston Marathon bombers, Dzhokhar and Tamerlan Tsarnaev, to argue against immigration, amnesty for illegals, and political asylum for Muslims. He writes: "Even the most high-tech security systems imaginable will inevitably fail as they are overwhelmed by a flood of often hostile and dangerous immigrants."

The writer accepts all of the improbable government statements as proof that the brothers were guilty. The wounded brother who was unable to respond to the boat owner who discovered him and had to be put on life support somehow managed to write a confession on the inside of the boat.

As soon as the authorities have the brother locked up in a hospital on life support, "unnamed officials" and "authorities who remain anonymous" are planting the story in the media that the suspect is signing written confessions of his guilt while on life support. No one has seen any of these written confessions. But we know that they exist, because the government and media say so.

The conservative writer knows that Dzhokhar is guilty because he is Muslim and a Chechen. Therefore, it does not occur to the writer to wonder about the agenda of the unnamed sources who are busy at work creating belief in the brothers' guilt. This insures that no juror would dare vote for acquittal and have to explain it to family and friends. Innocent until proven guilty in a court has been thrown out the window. This should disturb the conservative writer, but doesn't.

The conservative writer sees Chechen ethnicity as an indication of guilt even though the brothers grew up in the US as normal Americans, because Chechens are "engaged in anti-Russian jihad." But Chechens have no reason for hostility against the US. As evidence indicates, Washington supports the Chechens in their conflict with Russia. By supporting Chechen terrorism, Washington violates all of the laws that it ruthlessly applies to compassionate Americans who give donations to Palestinian charities that Washington alleges are run by Hamas, a Washington-declared terrorist organization.

It doesn't occur to the conservative writer that something is amiss when martial law is established over one of America's main cities and its metropolitan area, 10,000 heavily armed troops are put on the streets with tanks, and citizens are ordered out of their homes with their hands over their heads, all of this just to search for one wounded 19-year old suspect. Instead the writer blames the "surveillance state" on "the inevitable consequences of suicidal liberalism" which has embraced "the oldest sin in the world: rebellion against authority." The writer is so pleased to use the government's story line as a way of indulging the conservative's romance with authority and striking a blow at liberalism that he does not notice that he has lined up against the Founding Fathers who signed the Declaration of Independence and rebelled against authority.

I could just as easily have used a left-wing writer to illustrate the point that improbable explanations are acceptable if they fit with predispositions and can be employed in behalf of an agenda.

Think about it. Do you not think that it is extraordinary that the only investigations we have of such events as 9/11 and the Boston Marathon bombing are private investigations, such as this investigation of the backpacks [1].

There was no investigation of 9/11. Indeed, the White House resisted any inquiry at all for one year despite the insistent demands from the 9/11 families. NIST did not investigate anything. NIST simply constructed a computer model that was consistent with the government's story. The 9/11 Commission simply sat and listened to the government's explanation and wrote it down. These are not investigations.

The only investigations have come from a physicist who proved that WTC 7 came down at free fall and was thus the result of controlled demolition, from a team of scientists who examined dust from the WTC towers and found nanothermite, from high-rise architects and

4

structural engineers with decades of experience, and from first responders and firefighters who were in the towers and experienced explosions throughout the towers, even in the sub-basements.

We have reached the point where evidence is no longer required. The government's statements suffice. Only conspiracy kooks produce real evidence.

In America, government statements have a unique authority. This authority comes from the white hat that the US wore in World War II and in the subsequent Cold War. It was easy to demonize Nazi Germany, Soviet Communism and Maoist China. Even today when Russian publications interview me about the perilous state of civil liberty in the US and Washington's endless illegal military attacks abroad, I sometimes receive reports that some Russians believe that it was an impostor who was interviewed, not the real Paul Craig Roberts. There are Russians who believe that it was President Reagan who brought freedom to Russia, and as I served in the Reagan administration these Russians associate me with their vision of America as a light unto the world. Some Russians actually believe that Washington's wars are truly wars of liberation.

The same illusions reign among Chinese dissidents. Chen Guangcheng is the Chinese dissident who sought refuge in the US Embassy in China. Recently he was interviewed by the BBC World Service. Chen Guangcheng believes that the US protects human rights while China suppresses human rights. He complained to the BBC that in China police can arrest citizens and detain them for as long as six months without accounting for their detainment. He thought that the US and UK should publicly protest this violation of due process, a human right. Apparently, Chen Guangcheng is unaware that US citizens are subject to indefinite detention without due process and even to assassination without due process.

The Chinese government allowed Chen Guangcheng safe passage to leave China and live in the US. Chen Guangcheng is so dazzled by his illusions of America as a human rights beacon that it has never occurred to him that the oppressive, human rights-violating Chinese government gave him safe passage, but that Julian Assange, after being given political asylum by Ecuador is still confined to the Ecuadoran embassy in London, because Washington will not allow its UK puppet state to permit his safe passage to Ecuador.

Perhaps Chen Guangcheng and the Chinese and Russian dissidents who are so enamored of the US could gain some needed perspective if they were to read US soldier Terry Holdbrooks' book about the treatment given to the Guantanamo prisoners. Holdbrooks was there on the scene, part of the process, and this is what he told RT: "The torture and information extraction methods that we used certainly created a great deal of doubt and questions in my mind to whether or not this was my America. But when I thought about what we were doing there and how we go about doing it, it did not seem like the America I signed up to defend. It did not seem like the America I grew up in. And that in itself was a very disillusioning experience."

In a May 17 Wall Street Journal.com article, Peggy Noonan wrote that President Obama has lost his patina of high-mindedness. What did Obama do that brought this loss upon himself? Is it because he sits in the Oval Office approving lists of US citizens to be assassinated without due process of law? Is it because he detains US citizens indefinitely in violation of habeas corpus? Is it because he has kept open the torture prison at Guantanamo? Is it because he continued the war that the neoconservatives started, despite his promise to end it, and started new wars?

Is it because he attacks with drones people in their homes, medical centers, and work places in countries with which the US is not at war? Is it because his corrupt administration spies on American citizens without warrants and without cause?

No. It is none of these reasons. In Noonan's view these are not offenses for which presidents, even Democratic ones, lose their high-minded patina. Obama can no longer be trusted, because the IRS hassled some conservative political activists.

Noonan is a Republican, and what Obama did wrong was to use the IRS against some Republicans. Apparently, it has not occurred to Noonan that if Obama – or any president – can use the IRS against opponents, he can use Homeland Security and the police state against them. He can use indefinite detention against them. He can use drones against them.

All of these are much more drastic measures. Why isn't Peggy Noonan concerned?

Because she thinks these measures will only be used against terrorists, just as the IRS is only supposed to be used against tax evaders.

When a public and the commentators who inform it accept the collapse of the Constitution's authority and the demise of their civil liberties, to complain about the IRS is pointless.

First published on May 23, 2013.

[1]. "Official Story has Odd Wrinkles: A Pack of Questions about the Boston Bombing Backpacks"
https://whowhatwhy.org/politics/government-integrity/official-story-has-odd-wrinkles-a-pack-of-questions-about-the-boston-bombing-backpacks/

Truth Is Offensive

In America truth is offensive. If you tell the truth, you are offensive.

I am offensive. Michael Hudson is offensive. Gerald Celente is offensive. Herman Daly is offensive. Nomi Prins is offensive. Pam Martens is offensive. Chris Hedges is offensive. Chris Floyd is offensive. John Pilger is offensive. Noam Chomsky is offensive. Harvey Silverglate is offensive. Naomi Wolf is offensive. Stephen Lendman is offensive. David Ray Griffin is offensive. Ellen Brown is offensive.

Fortunately, many others are offensive. But how long before being offensive becomes being "an enemy of the state"?

Throughout history truth tellers have suffered and court historians have prospered. It is the same today. Gerald Celente illustrates this brilliantly in the next issue of the Trends Journal.

Over the past 35 years I have learned this lesson as a columnist. If you tell readers what is really going on, they want to know why you can't be positive. Why are you telling us that there are bad happenings that can't be remedied? Don't you know that God gave Americans the power to fix all wrongs? What are you? Some kind of idiot, an anti-American, a pinko-liberal-commie? If you hate America so much, why don't you move to Cuba, Iran or China (or to wherever the current bogyman is located)?

The ancient Greeks understood this well. In Greek mythology, Cassandra was the prophetess who no one believed despite her 100 percent record of being right. Telling the truth to Americans or to Europeans is just as expensive as telling the truth to the Greeks in ancient mythology.

In America and everywhere in the Western world or the entire world, telling the truth is unpopular. Indeed, in the USA telling the truth has been criminalized. Look for example at Bradley Manning, held for two years in prison without bail and without a trial in violation of the US Constitution, tortured for one year of his illegal confinement in violation of US and international law, and now put on trial by corrupt prosecutors for aiding "enemies of the US" by revealing the truth, as required of him by the US military code. US soldiers are required to report war crimes. When Bradley Manning's superiors showed themselves to be indifferent to war crimes, Manning reported the crimes via WikiLeaks. What else does a soldier with a sense of duty and a moral conscience do when the chain of command is corrupt?

Julian Assange is another example. WikiLeaks has taken up the reporting function that the Western media has abandoned. Remember, the New York Times did publish the Pentagon Papers in 1971, which undermined the lies Washington had told both to the public and to Congress to justify the costly Vietnam War. But today no newspaper or TV channel any longer accepts the responsibility to truthfully inform the public. Julian Assange stepped into the vacuum and was immediately demonized, not merely by Washington but also by left-wing and right-wing media, including Internet. It was a combination of jealousy, ignorance, and doing Washington's bidding.

Without WikiLeaks and Assange the world would know essentially nothing. Spin from Washington, the presstitute media, and the puppet state medias would prevail. So the word went out to destroy Julian Assange.

It is amazing how many people and Internet sites obeyed Washington's command. Assange has been so demonized that even though he has been granted political asylum by Ecuador, the British government, obeying its Washington master, refuses to allow him safe passage out of the London Ecuador Embassy. Is Assange destined to live out his life inside the Ecuador Embassy in London?

Will Assange be a replay of Cardinal Jozsef Mindszenty who on November 4, 1956, sought asylum in the US embassy in Budapest as Soviet tanks poured into Hungary to put down the anti-communist revolution? Cardinal Mindszenty lived for 15 years in the US embassy. Today it is "freedom and democracy" Amerika that is copying Soviet practices during the cold war.

In contrast with "freedom and democracy" US and UK, the "authoritarian," "communist," "oppressive" Chinese government when confronted with Chinese dissident Chen Guangcheng's defection to the US embassy in Beijing, let him go.

It is an upside down world when America and the British refuse to obey international law, but the Chinese communists uphold international law.

Insouciant Americans are undisturbed that alleged terrorists are tortured, held indefinitely in prison without due process, and executed on the whim of some executive branch official without due process of law. Most Americans go along with unaccountable murder, torture, and detention without evidence, which proclaims their gullibility to the entire world. There has never in history been a population as unaware as Americans. The world is amazed that an insouciant people became, if only for a short time, a superpower.

The world needs intelligence and leadership in order to avoid catastrophe, but America can provide neither intelligence nor leadership. America is a lost land where nuclear weapons are in the hands of those who are concerned only with their own power. Washington is the enemy of the entire world and encompasses the largest concentration of evil on the planet.

Where is the good to rise up against the evil?

First published on March 31, 2013.

Fake News A US Media Specialty

The American media specializes in fake news. Indeed, since the Clinton regime the American media has produced nothing but fake news. Do you remember the illegal US bombing and destruction of Yugoslavia? Do you remember "war criminal" Slobodan Milosevic, the Serbian president branded "the butcher of the Balkans," who was compared to Hitler until Hillary passed the title on to the President of Russia? Milosevic, not Bill Clinton, was arrested and placed on trial at the International Criminal Tribunal. He died in prison, some say murdered, before he was cleared of charges by the International Criminal Tribunal.

Do you remember the destruction of Iraq justified by the orchestrated propaganda, known by the criminal George W. Bush regime to be an outright lie, about Saddam Hussein's "weapons of mass destruction," weapons that the UN arms inspectors verified did not exist? Iraq was destroyed. Millions of Iraqis were killed, orphaned, widowed, and displaced. Saddam Hussein was subjected to a show trial more transparent than Stalin's trial of Bukharin and then murdered under the pretext of judicial execution.

Do you remember the destruction of Libya based entirely on Washington's lies and the criminal misuse of the UN no-fly resolution by turning it into a NATO bombing of Libya's military so that the CIA-armed jihadists could overthrow and murder Muammar Gaddafi? Do you remember the killer bitch Hillary gloating, "we came, we saw, he died!"

Do you remember the lies that the criminal Obama regime told about Assad of Syria and the planned US invasion of Syria that was blocked by the UK Parliament and the Russian government? Do you remember that Obama and the killer bitch sent ISIS to do the job that US troops were prevented from doing? Do you remember General Flynn revealing on TV that it was a "willful decision" of the criminal Obama regime to send ISIS to Syria over his objection as Director of the Defense Intelligence Agency? This bit of told truth is why Gen. Flynn is hated by the Washington criminals who forced him out as Trump's National Security Adviser.

Do you remember the US coup in Ukraine against the democratically elected government and its replacement with a neo-Nazi regime? Do you remember that Washington's crime against Ukrainian democracy was quickly hidden behind false charges of "Russian invasion"?

Can you think of any truthful report in the American news in the past two decades?

All of the lies leading to the death of millions told by the criminal Clinton, George W. Bush, and Obama regimes were transparent. The US media could easily have exposed them and saved the lives of millions of peoples and saved seven countries from destruction in whole or part. But the presstitutes cheered on the gratuitous and criminal destruction of countries and peoples. Every one of the presstitutes is a war criminal under the standards set by US Supreme Court Justice Robert Jackson at the Nuremberg trials.

We cannot even get a truthful jobs report. Yesterday (Aug. 4) the Bureau of Labor Statistics (BLS) reported 205,000 new private sector jobs in July and a drop in the unemployment rate to 4.3%. This is fake news.

The Associated Press's Christopher Rugaber rah-rahs the fake news, adding that many economists think "robust hiring could continue for many more months, or even years." Let's think about that for a moment. Generally speaking economists regard full employment to be a 5% rate of unemployment. There can never be a zero rate of unemployment because of frictions in the job market. For example, there are people between jobs who have lost or quit a job and are looking for a new one, and there are people who have dropped out of the work force, perhaps to spend more time parenting or to care for an aged and ill parent, and have reentered the work force. Economists also believe that employment cannot go too low without pushing up inflation.

Assuming economists have not suddenly changed their minds about what rate of unemployment is full employment, if the unemployment rate is currently 4.3%, it is already below the full employment rate. How can the rate continue to fall for years when the economy is already at full employment? Apparently, this question did not occur to the AP reporter or to the "many economists."

Of course, the 4.3% unemployment rate is fake news. It does not include millions of discouraged workers. When these workers who have not looked for jobs within the last four weeks are included, the unemployment rate jumps to 22-23%.

Now consider the alleged 205,000 July new jobs. Probably about half of these jobs are due to the add-ons from the birth-death model, and the other half from manipulations of seasonal adjustments. John Williams at shadowstats.com will tell us. However, let's assume the jobs are really there. Where does the BLS tell us the jobs are?

Eighty-nine percent of the jobs are in services, essentially domestic non-tradable services.

Professional and business services account for 49,000 of the jobs, of which 30,000 are in administrative and waste services (garbage collection) and 14,700 are in temporary help services.

54,000 of the jobs are in education and health services, of which ambulatory health care services, home health care services and social assistance account for 46,900 of the jobs.

62,000 of the jobs are in leisure and hospitality, of which waitresses and bartenders account for 53,100 of the jobs and amusements, gambling, and recreation account for 5,900 jobs.

This picture of American employment has been holding for about two decades. It is a portrait of a third world labor force. The jobs are not in export industries. The jobs are not in high productivity, high value-added occupations that produce a middle class income. The jobs are in lowly paid, often part-time domestic services.

The jobs do not produce incomes that provide discretionary spending to drive up business profits. So why did the stock market hit new highs? The answer is that corporate executives are taking advantage of the Federal Reserve's zero interest rates to borrow money with which to buy back their companies' shares in order to drive up their bonuses, the main component of their pay.

But these undeniable facts about employment did not prevent Christopher Rugaber and the other financial presstitutes or newspaper headline writers or "many economists" from asking "How much better can it get?" (Atlanta Journal-Constitution front page, Aug. 5, 2017).

It is not only seven Muslim countries that Washington and its presstitutes have destroyed in whole or part with lies. Washington's lies have also destroyed the American economy and the American work force.

First published on August 5, 2017.

Truth is an Endangered Species

My columns and those of guests generate a lot of appreciation and also a lot of demonization and expressions of hatred toward me. The slightest criticism of Israel labels one an anti-Semite. People who are aware understand that this word is so over-used that it has become meaningless, but the insouciant conclude that if you are labeled an anti-Semite you are some kind of monster who wants to harm Jews. If you point out the double-standards that white people suffer, you get branded a "racist white supremacist." If you point out that #MeToo feminists are criminalizing heterosexual sexual attraction, you become a misogynist. If you expose the official lies fed to the American people – Saddam Hussein's weapons of mass destruction, Assad's use of chemical weapons, Iranian nukes, Russian invasion of Ukraine, 9/11, Gulf of Tonkin, and so on – you are dismissed as a "conspiracy theorist" who hates America. Instead of seeing you as someone who is trying to rescue America, morons ask "If you hate America so much, why don't you move to Russia?" or Iran, or China, or Venezuela, or to whatever is the demonized and attacked country that the moron believes is getting its just reward.

Every year it becomes harder to tell the truth about anything. If you do too much truth-telling, as I am inclined to do, they come after you in droves. I had to stop websites that reproduce my columns, at least the ones I know about, from posting comments, because all sorts of paid trolls libel me and then spread the libel all over social media. Their purpose is to discredit me and to scare readers away from my website. It does work. When the mysterious site PropOrNot, financed by no one knows who, put me on a list of "Russian agents and Putin stooges," thousands dropped off the newsletter list.

Then they use Wikipedia, being an open biographical source that permits anyone to control your public image, to brand you an anti-Semite, a conspiracy theorist, and a holocaust denier. Perhaps you remember my column, "The Lies About WWII," a review of David

Irving's World War II histories – Churchill's War and Hitler's War. These are not the standard victor's history written to make us feel good about ourselves. To the contrary, Irving's histories are based on decades of historical investigation and on official documents, speeches, letters, and memoirs. Irving went around the world interviewing those who lived the experience. He found documents such as Rommel's and Goebbels' diaries, examined every document concerning the German government's Jewish policy, disproved the fake Hitler diaries, and so on. His books are regarded by objective historians as masterpieces. Yet, he was shut down. He told too much truth, an unacceptable sin.

In my extensive review of Irving's histories, I gave a summary paragraph of documentary evidence Irving provides of massacres of Jews and reported his conclusion that there was a holocaust of sorts but one different from the official picture. The definition of the Holocaust is the official Zionist story. To provide a holocaust description that differs from the official one makes a person a Holocaust Denier even if he describes a holocaust. And thus Irving's account makes him a Holocaust Denier. What Wikipedia did to me was to misrepresent my description of Irving's views as my own views and put me in the category of Holocaust Denier. It took forever to get the misrepresentation corrected. There are still problems with my biography in Wikipedia, but I have given up. Every time corrections are made they are erased. An open sourced biography requires far more integrity than exists, and this is the reason that Wikipedia is unreliable. You can only dare rely on Wikipedia for people and issues devoid of controversy. Basically, in my experience, Wikipedia is a mechanism for discrediting people who tell the truth.

As I often report, the vast majority of people are brainwashed by the propaganda that serves the ruling interests. They are too weak both mentally and emotionally to handle anything that is not the established view. It simply scares them and they run away. So when you write you know you are writing only for a select few.

The only way you can do this is to believe Margaret Mead that it only takes a few people to change the world. I think this was once true. Lenin and the Bolsheviks were a very few, and so were the Founding Fathers of the United States. But today our rulers have such extraordinary control mechanisms. Not that long ago the Internet was believed to be an instrument for freedom of speech, but they can shut you out and make you invisible. Alex Jones, for example, has been severed from YouTube and social media as have others. Google's search engine is instructed not to find disapproved commentators in searches. Large well-funded Internet sites funded by ruling interests can, along with the print and TV media, demonize you, as has been done to Julian Assange and Manning and even to the Presidents of the United States and Russia. I have already noticed that some dissident websites that were credible and resisting The Matrix have pulled in their horns. They fear that too much truth will marginalize them.

The Saker describes the censorship: "What we are witnessing today is a new age of censorship in which government and corporations work hand in hand to crush (ban, censor, demonetize, algorithmically purge and otherwise silence) all those who challenge the official ideology and its many narratives. It would be naïve to the extreme to assume that the so-called 'alternative media' and blogosphere have been spared such an effort at silencing heresies."

It has always been the case that the messenger is shot, but at least in former times the message could be heard. Today you can be shot and the message thrown down the Memory Hole.

I am tiring of the slings and arrows and all the ignorant, narcissistic, and rude emails that I receive. These letters don't come from my readers. They come from the paid trolls. The Saker describes their function: "These are the folks whose task it is to obfuscate the real issues, to bury them under tons of vapid ideological nonsense; the best way to do that is to misdirect any discussion away from the original topic and sidetrack it into either a barrage ad hominems or ideological clichés."

Some are not content to convince me once or even twice that they are blithering idiots, but insist on doing so every day. It is extraordinary how proud some are to demonstrate themselves as fools incapable of comprehending what they read. As an example, my recent columns about the use of the El Paso mass shooting to demonize white people, in which I quote people calling for the extermination of the white race, have resulted in me being denounced on other websites for "preaching hate," when in fact I am quoting those who are preaching hate and asking why are they doing so.

So, if you want to stop supporting this website, I won't cry. Indeed, I will be relieved of a burden, and can insulate myself from the stupidity of people. I have just about arrived at the conclusion that "intelligent American" is an oxymoron. Many readers have shared their frustrations of trying to inform friends and relatives that CNN doesn't always have the facts. I have the same experience with some friends and relatives. When I get questions from persons too brainwashed for truth to penetrate, I reply that I don't know, ask CNN.

This website is a contract between me and readers. As long as readers support the site, I will write what I think is the truth as long as I have the mental acuity and energy to do so. My agenda is the truth. Truth is truth. It is not race-truth, class-truth, gender- and transgender-truth, Identity Politics-truth, Republican-truth, Democratic-truth, liberal-truth, conservative-truth, libertarian-truth, leftwing-truth or any other kind of hyphenated truth.

If you are more interested in my typos than my content, find something else to read. Keep in mind that my fingers are aging and at times suffer from arthritis, my keyboard is worn out, new ones don't fit my computer, and typos result. After the millions of words I have written in my lifetime, it is impossible to proof read myself, and I don't always have a proof reader at hand. I have turned off the spellcheck, because Apple also substitutes words for you, and if you don't notice because you are focused on content, you can end up with puzzling sentences. The digital revolution is not the blessing that you are brainwashed to believe.

September is always the worst month for an appeal, but if you use the calendar year, that is where the quarter falls. I know you are busted. You blew it on a summer vacation and on the Labor Day 3-day weekend fling. But keep in mind that my energy and my will are what your support energizes.

The ruling elite have the American people so well insulated from reality behind empty patriotic and democratic slogans that not many of them can be reached. To be rescued from The Matrix you have to already be extraordinary. I am not a savior who can rescue you, but I can push you toward self-rescue. If you want to have a free mind, you can achieve it, but you must have the emotional strength for it. Things are not as you have been trained to perceive them. There is evil and corruption all around you. And it is in places and words that you have been taught to respect.

From the beginning of time there have been humans who have wanted to know the truth about things. Truth was the purpose of early philosophy. The scientific revolution gave humans a chance at some natural truths, and they had to be fought for. Today money is the main determinant of "truth." "Truth" is what money says, and money has the power to enforce "truth." Real truth, such as I attempt to tell, is not welcome today by any government or ruling interest anywhere in the Western World or in those countries that have been corrupted by the Western World. Indeed, the enemy of truth today is no longer in Moscow or China. The enemy is in Washington, New York, and Hollywood, in CNN, MSNBC, NPR, New York Times, Washington Post, and in the universities and scientists who lie for money, and in the superrich who control these entities, including Congress, the Executive Branch and Oval Office, and Judiciary.

Of all the endangered species, Truth is the most endangered. I am watching it go out.

First published on September 4, 2019.

Will Truth Be Criminalized?

The Establishment's determination to close down narrative-challenger Alex Jones has put Sandy Hook back in the news. As First Amendment protection is fading, I checked to see what I had written about Sandy Hook. I was relieved to see that I had only reported on the skepticism and asked questions.

My search of the IPE archives brought up my articles on other controversial shootings – Las Vegas and Orlando – and the Oklahoma City Bombing. The common thread in all of these incidents is that the narrative is established the minute the news is reported, and officials and media never vary from the narrative. As soon as it happens, the government and the media already know what happened. No investigation ever takes place. It was the same for President Kennedy's assassination, his brother's assassination, 9/11, the Gulf of Tonkin, Saddam Hussein's weapons of mass destruction, Assad's use of chemical weapons, the Israeli attack on the USS Liberty, etc.

Legitimate questions about the narratives are ignored by officials and media who seem to be involved in a conspiracy to bury the truth. Skeptics, no matter how prominent or fact-based are demonized as "conspiracy theorists" unworthy of attention.

Clearly, America no longer has a media watchdog. America has a propaganda ministry for official narratives.

What this tells us should shock every American, every US puppet government, and Washington's chosen enemies – Russia, China, and Iran – respect for truth is hard to find in the American media and the American government.

In the not distant future, it will become actionable to doubt the presstitues and the government on the grounds that doubt implies disbelief and disbelief is a crime or proves that you are a foreign agent.

Slander and libel will evolve to apply to media and government as institutions. As we are so gullible, so trusting, we are going to be reduced to silence or praise. Silence will bring official suspicion. Praise of the false narratives will bring career success and rewards. This is the stark situation that we face.

It is unclear that anything can be done to rectify this situation. Older Americans generally are comfortable with the idea that government and media have integrity. This is their picture of the bygone world that they grew up in. Younger people have been indoctrinated in schools that government and media protect blacks, homosexuals, and transgendered from racist, homophobic and transphobic white people who use normality as an illegitimate standard of approval. Sodom and Gomorrah are approved, but not the white family unit.

Can we believe that there is a future for freedom in America when Democrats, media, CIA, FBI, and NSA can create a narrative of President Donald Trump as a Russian agent?

Can we believe that there is a future for freedom in America when the same collection of schemers can create a show trial of the President of the United States planning a coup by a couple of hundred unarmed supporters seizing the government of the United States by walking around in the Capitol and sitting in Nancy Pelosi's chair?

Can we believe that Americans sufficiently stupid to believe such implausible narratives have any possibility of holding on to their freedom?

First published August 5, 2022.

Is the Saudi 9/11 Story Part Of The Deception?

James Jesus Angleton, head of CIA counterintelligence for three decades, long ago explained to me that intelligence services create stories inside stories, each with its carefully constructed trail of evidence, in order to create false trails as diversions. Such painstaking work can serve a variety of purposes. It can be used to embarrass or discredit an innocent person or organization that has an unhelpful position on an important issue and is in the way of an agenda. It can be used as a red herring to draw attention away from a failing explanation of an event by producing an alternative false explanation. I forget what Angleton called them, but the strategy is to have within a false story other stories that are there but withheld because of "national security" or "politically sensitive issues" or some such. Then if the official story gets into trouble, the backup story can be released in order to deflect attention into a new false story or to support the original story. Angleton said that intelligence services protect their necessary misdeeds by burying the misdeed in competing explanations.

Watching the expert craftsmanship of the "Saudis did 9/11" story, I have been wondering if the Saudi story is what Angleton described as a story within a story.

The official 9/11 story has taken too many hits to remain standing. The collapse of Building 7, which, if memory serves, was not mentioned at all in the 9/11 Commission Report, has been proven to have been a controlled demolition. Building 7 collapsed at free fall acceleration, which can only be achieved with controlled demolition.

Over 100 firemen, policemen, and building maintenance personnel who were inside the two towers prior to their collapse report hearing and experiencing multiple explosions. According to William Rodriguez, a maintenance employee in the north tower, there were explosions in the sub-basements of the tower prior to the time airplanes are said to have hit the towers.

An international team of scientists found in the dust of the towers both reacted and unreacted residues of explosives and substances capable of instantly producing the extreme temperatures that cut steel.

A large number of pilots, both commercial and military, have questioned the ability of alleged hijackers with substandard flight skills to conduct the maneuvers required by the flight paths.

2,500 architects and engineers have called for an independent investigation of the failure of the towers that were certified to be capable of withstanding a hit by airplanes.

The revelation that the 9/11 attack was financed by the Saudi government has the effect of bolstering the sagging official story while simultaneously satisfying the growing recognition that something is wrong with the official story.

Commentators and media are treating the story of Saudi financing of 9/11 as a major revelation that damns the Bush regime, but the revelation not only leaves in place but also strengthens the official story that Osama bin Laden carried out the attack with precisely the hijackers identified in the original story. The Bush regime is damned merely for protecting its Saudi friends and withholding evidence of Saudi financing.

The evidence of Saudi financing is what restores the credibility of the original story. Nothing changes in the story of the collapse of the three WTC buildings, the attack on the Pentagon, and the crashed airliner in Pennsylvania. American anger is now directed at the Saudis for financing the successful attacks.

To hype the Saudi story is to support the official story. A number of commentators who are usually suspicious of government are practically jumping up and down for joy that now they have something to pin on Bush. They haven't noticed that what they are pinning on him supports the official 9/11 story.

Moreover, they have not explained why the Saudi government would finance an attack on the country that protects it. Saudi Arabia is a long-time partner. They accept pieces of paper for their oil and then use the paper to finance the US Treasury's debt and to purchase US weapons systems, purchases that lead to larger weapons sales, thus spreading R&D costs over larger volume.

What do the Saudis have to gain from embarrassing the US by demonstrating the total failure of US national security? Really, if a few hijackers can outfox the NSA, the CIA, and the national security state, we clearly aren't getting our money's worth and are giving up our civil liberties for nothing.

Saudi financing does not explain who had access to wire the buildings for demolition, or to schedule on 9/11 a simulated attack that the actual attack modeled, thus causing confusion among some authorities about what was real and what was not.

Saudi financing does not explain the dancing Israelis who were apprehended filming the attacks on the towers and who later said on Israeli TV that they were sent to New York to film the attack. How did the Israelis know? Did Prince Bandar tell them? Bush didn't tell us about the Saudis, and the Israelis didn't tell us about the attack. Which is worse?

This Saudi revelation is too convenient for the official story. How do we know that it was not devised as a story inside the story to be used when the story got into trouble? The Saudis would be a logical choice to be put in such a position as the original neoconservative plan for overthrowing Middle Eastern governments included overthrowing Saudi Arabia. Now we have an excuse.

I have doubts that the alleged hijackers played any role other than cover for bringing down buildings by controlled demolition. Possibly the hijackers and the Saudis who financed them, if the evidence is real and not concocted, were not aware of their role and thought they were participating in a different deception.

Are we being deceived again with a story inside a story? Will it succeed along the lines that Angleton explained? Or will it possibly backfire? If the US government will hide some of the truth from us for 13 years, why not all of the truth? What else in the official story is false?

First published July 10, 2016.

CHAPTER 2
ECONOMIC
DECEPTION

Recovery or Collapse? Bet on Collapse

The US financial system and, probably, the financial system of Europe, like the police, no longer serves a useful social purpose.

In the US the police have proven themselves to be a greater threat to public safety than private sector criminals. I just Googled "police brutality" and up came 183,000,000 results.

The cost to society of the private financial system is even higher. Writing in CounterPunch (May 18), Rob Urie reports that two years ago Andrew Haldane, executive Director for Financial Stability at the Bank of England (the UK's version of the Federal Reserve) said that the financial crisis, now four years old, will in the end cost the world economy between $60 trillion and $200 trillion in lost GDP. If Urie's report is correct, this is an astonishing admission from a member of the ruling elite.

Try to get your mind around these figures. The US GDP, the largest in the world, is about 15 trillion. What Haldane is telling us is that the financial crisis will end up costing the world lost real income between 4 and 13 times the size of the current Gross Domestic Product of the United States. This could turn out to be an optimistic forecast.

In the end, the financial crisis could destroy Western civilization.

Even if Urie's report, or Haldane's calculation, is incorrect, the obvious large economic loss from the financial crisis is still unprecedented. The enormous cost of the financial crisis has one single source – financial deregulation. Financial deregulation is likely to prove to be the mistake that destroys Western civilization. While we quake in our boots from fear of "Muslim terrorists," it is financial deregulation that is destroying us, with help from jobs offshoring. Keep in mind that Haldane is a member of the ruling elite, not a critic of the system like myself, Gerald Celente, Michael Hudson, Pam

Martins, and Nomi Prins. (This is not meant to be an exhaustive list of critics.)

Financial deregulation has had dangerous and adverse consequences. Deregulation permitted financial concentration that produced "banks too big to fail," thus requiring the general public to absorb the costs of the banks' mistakes and reckless gambling.

Deregulation permitted banks to leverage a small amount of capital with enormous debt in order to maximize return on equity, thereby maximizing the instability of the financial system and the cost to society of the banks' bad bets.

Deregulation allowed financial institutions to sweep aside the position limits on speculators and to dominate commodity markets, turning them into a gambling casino and driving up the prices of energy and food.

Deregulation permits financial institutions to sell naked shorts, which means to sell a company's stock or gold and silver bullion that the seller does not possess into the market in order to drive down the price.

The informed reader can add more items to this list.

The dollar in its role as world reserve currency is the source of Washington's power. It allows Washington to control the international payments system and to exclude from the financial system those countries that do not do Washington's bidding. It allows Washington to print money with which to pay its bills and to purchase the cooperation of foreign governments or to fund opposition within those countries whose governments Washington is unable to purchase, such as Iran, Russia, and China. If the dollar was not the world reserve currency and actually reflected its true depreciated value from the mounting US debt and running of the printing press, Washington's power would be dramatically curtailed.

The US dollar has come close to its demise several times recently. In 2011 the dollar's value fell as low as 72 Swiss cents. Investors seeking safety for the value of their money flooded into Swiss francs, pushing the value of the franc so high that Switzerland's exports began to suffer. The Swiss government responded to the inflow of dollars and euros seeking refuge in the franc by declaring that it would in the future print new francs to offset the inflows of foreign currency in order to prevent the rise in the value of the franc. In other words, currency flight from the US and Europe forced the Swiss to inflate in order to prevent the continuous rise in the exchange value of the Swiss currency.

Prior to the sovereign debt crisis in Europe, the dollar was also faced with a run-up in the value of the euro as foreign central banks and OPEC members shifted their reserves into euros from dollars. The euro was on its way to becoming an alternative reserve currency. However, Goldman Sachs, whose former employees dominate the US Treasury and financial regulatory agencies and also the European Central Bank and governments of Italy and, indirectly, Greece, helped the Greek government to disguise its true deficit, thus deceiving the private European banks who were purchasing the bonds of the Greek government. Once the European sovereign debt crisis was launched, Washington had an interest in keeping it going, as it sends holders of euros fleeing into "safe" dollars, thus boosting the exchange value of the dollar, despite the enormous rise in Washington's own debt and the doubling of the US money supply.

Last year gold and silver were rapidly rising in price (measured in US dollars), with gold hitting $1,900 an ounce and on its way to $2,000 when suddenly short sales began dominating the bullion markets. The naked shorts of gold and silver bullion succeeded in driving the price of gold down $350 per ounce from its peak. Many informed observers believe that the reason Washington has not prosecuted the banksters for their known financial crimes is that the banksters serve as an auxiliary to Washington by protecting the value of the dollar by shorting bullion and rival currencies.

What happens if Greece exits the EU on its own or by the German boot? What happens if the other EU members reject German Chancellor Merkel's austerity, as the new president of France promised to do? If Europe breaks apart, do more investors flee to the doomed US dollar?

Will a dollar bubble become the largest bubble in economic history?

When the dollar goes, interest rates will escalate, and bond prices will collapse. Everyone who sought safety in US Treasuries will be wiped out. We should all be aware that such outcomes are not part of the public debate.

Recently Bill Moyers interviewed Simon Johnson, formerly chief economist of the International Monetary Fund and currently professor at MIT. It turns out that deregulation, which abolished the separation of investment banks from commercial banks, permitted Jamie Dimon's JPMorganChase to gamble with federally insured deposits. Despite this, Moyers reports that Republicans remain determined to kill the weak Dodd-Frank law and restore full deregulation.

Simon Johnson says: "I think it [deregulation] is a recipe for disaster." The problem is, Johnson says, that correct economic policy is blocked by the enormous donations banks make to political campaigns. This means Wall Street's attitudes and faulty risk models will result in an even bigger financial crisis than the one from which we are still suffering. And it will happen prior to recovery from the current crisis.

Johnson warns that the Republicans will distract everyone from the real crisis by concocting another "crisis" over the debt ceiling.

Johnson says that "a few people, particularly in and around the financial system, have become too powerful. They were allowed to take a lot of risk, and they did massive damage to the economy – more than eight million jobs lost. We're still struggling to get back anywhere close to employment levels where we were before 2008. And they've done massive damage to the budget. This damage to the budget is long lasting; it undermines the budget when we need it to be stronger because the society is aging. We need to support Social Security and support Medicare on a fair basis. We need to restore and rebuild revenue, revenue that was absolutely devastated by the financial crisis. People need to understand the link between what the banks did and the budget. And too many people fail to do that."

Consequently, Johnson says, the banksters continue to receive mega-benefits while imposing enormous social costs on society.

Few Americans and no Washington policymakers understand the dire situation. They are too busy hyping a non-existent recovery and the next war. Statistician John Williams reports that when correctly measured as a cost of living indicator, which the CPI no longer is, the current inflation rate in the US is 5 to 7 percentage points higher than the officially reported rate, as every consumer knows. The unemployment rate falls because, and only because, people unable to find jobs drop out of the labor force and are no longer counted as unemployed. Every informed person knows that the official inflation and unemployment rates are fictions; yet, the presstitute media continue to report the rates with a straight face as fact.

The way the government has rigged the measure of unemployment, it is possible for the US to have a zero rate of unemployment and not a single person employed or in the work force.

The way the government has the measure of inflation rigged, it is possible for your living standing to fall while the government reports that you are better off.

Financial deregulation raises the returns from speculative schemes above the returns from productive activity. The highly leveraged debt and derivatives that gave us the financial crisis have nothing to do with financing businesses. The banks are not only risking their customers' deposits on gambling bets but also jeopardizing the country's financial stability and economic future.

With an eye on the approaching dollar crisis, which will wreck the international financial system, the presidents of China, Russia, Brazil, South Africa, and the prime minister of India met last month to discuss forming a new bank that would shield their economies and commerce from mistakes made by Washington and the European Union. The five countries, known as the BRICS, intend to settle their trade with one another in their own currencies and cease relying on the dollar. The fact that Russia, the two Asian giants, and the largest economies in Africa and South America are leaving the dollar's orbit sends a powerful message of lack of confidence in Washington's handling of financial matters.

It is ironic that the outcome of financial deregulation in the US is the opposite of what its free market advocates promised. In place of highly competitive financial firms that live or die by their wits alone without government intervention, we have unprecedented financial concentration. Massive banks, "too big to fail," now send their multi-trillion dollar losses to Washington to be paid by heavily indebted US taxpayers whose real incomes have not risen in 20 years. The banksters take home fortunes in annual bonuses for their success in socializing the "free market" banks' losses and privatizing profits to the point of not even paying income taxes.

In the US free market economists unleashed avarice and permitted it to run amuck. Will the disastrous consequences discredit capitalism to the extent that the Soviet collapse discredited socialism?

Will Western civilization itself survive the financial tsunami that deregulated Wall Street has produced?

Ironic, isn't it, that the United States, the home of the "indispensable people," stands before us as the likely candidate whose government will be responsible for the collapse of the West.

First published on May 20, 2012.

America's Descent into Poverty

The United States has collapsed economically, socially, politically, legally, constitutionally, and environmentally. The country that exists today is not even a shell of the country into which I was born. In this article I will deal with America's economic collapse. In subsequent articles, I will deal with other aspects of American collapse.

Economically, America has descended into poverty. As Peter Edelman says, "Low-wage work is pandemic." Today in "freedom and democracy" America, "the world's only superpower," one fourth of the work force is employed in jobs that pay less than $22,000, the poverty line for a family of four. Some of these lowly-paid persons are young college graduates, burdened by education loans, who share housing with three or four others in the same desperate situation. Other of these persons are single parents only one medical problem or lost job away from homelessness.

Others might be Ph.Ds. teaching at universities as adjunct professors for $10,000 per year or less. Education is still touted as the way out of poverty, but increasingly is a path into poverty or into enlistments into the military services.

Edelman, who studies these issues, reports that 20.5 million Americans have incomes less than $9,500 per year, which is half of the poverty definition for a family of three.

There are six million Americans whose only income is food stamps. That means that there are six million Americans who live on the streets or under bridges or in the homes of relatives or friends. Hard-hearted Republicans continue to rail at welfare, but Edelman says, "basically welfare is gone."

In my opinion as an economist, the official poverty line is long out of date. The prospect of three people living on $19,000 per year is farfetched. Considering the prices of rent, electricity, water, bread and fast food, one person cannot live in the US on $6,333.33 per year. In Thailand, perhaps, until the dollar collapses, it might be done, but not in the US.

As Dan Ariely (Duke University) and Mike Norton (Harvard University) have shown empirically, 40% of the US population, the 40% less well off, own 0.3%, that is, three-tenths of one percent, of America's personal wealth. Who owns the other 99.7%? The top 20% have 84% of the country's wealth. Those Americans in the third and fourth quintiles – essentially America's middle class – have only 15.7% of the nation's wealth. Such an unequal distribution of income is unprecedented in the economically developed world.

In my day, confronted with such disparity in the distribution of income and wealth, a disparity that obviously poses a dramatic problem for economic policy, political stability, and the macro management of the economy, Democrats would have demanded corrections, and Republicans would have reluctantly agreed.

But not today. Both political parties whore for money.

The Republicans believe that the suffering of poor Americans is not helping the rich enough. Paul Ryan and Mitt Romney are committed to abolishing every program that addresses needs of what Republicans deride as "useless eaters."

The "useless eaters" are the working poor and the former middle class whose jobs were offshored so that corporate executives could receive multi-millions of dollars in performance pay compensation and their shareholders could make millions of dollars on capital gains. While a handful of executives enjoy yachts and Playboy playmates, tens of millions of Americans barely get by.

In political propaganda, the "useless eaters" are not merely a burden on society and the rich. They are leeches who force honest taxpayers to pay for their many hours of comfortable leisure enjoying life, watching sports events, and fishing in trout streams, while they push around their belongings in grocery baskets or sell their bodies for the next MacDonald burger.

The concentration of wealth and power in the US today is far beyond anything my graduate economic professors could image in the 1960s. At four of the world's best universities that I attended, the opinion was that competition in the free market would prevent great disparities in the distribution of income and wealth. As I was to learn, this belief was based on an ideology, not on reality.

Congress, acting on this erroneous belief in free market perfection, deregulated the US economy in order to create a free market. The immediate consequence was resort to every previous illegal action to monopolize, to commit financial and other fraud, to destroy the productive basis of American consumer incomes, and to redirect income and wealth to the one percent.

The "democratic" Clinton administration, like the Bush and Obama administrations, was suborned by free market ideology. The Clinton sell-outs to Big Money essentially abolished Aid to Families with Dependent Children. But this sell-out of struggling Americans was not enough to satisfy the Republican Party. Mitt Romney and Paul Ryan want to cut or abolish every program that cushions poverty-stricken Americans from starvation and homelessness.

Republicans claim that the only reason Americans are in need is because the government uses taxpayers' money to subsidize Americans who are unwilling to work. As Republicans see it, while we hard-workers sacrifice our leisure and time with our families, the welfare rabble enjoy the leisure that our tax dollars provide them.

This cock-eyed belief, on top of corporate CEOs maximizing their incomes by offshoring the middle class jobs of millions of Americans, has left Americans in poverty and cities, counties, states, and the federal government without a tax base, resulting in bankruptcies at the state and local level and massive budget deficits at the federal level that threaten the value of the dollar and its role as reserve currency.

The economic destruction of America benefitted the mega-rich with multi-billions of dollars with which to enjoy life and its high-priced accompaniments wherever the mega-rich wish. Meanwhile, away from the French Rivera, Homeland Security is collecting sufficient ammunition to keep dispossessed Americans under control.

First published on August 24, 2012.

Collapse At Hand

Ever since the beginning of the financial crisis and quantitative easing, the question has been before us: How can the Federal Reserve maintain zero interest rates for banks and negative real interest rates for savers and bond holders when the US government is adding $1.5 trillion to the national debt every year via its budget deficits? Not long ago the Fed announced that it was going to continue this policy for another 2 or 3 years. Indeed, the Fed is locked into the policy. Without the artificially low interest rates, the debt service on the national debt would be so large that it would raise questions about the US Treasury's credit rating and the viability of the dollar, and the trillions of dollars in Interest Rate Swaps and other derivatives would come unglued.

In other words, financial deregulation leading to Wall Street's gambles, the US government's decision to bail out the banks and to keep them afloat, and the Federal Reserve's zero interest rate policy have put the economic future of the US and its currency in an untenable and dangerous position. It will not be possible to continue to flood the bond markets with $1.5 trillion in new issues each year when the interest rate on the bonds is less than the rate of inflation. Everyone who purchases a Treasury bond is purchasing a depreciating asset. Moreover, the capital risk of investing in Treasuries is very high. The low interest rate means that the price paid for the bond is very high. A rise in interest rates, which must come sooner or later, will collapse the price of the bonds and inflict capital losses on bond holders, both domestic and foreign.

The question is: when is sooner or later? The purpose of this article is to examine that question.

Let us begin by answering the question: how has such an untenable policy managed to last this long?

A number of factors are contributing to the stability of the dollar and the bond market. A very important factor is the situation in Europe. There are real problems there as well, and the financial press keeps our focus on Greece, Europe, and the euro. Will Greece exit the European Union or be kicked out? Will the sovereign debt problem spread to Spain, Italy, and essentially everywhere except for Germany and the Netherlands?

Will it be the end of the EU and the euro? These are all very dramatic questions that keep focus off the American situation, which is probably even worse.

The Treasury bond market is also helped by the fear individual investors have of the equity market, which has been turned into a gambling casino by high-frequency trading.

High-frequency trading is electronic trading based on mathematical models that make the decisions. Investment firms compete on the basis of speed, capturing gains on a fraction of a penny, and perhaps holding positions for only a few seconds. These are not long-term investors. Content with their daily earnings, they close out all positions at the end of each day.

High-frequency trades now account for 70-80% of all equity trades. The result is major heartburn for traditional investors, who are leaving the equity market. They end up in Treasuries, because they are unsure of the solvency of banks who pay next to nothing for deposits, whereas 10-year Treasuries will pay about 2% nominal, which means, using the official Consumer Price Index, that they are losing 1% of their capital each year. Using John Williams' (shadowstats.com) correct measure of inflation, they are losing far more. Still, the loss is about 2 percentage points less than being in a bank, and unlike banks, the Treasury can have the Federal Reserve print the money to pay off its bonds. Therefore, bond investment at least returns the nominal amount of the investment, even if its real value is much lower.

The presstitute financial media tells us that flight from European sovereign debt, from the doomed euro, and from the continuing real estate disaster into US Treasuries provides funding for Washington's $1.5 trillion annual deficits. Investors influenced by the financial press might be responding in this way. Another explanation for the stability of the Fed's untenable policy is collusion between Washington, the Fed, and Wall Street. We will be looking at this as we progress.

Unlike Japan, whose national debt is the largest of all, Americans do not own their own public debt. Much of US debt is owned abroad, especially by China, Japan, and OPEC, the oil exporting countries. This places the US economy in foreign hands. If China, for example, were to find itself unduly provoked by Washington, China could dump up to $2 trillion in US dollar-dominated assets on world markets. All sorts of prices would collapse, and the Fed would have to rapidly create the money to buy up the Chinese dumping of dollar-denominated financial instruments.

The dollars printed to purchase the dumped Chinese holdings of US dollar assets would expand the supply of dollars in currency markets and drive down the dollar exchange rate. The Fed, lacking foreign currencies with which to buy up the dollars would have to appeal for currency swaps to sovereign debt-troubled Europe for euros, to Russia, surrounded by the US missile system, for rubles, to Japan, a country over its head in American commitment, for yen, in order to buy up the dollars with euros, rubles, and yen.

These currency swaps would be on the books, unredeemable and making additional use of such swaps problematical. In other words, even if the US government can pressure its allies and puppets to swap their harder currencies for a depreciating US currency, it would not be a repeatable process. The components of the American Empire don't want to be in dollars any more than do the BRICS.

However, for China, for example, to dump its dollar holdings all at once would be costly as the value of the dollar-denominated assets would decline as they dumped them. Unless China is faced with US military attack and needs to defang the aggressor, China as a rational economic actor would prefer to slowly exit the US dollar. Neither do Japan, Europe, nor OPEC wish to destroy their own accumulated wealth from America's trade deficits by dumping dollars, but the indications are that they all wish to exit their dollar holdings.

Unlike the US financial press, the foreigners who hold dollar assets look at the annual US budget and trade deficits, look at the sinking US economy, look at Wall Street's uncovered gambling bets, look at the war plans of the delusional hegemon and conclude: "I've got to carefully get out of this."

US banks also have a strong interest in preserving the status quo. They are holders of US Treasuries and potentially even larger holders. They can borrow from the Federal Reserve at zero interest rates and purchase 10-year Treasuries at 2%, thus earning a nominal profit of 2% to offset derivative losses. The banks can borrow dollars from the Fed for free and leverage them in derivative transactions. As Nomi Prins puts it, the US banks don't want to trade against themselves and their free source of funding by selling their bond holdings. Moreover, in the event of foreign flight from dollars, the Fed could boost the foreign demand for dollars by requiring foreign banks that want to operate in the US to increase their reserve amounts, which are dollar based.

I could go on, but I believe this is enough to show that even actors in the process who could terminate it have themselves a big stake in not rocking the boat and prefer to quietly and slowly sneak out of dollars before the crisis hits. This is not possible indefinitely as the process of gradual withdrawal from the dollar would result in continuous small declines in dollar values that would end in a rush to exit, but Americans are not the only delusional people.

The very process of slowly getting out can bring the American house down. The BRICS – Brazil, the largest economy in South America, Russia, the nuclear armed and energy independent economy on which Western Europe (Washington's NATO puppets) are dependent for energy, India, nuclear armed and one of Asia's two rising giants, China, nuclear armed, Washington's largest creditor (except for the Fed), supplier of America's manufactured and advanced technology products, and the new bogyman for the military-security complex's next profitable cold war, and South Africa, the largest economy in Africa – are in the process of forming a new bank. The new bank will permit the five large economies to conduct their trade without use of the US dollar.

In addition, Japan, an American puppet state since WWII, is on the verge of entering into an agreement with China in which the Japanese yen and the Chinese yuan will be directly exchanged. The trade between the two Asian countries would be conducted in their own currencies without the use of the US dollar. This reduces the cost of foreign trade between the two countries, because it eliminates payments for foreign exchange commissions to convert from yen and yuan into dollars and back into yen and yuan.

Moreover, this official explanation for the new direct relationship avoiding the US dollar is simply diplomacy speaking. The Japanese are hoping, like the Chinese, to get out of the practice of accumulating ever more dollars by having to park their trade surpluses in US Treasuries. The Japanese US puppet government hopes that the Washington hegemon does not require the Japanese government to nix the deal with China.

Now we have arrived at the nitty and gritty. The small percentage of Americans who are aware and informed are puzzled why the banksters have escaped with their financial crimes without prosecution. The answer might be that the banks "too big to fail" are adjuncts of Washington and the Federal Reserve in maintaining the stability of the dollar and Treasury bond markets in the face of an untenable Fed policy.

Let us first look at how the big banks can keep the interest rates on Treasuries low, below the rate of inflation, despite the constant increase in US debt as a percent of GDP – thus preserving the Treasury's ability to service the debt.

The imperiled banks too big to fail have a huge stake in low interest rates and the success of the Fed's policy. The big banks are positioned to make the Fed's policy a success. JPMorgan Chase and other giant-sized banks can drive down Treasury interest rates and, thereby, drive up the prices of bonds, producing a rally, by selling Interest Rate Swaps (IRSwaps).

A financial company that sells IRSwaps is selling an agreement to pay floating interest rates for fixed interest rates. The buyer is purchasing an agreement that requires him to pay a fixed rate of interest in exchange for receiving a floating rate.

The reason for a seller to take the short side of the IRSwap, that is, to pay a floating rate for a fixed rate, is his belief that rates are going to fall. Short-selling can make the rates fall, and thus drive up the prices of Treasuries. When this happens, as these charts illustrate, there is a rally in the Treasury bond market that the presstitute financial media attributes to "flight to the safe haven of the US dollar and Treasury bonds." In fact, the circumstantial evidence (see the charts in the link above) is that the swaps are sold by Wall Street whenever the Federal Reserve needs to prevent a rise in interest rates in order to protect its otherwise untenable policy. The swap sales create the impression of a flight to the dollar, but no actual flight occurs. As the IRSwaps require no exchange of any principal or real asset, and are only a bet on interest rate movements, there is no limit to the volume of IRSwaps.

This apparent collusion suggests to some observers that the reason the Wall Street banksters have not been prosecuted for their crimes is that they are an essential part of the Federal Reserve's policy to preserve the US dollar as world currency. Possibly the collusion between the Federal Reserve and the banks is organized, but it doesn't have to be. The banks are beneficiaries of the Fed's zero interest rate policy. It is in the banks' interest to support it. Organized collusion is not required.

Let us now turn to gold and silver bullion. Based on sound analysis, Gerald Celente and other gifted seers predicted that the price of gold would be $2000 per ounce by the end of last year. Gold and silver bullion continued during 2011 their ten-year rise, but in 2012 the price of gold and silver have been knocked down, with gold being $350 per ounce off its $1900 high.

In view of the analysis that I have presented, what is the explanation for the reversal in bullion prices? The answer again is shorting. Some knowledgeable people within the financial sector believe that the Federal Reserve (and perhaps also the European Central Bank) places short sales of bullion through the investment banks, guaranteeing any losses by pushing a key on the computer keyboard, as central banks can create money out of thin air.

Insiders inform me that as a tiny percent of those on the buy side of short sells actually want to take delivery on the gold or silver bullion, and are content with the financial money settlement, there is no limit to short selling of gold and silver. Short selling can actually exceed the known quantity of gold and silver.

Some who have been watching the process for years believe that government-directed short-selling has been going on for a long time. Even without government participation, banks can control the volume of paper trading in gold and profit on the swings that they create. Recently short selling is so aggressive that it not merely slows the rise in bullion prices but drives the price down. Is this aggressiveness a sign that the rigged system is on the verge of becoming unglued?

In other words, "our government," which allegedly represents us, rather than the powerful private interests who elect "our government" with their multi-million dollar campaign contributions, now legitimized by the Republican Supreme Court, is doing its best to deprive us mere citizens, slaves, indentured servants, and "domestic extremists" from protecting ourselves and our remaining wealth from the currency debauchery policy of the Federal Reserve. Naked short selling prevents the rising demand for physical bullion from raising bullion's price.

Jeff Nielson explains another way that banks can sell bullion shorts when they own no bullion [1]. Nielson says that JP Morgan is the custodian for the largest long silver fund while being the largest short-seller of silver. Whenever the silver fund adds to its bullion holdings, JP Morgan shorts an equal amount. The short selling offsets the rise in price that would result from the increase in demand for physical silver. Nielson also reports that bullion prices can be suppressed by raising margin requirements on those who purchase bullion with leverage. The conclusion is that bullion markets can be manipulated just as can the Treasury bond market and interest rates.

How long can the manipulations continue? When will the proverbial hit the fan?

If we knew precisely the date, we would be the next mega-billionaires.

Here are some of the catalysts waiting to ignite the conflagration that burns up the Treasury bond market and the US dollar:

A war, demanded by the Israeli government, with Iran, beginning with Syria, that disrupts the oil flow and thereby the stability of the Western economies or brings the US and its weak NATO puppets into armed

46

conflict with Russia and China. The oil spikes would degrade further the US and EU economies, but Wall Street would make money on the trades.

An unfavorable economic statistic that wakes up investors as to the true state of the US economy, a statistic that the presstitute media cannot deflect.

An affront to China, whose government decides that knocking the US down a few pegs into third world status is worth a trillion dollars.

More derivate mistakes, such as JPMorgan Chase's recent one, that send the US financial system again reeling and reminds us that nothing has changed.

The list is long. There is a limit to how many stupid mistakes and corrupt financial policies the rest of the world is willing to accept from the US. When that limit is reached, it is all over for "the world's sole superpower" and for holders of dollar-denominated instruments.

Financial deregulation converted the financial system, which formerly served businesses and consumers, into a gambling casino where bets are not covered. These uncovered bets, together with the Fed's zero interest rate policy, have exposed Americans' living standard and wealth to large declines. Retired people living on their savings and investments, IRAs and 401(k)s can earn nothing on their money and are forced to consume their capital, thereby depriving heirs of inheritance. Accumulated wealth is consumed.

As a result of jobs offshoring, the US has become an import-dependent country, dependent on foreign made manufactured goods, clothing, and shoes. When the dollar exchange rate falls, domestic US prices will rise, and US real consumption will take a big hit. Americans will consume less, and their standard of living will fall dramatically.

The serious consequences of the enormous mistakes made in Washington, on Wall Street, and in corporate offices are being held at bay by an untenable policy of low interest rates and a corrupt financial press, while debt rapidly builds. The Fed has been through this experience once before. During WWII the Federal Reserve kept interest rates low in order to aid the Treasury's war finance by minimizing the interest burden of the war debt. The Fed kept the interest rates low by buying the debt issues. The postwar inflation that resulted led to the Federal Reserve-Treasury Accord in 1951, in which agreement was reached that the Federal Reserve would cease monetizing the debt and permit interest rates to rise.

Fed chairman Bernanke has spoken of an "exit strategy" and said that when inflation threatens, he can prevent the inflation by taking the money back out of the banking system. However, he can do that only by selling Treasury bonds, which means interest rates would rise. A rise in interest rates would threaten the derivative structure, cause bond losses, and raise the cost of both private and public debt service. In other words, to prevent inflation from debt monetization would bring on more immediate problems than inflation. Rather than collapse the system, wouldn't the Fed be more likely to inflate away the massive debts?

Eventually, inflation would erode the dollar's purchasing power and use as the reserve currency, and the US government's credit worthiness would waste away. However, the Fed, the politicians, and the financial gangsters would prefer a crisis later rather than sooner. Passing the sinking ship on to the next watch is preferable to going down with the ship oneself. As long as interest rate swaps can be used to boost Treasury bond prices, and as long as naked shorts of bullion can be used to keep silver and gold from rising in price, the false image of the US as a safe haven for investors can be perpetuated.

However, the $230,000,000,000,000,000 in derivative bets by US banks might bring its own surprises. JPMorgan Chase has had to admit that its recently announced derivative loss of $2 billion is more than that.

How much more remains to be seen. According to the Comptroller of the Currency the five largest banks hold 95.7% of all derivatives. The five banks holding $226 trillion in derivative bets are highly leveraged gamblers. For example, JPMorgan Chase has total assets of $1.8 trillion but holds $70 trillion in derivative bets, a ratio of $39 in derivative bets for every dollar of assets. Such a bank doesn't have to lose very many bets before it is busted.

Assets, of course, are not risk-based capital. According to the Comptroller of the Currency report, as of December 31, 2011, JPMorgan Chase held $70.2 trillion in derivatives and only $136 billion in risk-based capital. In other words, the bank's derivative bets are 516 times larger than the capital that covers the bets.

It is difficult to imagine a more reckless and unstable position for a bank to place itself in, but Goldman Sachs takes the cake. That bank's $44 trillion in derivative bets is covered by only $19 billion in risk-based capital, resulting in bets 2,295 times larger than the capital that covers them.

Bets on interest rates comprise 81% of all derivatives. These are the derivatives that support high US Treasury bond prices despite massive increases in US debt and its monetization.

US banks' derivative bets of $230 trillion, concentrated in five banks, are 15.3 times larger than the US GDP. A failed political system that allows unregulated banks to place uncovered bets 15 times larger than the US economy is a system that is headed for catastrophic failure. As the word spreads of the fantastic lack of judgment in the American political and financial systems, the catastrophe in waiting will become a reality.

Everyone wants a solution, so I will provide one. The US government should simply cancel the $230 trillion in derivative bets, declaring them null and void. As no real assets are involved, merely gambling on notional values, the only major effect of closing out or netting all the swaps (mostly over-the-counter contracts between counter-parties) would be to take $230 trillion of leveraged risk out of the financial system. The financial gangsters who want to continue enjoying betting gains while the public underwrites their losses would scream and yell about the sanctity of contracts. However, a government that can murder its own citizens or throw them into dungeons without due process can abolish all the contracts it wants in the name of national security. And most certainly, unlike the war on terror, purging the financial system of the gambling derivatives would vastly improve national security.

First published on June 5, 2012.

[1]. "SLV And Silver Manipulation" https://www.gold-eagle.com/article/slv-and-silver-manipulation

The Hows and Whys of Gold Price Manipulation

The deregulation of the financial system during the Clinton and George W. Bush regimes had the predictable result: financial concentration and reckless behavior. A handful of banks grew so large that financial authorities declared them "too big to fail." Removed from market discipline, the banks became wards of the government requiring massive creation of new money by the Federal Reserve in order to support through the policy of Quantitative Easing the prices of financial instruments on the banks' balance sheets and in order to finance at low interest rates trillion dollar federal budget deficits associated with the long recession caused by the financial crisis.

The Fed's policy of monetizing one trillion dollars of bonds annually put pressure on the US dollar, the value of which declined in terms of gold. When gold hit $1,900 per ounce in 2011, the Federal Reserve realized that $2,000 per ounce could have a psychological impact that would spread into the dollar's exchange rate with other currencies, resulting in a run on the dollar as both foreign and domestic holders sold dollars to avoid the fall in value. Once this realization hit, the manipulation of the gold price moved beyond central bank leasing of gold to bullion dealers in order to create an artificial market supply to absorb demand that otherwise would have pushed gold prices higher. The manipulation consists of the Fed using bullion banks as its agents to sell naked gold shorts in the New York Comex futures market. Short selling drives down the gold price, triggers stop-loss orders and margin calls, and scares participants out of the gold trusts. The bullion banks purchase the deserted shares and present them to the trusts for redemption in bullion. The bullion can then be sold in the London physical gold market, where the sales both ratify the lower price that short-selling achieved on the Comex floor and provide a supply of bullion to meet Asian demands for physical gold as opposed to paper claims on gold.

The evidence of gold price manipulation is clear. In this article we present evidence and describe the process. We conclude that ability to manipulate the gold price is disappearing as physical gold moves from New York and London to Asia, leaving the West with paper claims to gold that greatly exceed the available supply.

The primary venue of the Fed's manipulation activity is the New York Comex exchange, where the world trades gold futures. Each gold futures contract represents one gold 100 ounce bar. The Comex is referred to as a paper gold exchange because of the use of these futures contracts. Although several large global banks are trading members of the Comex, JP Morgan, HSBC and Bank Nova Scotia conduct the majority of the trading volume. Trading of gold (and silver) futures occurs in an auction-style market on the floor of the Comex daily from 8:20 a.m. to 1:30 p.m. New York time. Comex futures trading also occurs on what is known as Globex. Globex is a computerized trading system used for derivatives, currency and futures contracts. It operates continuously except on weekends. Anyone anywhere in the world with access to a computer-based futures trading platform has access to the Globex system.

In addition to the Comex, the Fed also engages in manipulating the price of gold on the far bigger – in terms of total dollar value of trading – London gold market. This market is called the LBMA (London Bullion Marketing Association) market. It is comprised of several large banks who are LMBA market makers known as "bullion banks" (Barclays, Credit Suisse, Deutsche Bank, Goldman Sachs, HSBC, JPMorganChase, Merrill Lynch/Bank of America, Mitsui, Societe Generale, Bank of Nova Scotia and UBS). Whereas the Comex is a "paper gold" exchange, the LBMA is the nexus of global physical gold trading and has been for centuries. When large buyers like Central Banks, big investment funds or wealthy private investors want to buy or sell a large amount of physical gold, they do this on the LBMA market.

The Fed's gold manipulation operation involves exerting forceful downward pressure on the price of gold by selling a massive amount of Comex gold futures, which are dropped like bombs either on the Comex floor during NY trading hours or via the Globex system. A recent example of this occurred on Monday, January 6, 2014. After rallying over $15 in the Asian and European markets, the price of gold suddenly plunged $35 at 10:14 a.m. In a space of less than 60 seconds, more than 12,000 contracts traded – equal to more than 10% of the day's entire volume during the 23 hour trading period in which gold futures trade. There was no apparent news or market event that would have triggered the sudden massive increase in Comex futures selling which caused the sudden steep drop in the price of gold. At the same time, no other securities market (other than silver) experienced any unusual price or volume movement. 12,000 contracts represents 1.2 million ounces of gold, an amount that exceeds by a factor of three the total amount of gold in Comex vaults that could be delivered to the buyers of these contracts.

This manipulation by the Fed involves the short-selling of uncovered Comex gold futures. "Uncovered" means that these are contracts that are sold without any underlying physical gold to deliver if the buyer on the other side decides to ask for delivery. This is also known as "naked short selling." The execution of the manipulative trading is conducted through one of the major gold futures trading banks, such as JPMorganChase, HSBC, and Bank of Nova Scotia. These banks do the actual selling on behalf of the Fed. The manner in which the Fed dumps a large quantity of futures contracts into the market differs from the way in which a bona fide trader looking to sell a big position would operate. The latter would try to work off his position carefully over an extended period of time with the goal of trying to disguise his selling and to disturb the price as little as possible in order to maximize profits or minimize losses. In contrast, the Fed's sales telegraph the intent to drive the price lower with no regard for preserving profits or fear or incurring losses, because the goal is to inflict as much damage as possible on the price and intimidate potential buyers.

The Fed also actively manipulates gold via the Globex system. The Globex market is punctuated with periods of "quiet" time in which the trade volume is very low. It is during these periods that the Fed has its agent banks bombard the market with massive quantities of gold futures over a very brief period of time for the purpose of driving the price lower. The banks know that there are very few buyers around during these time periods to absorb the selling. This drives the price lower than if the selling operation occurred when the market is more active.

A primary example of this type of intervention occurred on December 18, 2013, immediately after the FOMC announced its decision to reduce bond purchases by $10 billion monthly beginning in January 2014. With the rest of the trading world closed, including the actual Comex floor trading, a massive amount of Comex gold futures were sold on the Globex computer trading system during one of its least active periods. This selling pushed the price of gold down $23 dollars in the space of two hours. The next wave of futures selling occurred in the overnight period starting at 2:30 a.m. NY time on December 19th. This time of day is one of the least active trading periods during any 23 hour trading day (there's one hour when gold futures stop trading altogether). Over 4900 gold contracts representing 14.5 tonnes of gold were dumped into the Globex system in a 2-minute period from 2:40-2:41 a.m, resulting in a $24 decline in the price of gold. This wasn't the end of the selling. Shortly after the Comex floor opened later that morning, another 1,654 contracts were sold followed shortly after by another 2,295 contracts. This represented another 12.2 tonnes of gold. Then at 10:00 a.m. EST, another 2,530 contracts were unloaded on the market followed by an additional 3,482 contracts just six minutes later. These sales represented another 18.7 tonnes of gold.

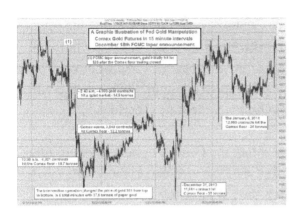

Altogether, in 6 minutes during an eight hour period, a total amount of 37.6 tonnes (a "tonne" is a metric ton – about 10% more weight than a US "ton") of gold future contracts were sold. The contracts sold during these 6 minutes accounted for 10% of the total volume during that 23 hours period of time. Four-tenths of one percent of the trading day accounted for 10% of the total volume. The gold represented by the futures contracts that were sold during these 6 minutes was a multiple of the amount of physical gold available to Comex for delivery.

The purpose of driving the price of gold down was to prevent the announced reduction in bond purchases (the so-called tapering) from sending the dollar, stock and bond markets down. The markets understand that the liquidity that Quantitative Easing provides is the reason for the high bond and stock prices and understand also that the gains from the rising stock market discourage gold purchases. Previously when the Fed had mentioned that it might reduce bond purchases, the stock market fell and bonds sold off. To neutralize the market scare, the Fed manipulated both gold and stock markets.

While the manipulation of the gold market has been occurring since the start of the bull market in gold in late 2000, this pattern of rampant manipulative short-selling of futures contracts has been occurring on a more intense basis over the last 2 years, during gold's price decline from a high of $1900 in September 2011. The attack on gold's price typically will occur during one of several key points in time during the

23 hour Globex trading period. The most common is right at the open of Comex gold futures trading, which is 8:20 a.m. New York time. To set the tone of trading, the price of gold is usually knocked down when the Comex opens. Here are the other most common times when gold futures are sold during illiquid Globex system time periods:

– 6:00 p.m NY time weekdays, when the Globex system re-opens after closing for an hour;
– 6:00 p.m. Sunday evening NY time when Globex opens for the week;
– 2:30 a.m. NY time, when Shanghai Gold Exchange closes
– 4:00 a.m. NY time, just after the morning gold "fix" on the London gold market (LBMA);
2:00 p.m. NY time any day but especially on Friday, after the Comex floor trading has closed – it's an illiquid Globex-only session and the rest of the world is still closed.

In addition to selling futures contracts on the Comex exchange in order to drive the price of gold lower, the Fed and its agent bullion banks also intermittently sell large quantities of physical gold in London's LBMA gold market. The process of buying and selling actual physical gold is more cumbersome and complicated than trading futures contracts. When a large supply of physical gold hits the London market all at once, it forces the market a lot lower than an equivalent amount of futures contracts would. As the availability of large amounts of physical gold is limited, these "physical gold drops" are used carefully and selectively and at times when the intended effect on the market will be most effective.

The primary purpose for short-selling futures contracts on Comex is to protect the dollar's value from the growing supply of dollars created by the Fed's policy of Quantitative Easing. The Fed's use of gold leasing to supply gold to the market in order to reduce the rate of rise in the gold price has drained the Fed's gold holdings and is creating a shortage in physical gold. Historically most big buyers would leave their gold for safe-keeping in the vaults of the Fed, Bank of England or private bullion banks rather than incur the cost of moving gold to local depositories. However, large purchasers of gold, such as China, now require actual delivery of the gold they buy.

Demands for gold delivery have forced the use of extraordinary and apparently illegal tactics in order to obtain physical gold to settle futures contracts that demand delivery and to be able to deliver bullion purchased on the London market (LBMA). Gold for delivery is obtained from opaque Central Bank gold leasing transactions, from "borrowing" client gold held by the bullion banks like JP Morgan in their LBMA custodial vaults, and by looting the gold trusts, such as GLD, of their gold holdings by purchasing large blocks of shares and redeeming the shares for gold.

Central Bank gold leasing occurs when Central Banks take physical gold they hold in custody and lease it to bullion banks. The banks sell the gold on the London physical gold market. The gold leasing transaction makes available physical gold that can be delivered to buyers in quantities that would not be available at existing prices. The use of gold leasing to manipulate the price of gold became a prevalent practice in the 1990's. While Central Banks admit to engaging in gold lease transactions, they do not admit to its purpose, which is to moderate rises in the price of gold, although Fed Chairman Alan Greenspan did admit during Congressional testimony on derivatives in 1998 that "Central banks stand ready to lease gold in increasing quantities should the price rise."

Another method of obtaining bullion for sale or delivery is known as "rehypothecation." Rehypothecation occurs when a bank or brokerage firm "borrows" client assets being held in custody by banks. Technically, bank/brokerage firm clients sign an agreement when they open an account in which the assets in the account might be pledged for loans, like margin loans. But the banks then take pledged assets and use them for their own purpose rather than the client's. This is rehypothecation. Although Central Banks fully disclose the practice of leasing gold, banks/brokers do not publicly disclose the details of their rehypothecation activities.

Over the course of the 13-year gold bull market, gold leasing and rehypothecation operations have largely depleted most of the gold in the vaults of the Federal Reserve, Bank of England, European Central Bank and private bullion banks such as JPMorganChase. The depletion of vault gold became a problem when Venezuela was the first country to repatriate all of its gold being held by foreign Central Banks, primarily the Fed and the BOE. Venezuela's request was provoked by rumors circulating the market that gold was being leased and hypothecated in increasing quantities. About a year later, Germany made a similar request. The Fed refused to honor Germany's request and, instead, negotiated a seven year timeline in which it would ship back 300 of Germany's 1500 tonnes. This made it apparent that the Fed did not have the gold it was supposed to be holding for Germany.

Why does the Fed need seven years in which to return 20 percent of Germany's gold? The answer is that the Fed does not have the gold in its vault to deliver. In 2011 it took four months to return Venezuela's 160 tonnes of gold. Obviously, the gold was not readily at hand and had to be borrowed, perhaps from unsuspecting private owners who mistakenly believe that their gold is held in trust.

Western central banks have pushed fractional gold reserve banking to the point that they haven't enough reserves to cover withdrawals. Fractional reserve banking originated when medieval goldsmiths learned that owners of gold stored in their vault seldom withdrew the gold. Instead, those who had gold on deposit circulated paper claims to gold. This allowed goldsmiths to lend gold that they did not have by issuing paper receipts. This is what the Fed has done. The Fed has created paper claims to gold that does not exist in physical form and sold these claims in mass quantities in order to drive down the gold price. The paper claims to gold are a large multiple of the amount of actual gold available for delivery. The Reserve Bank of India reports that the ratio of paper claims to gold exceed the amount of gold available for delivery by 93:1.

Fractional reserve systems break down when too many depositors or holders of paper claims present them for delivery. Breakdown is occurring in the Fed's fractional bullion operation. In the last few years the Asian markets – specifically and especially the Chinese – are demanding actual physical delivery of the bullion they buy. This has created a sense of urgency among the Fed, Treasury and the bullion banks to utilize any means possible to flush out as many weak holders of gold as possible with orchestrated price declines in order to acquire physical gold that can be delivered to Asian buyers.

The $650 decline in the price of gold since it hit $1900 in September 2011 is the result of a manipulative effort designed both to protect the dollar from Quantitative Easing and to free up enough gold to satisfy Asian demands for delivery of gold purchases.

Around the time of the substantial drop in gold's price in April, 2013, the Bank of England's public records showed a 1300 tonne decline in the amount of gold being held in the BOE bullion vaults. This is a fact that has not been denied or reasonably explained by BOE officials despite several published inquiries. This is gold that was being held in custody but not owned by the Bank of England. The truth is that the 1300 tonnes is gold that was required to satisfy delivery demands from the large Asian buyers. It is one thing for the Fed or BOE to sell, lease or rehypothecate gold out of their vault that is being safe-kept knowing the entitled owner likely won't ask for it anytime soon, but it is another thing altogether to default on a gold delivery to Asians demanding delivery.

Default on delivery of purchased gold would terminate the Federal Reserve's ability to manipulate the gold price. The entire world would realize that the demand for gold greatly exceeds the supply, and the price of gold would explode upwards. The Federal Reserve would lose control and would have to abandon Quantitative Easing. Otherwise, the exchange value of the US dollar would collapse, bringing to an end US financial hegemony over the world.

Last April, the major takedown in the gold price began with Goldman Sachs issuing a "technical analysis" report with an $850 price target (gold was around $1650 at that time). Goldman Sachs also broadcast to every major brokerage firm and hedge fund in New York that gold was going to drop hard in price and urged brokers to get their clients out of all physical gold holdings and/or shares in physical gold trusts like GLD. GLD and other gold ETFs are trusts that purchase physical gold/silver bullion and issue shares that represent claims on the bullion holdings. The shares are marketed as investments in gold, but represent claims that can only be redeemed in very large blocks of shares, such as 100,000, and perhaps only by bullion banks. GLD is the largest gold ETF (exchange traded fund), but not the only one. The purpose of Goldman Sachs' announcement was to spur gold sales that would magnify the price effect of the short-selling of futures contracts. Heavy selling of futures contracts drove down the gold price and forced sales of GLD and other ETF shares, which were bought up by the bullion banks and redeemed for gold.

At the beginning of 2013, GLD held 1350 tonnes of gold. By April 12th, when the heavy intervention operation began, GLD held 1,154 tonnes. After the series of successive raids in April, the removal of gold from GLD accelerated and currently there are 793 tonnes left in the trust. In a little more than one year, more than 41% of the gold bars held by GLD were removed – most of that after the mid-April intervention operation.

In addition, the Bank of England made its gold available for purchase by the bullion banks in order to add to the ability to deliver gold to Asian purchasers.

The financial media, which is used to discredit gold as a safe haven from the printing of fiat currencies, claims that the decline in GLD's physical gold is an indication that the public is rejecting gold as an investment. In fact, the manipulation of the gold price downward is being done systematically in order to coerce holders of GLD to unload their shares. This enables the bullion banks to accumulate the amount of shares required to redeem gold from the GLD Trust and ship that gold to Asia in order to meet the enormous delivery demands. For example, in the event described above on January 6th, 14% of GLD's total volume for the day traded in a 1-minute period starting at 10:14 a.m. The total volume on the day for GLD was almost 35% higher than the average trading volume in GLD over the previous ten trading days.

Before 2013, the amount of gold in the GLD vault was one of the largest stockpiles of gold in the world. The swift decline in GLD's gold inventory is the most glaring indicator of the growing shortage of physical gold supply that can be delivered to the Asian market and other large physical gold buyers. The more the price of gold is driven down in the Western paper gold market, the higher the demand for physical bullion in Asian markets. In addition, several smaller physical gold ETFs have experienced substantial gold withdrawals. Including the more than 100 tonnes of gold that has disappeared from the Comex vaults in the last year, well over 1,000 tonnes of gold has been removed from the various ETFs and bank custodial vaults in the last year. Furthermore, there is no telling how much gold that is kept in bullion bank private vaults on behalf of wealthy investors has been rehypothecated. All of this gold was removed in order to avoid defaulting on delivery demands being imposed by Asian commercial, investment and sovereign gold buyers.

The Federal Reserve seems to be trapped. The Fed is creating approximately 1,000 billion new US dollars annually in order to support the prices of debt related derivatives on the books of the few banks that have been declared to be "to big to fail" and in order to finance the large federal budget deficit that is now too large to be financed by the recycling of Chinese and OPEC trade surpluses into US Treasury debt. The problem with Quantitative Easing is that the annual creation of an enormous supply of new dollars is raising questions among American and foreign holders of vast amounts of US dollar-denominated financial instruments. They see their dollar holdings being diluted by the creation of new dollars that are not the result of an increase in wealth or GDP and for which there is no demand.

Quantitative Easing is a threat to the dollar's exchange value. The Federal Reserve, fearful that the falling value of the dollar in terms of gold would spread into the currency markets and depreciate the dollar, decided to employ more extreme methods of gold price manipulation. When gold hit $1,900, the Federal Reserve panicked. The manipulation of the gold price became more intense. It became more imperative to drive down the price, but the lower price resulted in higher Asian demand for which scant supplies of gold were available to meet.

Having created more paper gold claims than there is gold to satisfy, the Fed has used its dependent bullion banks to loot the gold exchange traded funds (ETFs) of gold in order to avoid default on Asian deliveries. Default would collapse the fractional bullion system that allows the Fed to drive down the gold price and protect the dollar from QE.

What we are witnessing is our central bank pulling out all stops on integrity and lawfulness in order to serve a small handful of banks that financial deregulation allowed to become "too big to fail" at the expense of our economy and our currency. When the Fed runs out of gold to borrow, to rehypothecate, and to loot from ETFs, the Fed will have to abandon QE or the US dollar will collapse and with it Washington's power to exercise hegemony over the world.

Dave Kranzler traded high yield bonds for Bankers Trust for a decade. As a co-founder and principal of Golden Returns Capital LLC, he manages the Precious Metals Opportunity Fund.

First published on January 17, 2014.

How Economists and Policymakers Murdered Our Economy

The economy has been debilitated by the offshoring of middle class jobs for the benefit of corporate profits and by the Federal Reserve's policy of Quantitative Easing in order to support a few oversized banks that the government protects from market discipline. Not only does QE distort bond and stock markets, it threatens the value of the dollar and has resulted in manipulation of the gold price.

When US corporations send jobs offshore, the GDP, consumer income, tax base, and careers associated with the jobs go abroad with the jobs. Corporations gain the additional profits at large costs to the economy in terms of less employment, less economic growth, reduced state, local and federal tax revenues, wider deficits, and impairments of social services.

When policymakers permitted banks to become independent of market discipline, they made the banks an unresolved burden on the economy. Authorities have provided no honest report on the condition of the banks. It remains to be seen if the Federal Reserve can create enough money to monetize enough debt to rescue the banks without collapsing the US dollar. It would have been far cheaper to let the banks fail and be reorganized.

US policymakers and their echo chamber in the economics profession have let the country down badly. They claimed that there was a "New Economy" to take the place of the "old economy" jobs that were moved offshore. As I have pointed out for a decade, US jobs statistics show no sign of the promised "New Economy."

The same policymakers and economists who told us that "markets are self-regulating" and that the financial sector could safely be deregulated also confused jobs offshoring with free trade. Hyped "studies" were put together designed to prove that jobs offshoring was good for the US economy. It is difficult to fathom how such destructive errors could consistently be made by policymakers and economists for more than a decade. Were these mistakes or cover for a narrow and selfish agenda?

In June, 2009 happy talk appeared about "the recovery," now 4.5 years old. As John Williams (shadowstats.com) has made clear, "the recovery" is entirely the artifact of the understated measure of inflation used to deflate nominal GDP. By under-measuring inflation, the government can show low, but positive, rates of real GDP growth. No other indicator supports the claim of economic recovery.

John Williams writes that consumer inflation, if properly measured, is running around 9%, far above the 2% figure that is the Fed's target and more in line with what consumers are actually experiencing. We have just had a 6.5% annual increase in the cost of a postage stamp.

The Fed's target inflation rate is said to be low, but Simon Black points out that the result of a lifetime of 2% annual inflation is the loss of 75% of the purchasing power of the currency. He uses the cost of sending a postcard to illustrate the decline in the purchasing power of median household income today compared to 1951. That year it cost one cent to send a post card. As household income was $4,237, the household could send 423,700 postcards. Today the comparable income figure is $51,017. As it costs 34 cents to send one postcard, today's household can only afford to send 150,050 postcards. Nominal income rose 12 times, and the cost of sending a postcard rose 34 times.

Just as the American people know that there is more inflation than is reported, they know that there is no recovery. A Gallup Poll reported this month that only 28% of Americans are satisfied with the economy.

From hard experience, Americans have also caught on that "free trade agreements" are nothing but vehicles for moving their jobs abroad. The latest effort by the corporations to loot and defraud the public is known

65

as the "Trans-Pacific Partnership." "Fast-tracking" the bill allowed the corporations to write the bill in secret without congressional input. Some research shows that 90% of Americans will suffer income losses under TPP, while wealth becomes even more concentrated at the top.

TPP affects every aspect of our lives from what we eat to the Internet to the environment. According to Kevin Zeese in Alternet, "the leak of the [TPP] Intellectual Property Chapter revealed that it created a path to patent everything imaginable, including plants and animals, to turn everything into a commodity for profit."

The secretly drafted TPP also creates authority for the executive branch to change existing US law to make the laws that were not passed in secret compatible with the secretly written trade bill. Buy American requirements and any attempt to curtail jobs offshoring would become illegal "restraints on trade."

If the House and Senate are willing to turn over their legislative function to the executive branch, they might as well abolish themselves.

The financial media has been helping the Federal Reserve and the banks to cover up festering problems with rosy hype, but realization that there are serious unresolved problems might be spreading. Last week interest rates on 30-day T-bills turned negative. That means people were paying more for a bond than it would return at maturity. Dave Kranzler sees this as a sign of rising uncertainty about banks. Reminiscent of the Cyprus banks' limits on withdrawals, last Friday (January 24) the BBC reported that the large UK bank HSBC is preventing customers from withdrawing cash from their accounts in excess of several thousand pounds.

If and when uncertainty spreads to the dollar, the real crisis will arrive, likely followed by high inflation, exchange controls, pension confiscations, and resurrected illegality of owning gold and silver.

Capitalist greed aided and abetted by economists and policymakers will have destroyed America.

First published on January 25, 2014.

How Junk Economists Help The Rich Impoverish The Working Class

Last week, I explained how economists and policymakers destroyed our economy for the sake of short-term corporate profits from jobs offshoring and financial deregulation.

That same week Business Week published an article, "Factory Jobs Are Gone. Get Over It," by Charles Kenny. Kenny expresses the view of establishment economists, such as Brookings Institute economist Justin Wolfers who wants to know "What's with the political fetish for manufacturing? Are factories really so awesome?"

"Not really," Kenny says. Citing Eric Fisher of the Cleveland Federal Reserve Bank, Kenny reports that wages rise most rapidly in those states that most quickly abandon manufacturing. Kenny cites Gary Hufbauer, once an academic colleague of mine now at the Peterson Institute, who claims that the 2009 tariffs applied to Chinese tire imports cost US consumers $1 billion in higher prices and 3,731 lost retail jobs. Note the precision of the jobs loss, right down to the last 31.

In support of the argument that Americans are better off without manufacturing jobs, Kenny cites MIT and Harvard academic economists to the effect that there is no evidence that manufacturing tends to cluster, thus disputing the view that there are economies from manufacturers tending to congregate in the same areas where they benefit from an experienced work force and established supply chains.

Perhaps the MIT and Harvard economists did their study after US manufacturing centers became shells of their former selves and Detroit lost 25% of its population, Gary Indiana lost 22% of its population, Flint Michigan lost 18% of its population, Cleveland lost 17% of its population, and St Louis lost 20% of its population. If the economists' studies were done after manufacturing had departed, they would not find manufacturing concentrated in locations where it formerly

68

flourished. MIT and Harvard economists might find this an idea too large to comprehend.

Kenny's answer to the displaced manufacturing workers is – you guessed it – jobs training. He cites MIT economist David Autor who thinks the problem is the federal government only spends $1 on retraining for every $400 that it spends on supporting displaced workers.

These arguments are so absurd as to be mindless. Let's examine them. What jobs are the displaced manufacturing workers to be trained for? Why, service jobs, of course. Kenny actually thinks that "service industries – hotels, hospitals, media, and accounting – have taken up the slack." (I don't know where he gets media and accounting from; scant sign of such jobs are found in the payroll jobs reports.) Moreover, service jobs have certainly not taken up the slack as the rising rate of long-term unemployment and declining labor force participation rate prove.

Nontradable service sector jobs such as hotel maids, hospital orderlies, retail clerks, waitresses and bartenders are low productivity, low value-added jobs that cannot pay incomes comparable to manufacturing jobs. The long term decline in real median family income relates to the movement offshore of manufacturing jobs and tradable professional service jobs, such as software engineering, IT, research and design.

Moreover, domestic service jobs do not produce exportable goods and services. A country without manufactures has little with which to earn foreign exchange in order to pay for its imports of its shoes, clothing, manufactured goods, high-technology products, Apple computers, and increasingly food. Therefore, that country's trade deficit widens as each year it owes more and more to foreigners.

A country whose best known products are fraudulent and toxic financial instruments and GMO foods that no one wants cannot pay for its imports except by signing over its existing assets. The foreigners buy up US assets with their trade surpluses. Consequently, income from rents, interest, dividends, capital gains, and profits leave US pockets for foreign pockets. It is a safe bet that Hufbauer did not include any of these costs, or maybe even the loss of US tire workers' wages and tire manufacturers' profits, when he concluded that trying to save US tire manufacturing jobs cost more than it was worth.

Eric Fisher's argument that the highest wage growth is found in areas where higher productivity manufacturing jobs are most rapidly replaced with lower productivity domestic service jobs is beyond absurd. (Possibly Fisher did not say this; I'm taking Kenny's word for it.) It has always been a foundation of labor economics that workers are paid the value of their contribution to output. Manufacturing employees working with technology embodied in plant and equipment produce more value per man hour than maids changing sheets and bartenders mixing drinks.

In my book, The Failure of Laissez Faire Capitalism And Economic Dissolution Of The West (2013), I point out the obvious mistakes in "studies" by Matthew Slaughter, a former member of the President's Council of Economic Advisors, and Harvard professor Michael Porter. These academic economists conclude on the basis of extraordinary errors and ignorance of empirical facts, that jobs offshoring is good for Americans. They were able to reach this conclusion despite the absence of any visibility of this good, and they hold to this absurd conclusion despite the inability of a "recovery" (or lack of one) that is 4.5 years old to get off the ground and get employment back up to where it was six years ago. They hold to their "education is the answer" solution despite the growing percentage of university graduates who cannot find employment.

Michael Hudson is certainly correct to call economists purveyors of "junk economics." Indeed, I wonder if economists even have junk value. But they are well paid by Wall Street and the offshoring corporations.

What the Brookings Institute's Justin Wolfers needs to ask himself is: what is the redefinition of economic development? For my lifetime the definition of a developed economy is an industrialized economy. It has always been "the industrialized countries" that occupy the status of "developed economies," contrasted with "undeveloped countries," "developing countries," and "emerging economies." How is an economy developed if it is shedding its industry and manufacturing? This is the reverse of the development process. Without realizing it, Kenny describes the unravelling of the US economy when he describes the decline of US manufacturing from 28 percent of US GDP in 1953 to 12% in 2012. The US now has the work force of a third world country, with the vast bulk of the population employed in lowly paid domestic services. The US work force no longer looks like the work force of a developed country. It looks like third world India's work force of three decades ago.

Kenny and junk economists speak of the decline of US manufacturing jobs as if they are not being offshored to countries where labor is cheap but replaced by automation. No doubt there has been automation, and more ways of replacing humans with machines will be found. But if manufacturing jobs are things of the past, why is China's sudden and rapid rise to economic power accompanied by 100 million manufacturing jobs? Apple computers are not made in China by robots. If robots are making Apple computers, it would be just as cheap to make the computers in the US. The Chinese manufacturing workforce is almost the size of the entire US work force.

US companies employ Americans to market the products that are produced abroad for sale in the US. This is why US corporations employ Americans mainly in service jobs. Foreigners make the goods, and Americans sell them.

Economic development has always been about acquiring the capital, technology, business knowledge, and trained workforce to make valuable things that can be sold at home and abroad. US capital and technology are being located abroad, and the trained domestic workforce is disappearing from disuse and abandonment. The US is falling out of the ranks of the industrialized countries and is on the path to becoming an undeveloped economy.

First published on January 28, 2014.

The Fed Is The Great Deceiver

Paul Craig Roberts and Dave Kranzler

Is the Fed "tapering"? Did the Fed really cut its bond purchases during the three month period November 2013 through January 2014? Apparently not if foreign holders of Treasuries are unloading them.

From November 2013 through January 2014 Belgium with a GDP of $480 billion purchased $141.2 billion of US Treasury bonds. Somehow Belgium came up with enough money to allocate during a 3-month period 29 percent of its annual GDP to the purchase of US Treasury bonds.

Certainly Belgium did not have a budget surplus of $141.2 billion. Was Belgium running a trade surplus during a 3-month period equal to 29 percent of Belgium GDP?

No, Belgium's trade and current accounts are in deficit.

Did Belgium's central bank print $141.2 billion worth of euros in order to make the purchase?

No, Belgium is a member of the euro system, and its central bank cannot increase the money supply.

So where did the $141.2 billion come from?

There is only one source. The money came from the US Federal Reserve, and the purchase was laundered through Belgium in order to hide the fact that actual Federal Reserve bond purchases during November 2013 through January 2014 were $112 billion per month.

In other words, during those 3 months there was a sharp rise in bond purchases by the Fed. The Fed's actual bond purchases for those three months are $27 billion per month above the original $85 billion monthly purchase and $47 billion above the official $65 billion monthly purchase at that time. (In March 2014, official QE was tapered to $55 billion per month and to $45 billion for May.)

Why did the Federal Reserve have to purchase so many bonds above the announced amounts and why did the Fed have to launder and hide the purchase?

Some country or countries, unknown at this time, for reasons we do not know dumped $104 billion in Treasuries in one week.

Another curious aspect of the sale and purchase laundered through Belgium is that the sale was not executed and cleared via the Fed's own National Book-Entry System (NBES), which was designed to facilitate the sale and ownership transfer of securities for Fed custodial customers. Instead, The foreign owner(s) of the Treasuries removed them from the Federal Reserve's custodial holdings and sold them through the Euroclear securities clearing system, which is based in Brussels, Belgium.

We do not know why or who. We know that there was a withdrawal, a sale, a drop in the Federal Reserve's "Securities held in Custody for Foreign Official and International Accounts," an inexplicable rise in Belgium's holdings, and then the bonds reappear in the Federal Reserve's custodial accounts.

What are the reasons for this deception by the Federal Reserve?

The Fed realized that its policy of Quantitative Easing initiated in order to support the balance sheets of "banks too big to fail" and to lower the Treasury's borrowing cost was putting pressure on the US dollar's value. Tapering was a way of reassuring holders of dollars and dollar-denominated financial instruments that the Fed was going to reduce and eventually end the printing of new dollars with which to support

74

financial markets. The image of foreign governments bailing out of Treasuries could unsettle the markets that the Fed was attempting to sooth by tapering.

A hundred billion dollar sale of US Treasuries is a big sale. If the seller was a big holder of Treasuries, the sale could signal the bond market that a big holder might be selling Treasuries in large chunks. The Fed would want to keep the fact and identity of such a seller secret in order to avoid a stampede out of Treasuries. Such a stampede would raise interest rates, collapse US financial markets, and raise the cost of financing the US debt. To avoid the rise in interest rates, the Fed would have to accept the risk to the dollar of purchasing all the bonds. This would be a no-win situation for the Fed, because a large increase in QE would unsettle the market for US dollars.

Washington's power ultimately rests on the dollar as world reserve currency. This privilege, attained at Bretton Woods following World War 2, allows the US to pay its bills by issuing debt. The world currency role also gives the US the power to cut countries out of the international payments system and to impose sanctions.

As impelled as the Fed is to protect the large banks that sit on the board of directors of the NY Fed, the Fed has to protect the dollar. That the Fed believed that it could not buy the bonds outright but needed to disguise its purchase by laundering it through Belgium suggests that the Fed is concerned that the world is losing confidence in the dollar.

If the world loses confidence in the dollar, the cost of living in the US would rise sharply as the dollar drops in value. Economic hardship and poverty would worsen. Political instability would rise.

If the dollar lost substantial value, the dollar would lose its reserve currency status. Washington would not be able to issue new debt or new dollars in order to pay its bills.

Its wars and hundreds of overseas military bases could not be financed.

The withdrawal from unsustainable empire would begin. The rest of the world would see this as the silver lining in the collapse of the international monetary system brought on by the hubris and arrogance of Washington.

First published on May 12, 2014.

Rigged Gold Price Distorts Perception of Economic Reality

Paul Craig Roberts and Dave Kranzler

The Federal Reserve and its bullion bank agents (JP Morgan, Scotia, and HSBC) have been using naked short-selling to drive down the price of gold since September 2011. The latest containment effort began in mid-July of this year, after gold had moved higher in price from the beginning of June and was threatening to take out key technical levels, which would have triggered a flood of buying from hedge funds.

The Fed and its agents rig the gold price in the New York Comex futures (paper gold) market. The bullion banks have the ability to print an unlimited supply of gold contracts which are sold in large volumes at times when Comex activity is light. Generally, on the other side of the trade the buyers of contracts are large hedge funds and other speculators, who use the contracts to speculate on the direction of the gold price. The hedge funds and speculators have no interest in acquiring physical gold and settle their bets in cash, which makes it possible for the bullion banks to sell claims to gold that they cannot back with physical metal. Contracts sold without underlying gold to back them are called "uncovered contracts" or "naked shorts." It is illegal to engage in naked shorting in the stock and bond markets, but it is permitted in the gold futures market.

The fact that the price of gold is determined in a futures market in which paper claims to gold are traded merely to speculate on price means that the Fed and its bank agents can suppress the price of gold even though demand for physical gold is rising. If there were strict requirements that gold shorts could not be naked and had to be backed by the seller's possession of physical gold represented by the futures contract, the Federal Reserve and its agents would be unable to control the price of gold, and the gold price would be much higher than it is now. Gold price manipulation is used when demand for delivery of gold bullion begins to put upward pressure on the price of gold and hedge funds speculate on the rising price of gold by purchasing large quantities of Comex futures contracts (paper gold). This speculation accelerates the upward move in the price of gold. The TF Metals Report provides a good description of this illegal manipulation of the gold market:

"Over a period of 10 weeks to begin the year, the Comex bullion banks were able to limit the rally to only 15% by supplying the "market" with 95,000 brand new naked short contracts. That's 9.5MM ounces of make-believe paper gold or about 295 metric tonnes.

"Over a period of just 5 weeks in June and July, the Comex bullion banks were able to limit the rally to only 7% by supplying the "market" with 79,000 brand new naked short contracts. That's 7.9MM ounces of make-believe paper gold or about 246 metric tonnes."

In previous columns, we have documented the heavy short-selling into light trading periods. The bullion banks do not have nearly enough gold in their possession to make deliveries to the buyers if the buyers decide to stand for delivery per the terms of the paper gold contract. The reason this scheme works is because the majority of the buyers of the contracts are speculators, not gold purchasers, and never demand delivery of the gold. Instead, they settle the contracts in cash. They are looking for short-term trading profits, not for a gold hedge against currency inflation. If a majority of the longs (the purchasers of the contracts) required delivery of the gold, the regulators would not tolerate the extent to which gold is shorted with uncovered contracts.

In our opinion, the manipulation is illegal, because it is insider trading. The bullion banks that short the gold market are clearing members of the Comex/NYMEX/CME. In that role, the bullion banks have access to the computer system used to clear and settle trades, which means that the bullion banks have access to all the trading positions, including those of the hedge funds. When the hedge funds are in the deepest, the bullion banks dump naked shorts on the Comex, driving down the futures price, which triggers selling from stop-loss orders and margin calls that drive the price down further. Then the bullion banks buy the contracts at a lower price than they sold and pocket the difference, simultaneously serving the Fed by protecting the dollar from the Fed's loose monetary policy by lowering the gold price and preventing the concern that a rising gold price would bring to the dollar.

Since mid-July, nearly every night in the US the price of gold remains steady or drifts higher. This is when the eastern hemisphere markets are open and the market players are busy buying physical gold for which delivery is mandatory. But as regular as clockwork, following the close of the Asian markets, the London and New York paper gold markets open, and the price of gold is immediately taken lower as paper gold contracts flood into the market setting a negative tone for the day's trading.

Gold serves as a warning for aware people that financial and economic trouble are brewing. For instance, from the period of time just before the tech bubble collapsed (January 2000) until just before the collapse of Bear Stearns triggered the Great Financial Crisis (March 2008), gold rose in value from $250 to $1020 per ounce, or just over 400%. Moreover, in the period since the Great Financial Collapse, gold has risen 61% despite claims that the financial system was repaired. It was up as much as 225% (September 2011) before the Fed began the systematic take-down and containment of gold in order to protect the dollar from the massive creation of new dollars required by Quantitative Easing.

The US economy and financial system are in worse condition than the Fed and Treasury claim and the financial media reports. Both public and private debt burdens are high. Corporations are borrowing from banks in order to buy back their own stocks. This leaves corporations with new debt but without income streams from new investments with which to service the debt. Retail stores are in trouble, including dollar store chains. The housing market is showing signs of renewed downturn. The September 16 release of the 2013 Income and Poverty report shows that real median household income has declined to the level in 1994 two decades ago and is actually lower than in the late 1960s and early 1970s. The combination of high debt and decline in real income means that there is no engine to drive the economy.

In the 21st century, US debt and money creation has not been matched by an increase in real goods and services. The implication of this mismatch is inflation. Without the price-rigging by the bullion banks, gold and silver would be reflecting these inflation expectations.

The dollar is also in trouble because its role as world reserve currency is threatened by the abuse of this role in order to gain financial hegemony over others and to punish with sanctions those countries that do not comply with the goals of US foreign policy. The Wolfowitz Doctrine, which is the basis of US foreign policy, says that it is imperative for Washington to prevent the rise of other countries, such as Russia and China, that can limit the exercise of US power.

Sanctions and the threat of sanctions encourage other countries to leave the dollar payments system and to abandon the petrodollar. The BRICS (Brazil, Russia, India, China, South Africa) have formed to do precisely that. Russia and China have arranged a massive long-term energy deal that avoids use of the US dollar. Both countries are settling their trade accounts with each other in their own currencies, and this practice is spreading. China is considering a gold-backed yuan, which would make the Chinese currency highly desirable as a reserve asset. It is possible that the Fed's attack on gold is also aimed at making Chinese and Russian gold accumulation less supportive of their currencies. A currency linked to a falling gold price is not the same as a currency linked to a rising gold price.

It is unclear whether the new Chinese gold exchange in Shanghai will displace the London and New York futures markets. Naked short-selling is not permitted in the Chinese gold exchange. The world could end up with two gold futures markets: one based on assessments of reality, and the other based on gambling and price-rigging.

The future will also determine whether the role of reserve currency has been overtaken by time. The US dollar took that role in the aftermath of World War II, a time when the US had the only industrial economy that had not been destroyed in the war. A stable means of settling international accounts was needed. Today there are many economies that have tradable currencies, and accounts can be settled between countries in their own currencies. There is no longer a need for a single reserve currency. As this realization spreads, pressure on the dollar's value will intensify.

For a period the Federal Reserve can support the dollar's exchange value by pressuring Japan and the European Central Bank to print their currencies with which to support the dollar with purchases in the foreign exchange market. Other countries, such as Switzerland, will print their own currencies so as not to endanger their exports by a rise in the dollar price of their exports. But eventually the large US trade deficits produced by offshoring the production of goods and services sold into US markets and the collapse of the middle class and tax base caused by jobs offshoring will destroy the value of the US dollar.

When that day arrives, US living standards, already endangered, will plummet. American power will have been destroyed by corporate greed and the Fed's policy of sacrificing the US economy in order to save four or five mega-banks, whose former executives control the Fed, the US Treasury, and the federal financial regulatory agencies.

First published on September 22, 2014.

A Global House Of Cards

As most Americans, if not the financial media, are aware, Quantitative Easing (a euphemism for printing money) has failed to bring back the US economy.

So why has Japan adopted the policy? Since the heavy duty money printing began in 2013, the Japanese yen has fallen 35% against the US dollar, a big cost for a country dependent on energy imports. Moreover, the Japanese economy has shown no growth in response to the QE stimulus to justify the rising price of imports.

Despite the economy's lack of response to the stimulus, last month the Bank of Japan announced a 60% increase in quantitative easing – from 50 to 80 trillion yen annually. Albert Edwards, a strategist at Societe Generale, predicts that the Japanese printing press will drive the yen down from 115 yen to the dollar to 145.

This is a prediction, but why risk the reality? What does Japan have to gain from currency depreciation? What is the thinking behind the policy?

An easy explanation is that Japan is being ordered to destroy its currency in order to protect the over-printed US dollar. As a vassal state, Japan suffers under US political and financial hegemony and is powerless to resist Washington's pressure.

The official explanation is that, like the Federal Reserve, the Bank of Japan professes to believe in the Phillips Curve, which associates economic growth with inflation. The supply-side economic policy implemented by the Reagan administration disproved the Phillips Curve belief that economic growth was inconsistent with a declining or a stable rate of inflation. However, establishment economists refuse to take note and continue with the dogmas with which they are comfortable.

In the US QE caused inflation in stock and bond prices as most of the liquidity provided went into financial markets instead of into consumers' pockets. There is more consumer price inflation than the official inflation measures report, as the measures are designed to under-report inflation, thereby saving money on COLA adjustments, but the main effect of QE has been unrealistic stock and bond prices.

The Bank of Japan's hopes are that raw material and energy import prices will rise as the exchange value of yen falls, and that these higher costs will be passed along in consumer prices, pushing up inflation and stimulating economic growth. Japan is betting its economy on a discredited theory.

The interesting question is why financial strategists expect the yen to collapse under QE, but did not expect the dollar to collapse under QE. Japan is the world's third largest economy, and until about a decade ago was going gangbusters despite the yen rising in value. Why should QE affect the yen differently from the dollar?

Perhaps the answer lies in the very powerful alliance between the US government and the banking/financial sector and on the obligation that Washington imposes on its vassal states to support the dollar as world reserve currency. Japan lacks the capability to neutralize normal economic forces. Washington's ability to rig markets has allowed Washington to keep its economic house of cards standing.

The Federal Reserve's announcement that QE is terminated has improved the outlook for the US dollar. However, as Nomi Prins makes clear, QE has not ended, merely morphed.

The Fed's bond purchases have left the big banks with $2.6 trillion in excess cash reserves on deposit with the Fed. The banks will now use this money to buy bonds in place of the Fed's purchases. When this money runs out, the Fed will find a reason to restart QE. Moreover, the Fed has announced that it intends to reinvest the interest and returning principle from its $4.5 trillion in holdings of mortgage backed instruments and Treasuries to continue purchasing bonds. Possibly also, interest rate swaps can be manipulated to keep rates down. So, despite the announced end of QE, purchases will continue to support high bond prices, and the high bond prices will continue to encourage purchases of stocks, thus perpetuating the house of cards.

As Dave Kranzler and I (and no doubt others) have pointed out, a stable or rising dollar exchange value is the necessary foundation to the house of cards. Until three years ago, the dollar was losing ground rapidly with respect to gold. Since that time massive sales of uncovered shorts in the gold futures market have been used to drive down the gold price.

That gold and silver bullion prices are rigged is obvious. Demand is high, and supply is constrained; yet prices are falling. The US mint cannot keep up with the demand for silver eagles and has suspended sales. The Canadian mint is rationing the supply of silver maple leafs. Asian demand for gold, especially from China, is at record levels.

The third quarter, 2014, was the 15th consecutive quarter of net purchases of gold by central banks. Dave Kranzler reports that in the past eight months, 101 tonnes have been drained from GLD, an indication that there is a gold shortage for delivery to physical purchasers. The declining futures price, which is established in a paper market where contracts are settled in cash, not in gold, is inconsistent with rising demand and constrained supply and is a clear indication of price rigging by US authorities.

The extent of financial corruption involving collusion between the mega-banks and the financial authorities is unfathomable. The Western financial system is a house of cards resting on corruption.

The house of cards has stood longer than I thought possible. Can it stand forever or are there so many rotted joints that some simultaneous collection of failures overwhelms the manipulation and brings on a massive crash? Time will tell.

First published on November 14, 2014.

Insider Trading and Financial Terrorism on Comex

July 16, 2014. The first two days this week gold was subjected to a series of computer HFT-driven "flash crashes" that were aimed at cooling off the big move higher gold has made since the beginning of June. During this move higher, the hedge funds, who typically "chase" the momentum of gold up or down, built up hefty long positions in gold futures over the last 6 weeks. In order to disrupt the upward momentum in the price of gold, the bullion banks short gold in the futures market by dumping large contracts that drive down the price and make money for the banks in the process.

As we explained in previous articles on this subject, the price of gold is not determined in markets where physical gold is bought and sold but in the paper futures market where contracts trade and speculators place bets on the price of gold. Most of the contracts traded on the Comex futures market are settled in cash. The value of the contracts used to short gold and drive down the price is well in excess of the actual amount of physical gold that is kept on the Comex and available for delivery. One might think that regulators would pay attention to a market in which the value of contracts outstanding exceeds by several multiples the amount of physical gold available for delivery.

The Comex gold futures market trades 23 hours per day on a global computer system called Globex and on the NYC trading floor from 8:20 a.m. EST to 1:30p.m. EST. The Comex floor trading session is the highest volume trading period during any 23 hour trading period because that is when most of the large U.S. financial institutions and other users of Comex futures (jewelry manufactures and gold mining companies) are open for business and therefore transact their Comex business during Comex floor hours in order to achieve the best trading execution at the lowest cost.

The big hedge funds primarily trade gold futures using computers and algorithm programs. When they buy, they set stop-loss orders which are used to protect their trading positions on the downside. A "stop-loss" order is an order to sell at a pre-specified price by a trader. A stop-loss order is automatically triggered and the position is sold when the market trades at the price which was pre-set with the stop-order.

The bullion banks who are members and directors of Comex have access to the computers used to clear Comex trades, which means they can see where the stop-loss orders are set. When they decide to short the market, they start selling Comex futures in large amounts to force the market low enough to trigger the stop-loss orders being used by the hedge fund computers. For instance, huge short-sell orders at 2:20 a.m. Monday morning triggered an avalanche of stop-loss selling, as shown in this graph of Monday's (July 14) action:

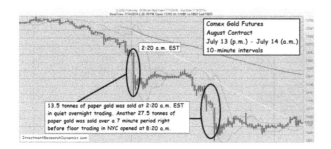

In the graph above, the first circled red bar shows the flash crash that was engineered at 2:20 a.m. EST, a typically low-volume, quiet period for gold trading. 13.5 tonnes of short-sales were unloaded into the Comex computer trading system. The second circled red bar shows a second engineered flash-crash right before the Comex floor opened at 8:20 a.m. EST. This was triggered by sales of futures contracts representing 27.5 tonnes of gold. A third hit (not shown) occurred at 9:01 a.m. This time contracts representing 40 tonnes of gold hit the market.

The banks use the selling from the hedge funds to cover the short positions they've amassed and book trading profits as they cover their short positions at price levels that are below the prices at which their short positions were established. This is insider trading and unrestrained financial terrorism at its finest.

As shown on the graph below, on Tuesday, July 15, another flash-crash in gold was engineered in the middle of Janet Yellen's very "dovish" Humphrey-Hawkins testimony. Contracts representing 45 tonnes of gold were sold in 3 minutes, which took gold down over $13 and below the key $1300 price level. There were no apparent news triggers or specific comments from Yellen that would have triggered a sudden sell-off in gold – just a massive dumping of gold futures contracts. No other related market (stocks, commodities) registered any unusual movement up or down when this occurred:

Between July 14 and July 15, contracts representing 126 tonnes of gold was sold in a 14-minute time window which took the price of gold down $43 dollars. No other market showed any unusual or extraordinary movement during this period.

To put contracts for 126 tonnes of gold into perspective, the Comex is currently reporting that 27 tonnes of actual physical gold are classified as being available for deliver should the buyers of futures contracts want delivery. But the buyers are the banks themselves who won't be taking delivery.

One motive of the manipulation is to operate and control Comex trading in a manner that helps the Fed contain the price of gold, thereby preventing its rise from signaling to the markets that problems festering in the U.S. financial system are growing worse by the day. This is an act of financial terrorism supported by federal regulatory authorities. Another motive is to help support the relative trading level of the U.S. dollar, as we've described in previous articles on this topic. And, of course, the banks make money from the manipulation of the futures market.

The Commodity Futures Trading Commission, the branch of government which was established to oversee the Comex and enforce long-established trading regulations, has been presented with the evidence of manipulation several times. Its near-automatic response is to disregard the evidence and look the other way. The only explanation for this is that the Government is complicit in the price suppression and manipulation of gold and silver and welcomes the insider trading that helps to achieve this result. The conclusion is inescapable: if illegality benefits the machinations of the US government, the US government is all for illegality.

First published on July 16, 2014.

US Resorts to Illegality to Protect Failed Policies

Paul Craig Roberts & Dave Kranzler

In a blatant and massive market intervention, the price of gold was smashed on Friday. Right after the Comex opened on Friday morning 7,008 paper gold contracts representing 20 tonnes of gold were dumped in the New York Comex futures market at 8:50 a.m. EST. At 12:35 a.m. EST 10,324 contracts representing 30 tonnes of gold were dropped on the Comex futures market:

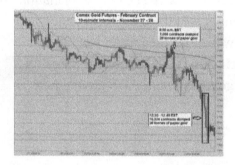

No relevant news or events occurred that would have triggered this sudden sell-off in gold. Furthermore, none of the other markets experienced any unusual movement (stocks, bonds, currencies).

The intervention in the gold market occurred on the Friday after the U.S. had observed its Thanksgiving Day holiday. It is one of the lowest volume trading days of the year on the Comex.

A rational person who wants to short gold because he believes the price will fall wants to obtain the highest price for the contracts he sells in order to maximize his profits when he settles the contracts. If his sale of contracts drives down the price of gold, he reduces the spread between the amount he receives for his contracts and the price at settlement, thus minimizing his profits, or if the price goes against him maximizing his losses. A bona fide seller speculating on the direction of the gold price would choose a more liquid market period and dribble out his contract sales so as not to cause a significant impact on the price.

As you can see from the price-action on the graph, massive sales concentrated within a few minutes minimize sales proceeds and are at odds with profit maximization. A rational seller would not behave in this way. What we are witnessing in the bullion futures market are short sales designed to drive down the price of bullion. This is price manipulation.

Here is the Security and Exchange Commission's definition of manipulation:

Manipulation is intentional conduct designed to deceive investors by controlling or artificially affecting the market for a security…[this includes] rigging quotes, prices or trades to create a false or deceptive picture of the demand for a security. Those who engage in manipulation are subject to various civil and criminal sanctions.

Why is manipulation of the price of gold in the futures market not investigated and prosecuted?
The manipulation has been blatant and repetitious since 2011.

The answer to the question is that suppressing the price of gold helps to protect the U.S. dollar's value from the excessive debt and money creation of the past six years. The attacks on gold also enable the bullion banks to purchase large blocks of shares in the GLD gold trust that can be redeemed in gold with which to supply Asian purchasers. Whether or not the Federal Reserve and the U.S. Treasury are instigators of the price manipulation, government authorities tolerate it as it supports the dollar's value in the face of an enormous creation of new dollars and new federal debt.

In other words, the illegal rigging of the price of gold in the futures market is deemed by the US government to be essential to the success of its economic policy, just as illegal torture, illegal military invasions and attacks on sovereign countries, unconstitutional violation of habeas corpus, unconstitutional spying on U.S. citizens, and illegal and unconstitutional murder of U.S. citizens by the executive branch are essential to the U.S. government's "war on terror."

The U.S. government resorts to massive illegality across the board in order to protect its failed policies. The rule of law and accountable government have been sacrificed to failed policies.

First published on December 1, 2014.

The Lawless Manipulation of Bullion Markets by Public Authorities

Paul Craig Roberts and Dave Kranzler

Note: In this article the times given are Eastern Standard Time. The software that generated the graph uses Mountain Standard Time. Therefore, read the x-axis two hours later than the axis indicates.

The Federal Reserve and its bullion bank agents are actively using uncovered futures contracts to illegally manipulate the prices of precious metals in order to keep interest rates below the market rate. The purpose of manipulation is to support the U.S. dollar's reserve status at a time when the dollar should be in decline from the over-supply created by QE and from trade and budget deficits.

Historically, the role of gold and silver has been to function as a means of exchange and a store of wealth during periods of economic and political turmoil. Since the bullion bull market began in late 2000, It rose almost non-stop until March 2008, ahead of the Great Financial Crisis, which started with the collapse of Bear Stearns. When Bear Stearns collapsed, gold was taken down over the course of the next 7 months from $1035 to $680, or 34%; silver from $21 to $8, or 62%. The most violent takedown occurred as Lehman collapsed and Goldman Sachs was about to collapse. This takedown occurred during a period of time when gold should have been going parabolic in price. The price of gold finally took off in late October 2008 from $680 to $1900 while the Government and the Fed were busy printing money to bail out the banks. While the price of gold rose nearly 300% from late 2008 to September 2011, the U.S. dollar lost over 17% of its value, falling from 89 on the dollar index to 73.50.

The current takedown of gold from $1900 to $1200 has occurred during a period of time when financial and political fraud and corruption becomes worse and more blatant by the day. Along with this, the intensity and openness with which the metals are systematically beat down seems to grow by the day.

Comex futures trade 23 hours a day via a global computerized trading system known as Globex. The heaviest period of trading occurs when the actual Comex floor operations are open, which is 8:20 a.m. to 1:30 p.m. EST. All other times Comex futures trade electronically via Globex. Gold and silver are smashed primarily during the Globex-only trading periods, when volume is often light to non-existent.

This graph of Comex futures trading on December 16th shows the sudden plunge in the price of silver.

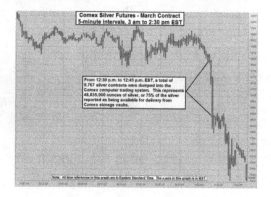

The second stage of the sharp price drop begins at 1:30 pm eastern time (11:30 mountain time), after the Comex floor trading operation was closed for the day. This is typically one of the lowest volume trading periods, during which orders to buy or sell can cause significant price disruption to the market. There were no news or events that would have triggered the sudden selling of bullion futures, and none of the other markets experienced unusual movements while gold and silver were quickly plunging in price.

To put in perspective the 9,767 silver contracts sold in 15 minutes, the total trading volume in Comex silver for the 23-hour global trading period for Comex contracts ending at 5:00 p.m. on December 15th was 149,964 contracts, or an average of 6,520 contracts per hour. The only type of market participant that would dump almost 10,000 contracts in a 15-minute period is a seller who's only motivation is to push the price of silver as low as possible. One entity that can afford to use capital like this is the Federal Reserve, because the Fed can create its own capital for free using the printing press.

In the background, the financial markets are becoming increasingly pressured by declines in emerging market currencies, insolvent sovereign governments – including here in the US – and perhaps a renewed derivatives crisis triggered by the collapse in the price of oil. The oil price decline could result in derivative problems larger than the subprime mortgage derivatives of the 2008 crisis.

The downward manipulation of the prices of precious metals prevents the "crisis warning transmission system" from properly functioning. More important, the decline in the price of gold/silver vs. the U.S. dollar conveys the illusion that the dollar is strong at a time when, in fact, the dollar should be under pressure from the over-issuance of dollars and dollar-denominated debt.

What we have been experiencing since the 2008 crisis is not only the subordination of US economic policy to the needs of banks "too big to fail," but also the subordination of law and the financial regulatory agencies to the interests of a few private banks. The manipulation of the bullion markets is illegal whether done by private parties or on public authority, and so we have the spectacle of the US government supporting a handful of banks via illegal means. Not only has economic accountability been set aside, but also legal accountability.

Just as Washington places itself above laws prohibiting torture and naked aggression in order to conduct its self-declared "war on terror" and above the Constitution in order to construct a domestic police state, Washington places itself above the laws prohibiting market manipulation.
Obviously, the government's claim to represent the rule of law is as false as all its other claims. The foul stench of corruption and

hypocrisy that emanates from Washington is the smell of a dying country.

First published on December 22, 2014.

Magic Growth Numbers

Everyone wants good news, so the government makes it up. The latest fiction is that US real GDP grew 4.6% in the second quarter and 5% in the third.

Where did this growth come from?

Not from rising real consumer incomes.

Not from rising consumer credit.

Not from rising real retail sales.

Not from the housing sector.

Not from a trade surplus.

The growth came from a Bureau of Economic Analysis survey of consumer spending on services. The BEA found that spending on Obamacare drove the US real GDP growth to 5% in the third quarter.

In America, unlike in other countries, a huge chunk of medical spending goes to insurance company profits, not to health care. Another big chunk goes to paperwork, which has a variety of purposes such as collecting personal information on patients and combating fraud (probably the paperwork costs more than fraud). Another chunk goes for tests and procedures in order to justify further procedures. For example, if a doctor thinks a patient's diagnosis requires a MRI, he must often first order an x-ray to establish that a cheaper procedure does not suffice. If a cancerous skin growth needs to come off, first a biopsy must be done to establish that it is a cancer so that a needless removal is not performed. And, of course, medical practicians must order unnecessary tests in order to protect themselves from the liability of relying on their medical judgment.

To regard any of these expenses as economic growth is farfetched.

There are sampling and other problems with the survey of personal consumption, and apparently Obamacare spending was all dumped into the third quarter. Why the third quarter?

The answer is that the illusion of economic recovery must be kept alive.

Real GDP growth of 5% in the third quarter is inconsistent with the sharp fall in key industrial commodity prices. It is not only oil (down 47%) but iron ore prices (down 49%), natural gas (down 30%), copper (down 15%). Pam and Russ Martens show that the fall in the producer price index for industrial commodities in 2014 is sharper than in 2008, the year of the crash [1].

With 30% of 30-year old Americans and almost 50% of 25-year olds living with parents, with debt-based derivative instruments impacted by falling oil and industrial commodity prices, with the likelihood that the US and EU economic attack on Russia will fail and perhaps produce retaliatory measures that could bring down the European banking system, look for 2015 to be the year that Washington will cease to get away with its economic lies.

The financial media and Wall Street economists by refusing to ask obvious questions have left the American people unprepared for another drop in their living standards and ability to cope.

First published on December 26, 2014.

[1]. "Oil Crash: Don't Believe the Happy Clatter"
http://wallstreetonparade.com/2014/12/oil-crash-dont-believe-the-happy-clatter

Are Big Banks Using Derivatives To Suppress Bullion Prices?

Paul Craig Roberts and Dave Kranzler

We have explained on a number of occasions how the Federal Reserve's agents, the bullion banks (principally JPMorganChase, HSBC, and Scotia) sell uncovered shorts ("naked shorts") on the Comex (gold futures market) in order to drive down an otherwise rising price of gold. By dumping so many uncovered short contracts into the futures market, an artificial increase in "paper gold" is created, and this increase in supply drives down the price.

This manipulation works because the hedge funds, the main purchasers of the short contracts, do not intend to take delivery of the gold represented by the contracts, settling instead in cash. This means that the banks who sold the uncovered contracts are never at risk from their inability to cover contracts in gold. At any given time, the amount of gold represented by the paper gold contracts ("open interest') can exceed the actual amount of physical gold available for delivery, a situation that does not occur in other futures markets.

In other words, the gold and silver futures markets are not a place where people buy and sell gold and silver. These markets are places where people speculate on price direction and where hedge funds use gold futures to hedge other bets according to the various mathematical formulas that they use. The fact that bullion prices are determined in this paper, speculative market, and not in real physical markets where people sell and acquire physical bullion, is the reason the bullion banks can drive down the price of gold and silver even though the demand for the physical metal is rising.

For example last Tuesday the US Mint announced that it was sold out of the American Eagle one ounce silver coin. It is a contradiction of the law of supply and demand that demand is high, supply is low, and the price is falling. Such an economic anomaly can only be explained by manipulation of prices in a market where supply can be created by printing paper contracts.

Obviously fraud and price manipulation are at work, but no heads roll. The Federal Reserve and US Treasury support this fraud and manipulation, because the suppression of precious metal prices protects the value and status of the US dollar as the world's reserve currency and prevents gold and silver from fulfilling their role as the transmission mechanism that warns of developing financial and economic troubles. The suppression of the rising gold price suppresses the warning signal and permits the continuation of financial market bubbles and Washington's ability to impose sanctions on other world powers that are disadvantaged by not being a reserve currency.

It has come to our attention that over-the-counter (OTC) derivatives also play a role in price suppression and simultaneously serve to provide long positions for the bullion banks that disguise their manipulation of prices in the futures market.

OTC derivatives are privately structured contracts created by the secretive large banks. They are a paper, or derivative, form of an underlying financial instrument or commodity. Little is known about them. Brooksley Born, the head of the Commodity Futures Trading Corporation (CFTC) during the Clinton regime said, correctly, that the derivatives needed to be regulated. However, Federal Reserve Chairman Alan Greenspan, Treasury Secretary and Deputy Secretary Robert Rubin and Lawrence Summers, and Securities and Exchange Commission (SEC) chairman Arthur Levitt, all de facto agents of the big banks, convinced Congress to prevent the CFTC from regulating OTC derivatives.

The absence of regulation means that information is not available that would indicate the purposes for which the banks use these derivatives. When JPMorgan was investigated for its short silver position on

Comex, the bank convinced the CFTC that its short position on Comex was a hedge against a long position via OTC derivatives. In other words, JPMorgan used its OTC derivatives to shield its attack on the silver price in the futures market.

During 2015 the attack on bullion prices has intensified, driving the prices lower than they have been for years. During the first quarter of this year there was a huge upward spike in the quantity of precious metal derivatives.

If these were long positions hedging the banks' Comex shorts, why did the price of gold and silver decline?

More evidence of manipulation comes from the continuing fall in the prices of gold and silver as set in paper future markets, although demand for the physical metals continues to rise even to the point that the US Mint has run out of silver coins to sell. Uncertainties arising from the Greek No vote increase systemic uncertainty. The normal response would be rising, not falling, bullion prices.

The circumstantial evidence is that the unregulated OTC derivatives in gold and silver are not really hedges to short positions in Comex but are themselves structured as an additional attack on precious metal prices.

If this supposition is correct, it indicates that seven years of bailing out the big banks that control the Federal Reserve and US Treasury at the expense of the US economy has threatened the US dollar to the extent that the dollar must be protected at all cost, including US regulatory tolerance of illegal activity to suppress gold and silver prices.

First published on July 8, 2015.

Supply and Demand in the Gold and Silver Futures Markets

Paul Craig Roberts and Dave Kranzler

This article establishes that the price of gold and silver in the futures markets in which cash is the predominant means of settlement is inconsistent with the conditions of supply and demand in the actual physical or current market where physical bullion is bought and sold as opposed to transactions in uncovered paper claims to bullion in the futures markets. The supply of bullion in the futures markets is increased by printing uncovered contracts representing claims to gold. This artificial, indeed fraudulent, increase in the supply of paper bullion contracts drives down the price in the futures market despite high demand for bullion in the physical market and constrained supply. We will demonstrate with economic analysis and empirical evidence that the bear market in bullion is an artificial creation.

The law of supply and demand is the basis of economics. Yet the price of gold and silver in the Comex futures market, where paper contracts representing 100 troy ounces of gold or 5,000 ounces of silver are traded, is inconsistent with the actual supply and demand conditions in the physical market for bullion. For four years the price of bullion has been falling in the futures market despite rising demand for possession of the physical metal and supply constraints.

We begin with a review of basics. The vertical axis measures price. The horizontal axis measures quantity. Demand curves slope down to the right, the quantity demanded increasing as price falls. Supply curves slope upward to the right, the quantity supplied rising with price. The intersection of supply with demand determines price. (Graph 1)

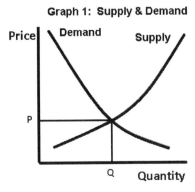

Graph 1: Supply & Demand

Supply and Demand Graph 1.

A change in quantity demanded or in the quantity supplied refers to a movement along a given curve. A change in demand or a change in supply refers to a shift in the curves. For example, an increase in demand (a shift to the right of the demand curve) causes a movement along the supply curve (an increase in the quantity supplied).

Changes in income and changes in tastes or preferences toward an item can cause the demand curve to shift. For example, if people expect that their fiat currency is going to lose value, the demand for gold and silver would increase (a shift to the right).

Changes in technology and resources can cause the supply curve to shift. New gold discoveries and improvements in gold mining technology would cause the supply curve to shift to the right. Exhaustion of existing mines would cause a reduction in supply (a shift to the left).

What can cause the price of gold to fall? Two things: The demand for gold can fall, that is, the demand curve could shift to the left, intersecting the supply curve at a lower price. The fall in demand results in a reduction in the quantity supplied. A fall in demand means that people want less gold at every price. (Graph 2)

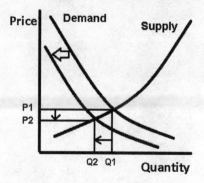

Graph 2: Decrease in Demand

Supply and Demand Graph 2.

Alternatively, supply could increase, that is, the supply curve could shift to the right, intersecting the demand curve at a lower price. The increase in supply results in an increase in the quantity demanded. An increase in supply means that more gold is available at every price. (Graph 3)

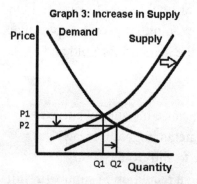

Graph 3: Increase in Supply

Supply and Demand Graph 3.

To summarize: a decline in the price of gold can be caused by a decline in the demand for gold or by an increase in the supply of gold.

A decline in demand or an increase in supply is not what we are observing in the gold and silver physical markets. The price of bullion in the futures market has been falling as demand for physical bullion increases and supply experiences constraints. What we are seeing in the physical market indicates a rising price. Yet in the futures market in

104

which almost all contracts are settled in cash and not with bullion deliveries, the price is falling.

For example, on July 7, 2015, the U.S. Mint said that due to a "significant" increase in demand, it had sold out of Silver Eagles (one ounce silver coin) and was suspending sales until some time in August. The premiums on the coins (the price of the coin above the price of the silver) rose, but the spot price of silver fell 7 percent to its lowest level of the year (as of July 7).

This is the second time in 9 months that the U.S. Mint could not keep up with market demand and had to suspend sales. During the first 5 months of 2015, the U.S. Mint had to ration sales of Silver Eagles. According to Reuters, since 2013 the U.S. Mint has had to ration silver coin sales for 18 months. In 2013 the Royal Canadian Mint announced the rationing of its Silver Maple Leaf coins: "We are carefully managing supply in the face of very high demand. . . . Coming off strong sales volumes in December 2012, demand to date remains very strong for our Silver Maple Leaf and Gold Maple Leaf bullion coins." During this entire period when mints could not keep up with demand for coins, the price of silver consistently fell on the Comex futures market. On July 24, 2015 the price of gold in the futures market fell to its lowest level in 5 years despite an increase in the demand for gold in the physical market. On that day U.S. Mint sales of Gold Eagles (one ounce gold coin) were the highest in more than two years, yet the price of gold fell in the futures market.

How can this be explained? The financial press says that the drop in precious metals prices unleashed a surge in global demand for coins. This explanation is nonsensical to an economist. Price is not a determinant of demand but of quantity demanded. A lower price does not shift the demand curve. Moreover, if demand increases, price goes up, not down.

Perhaps what the financial press means is that the lower price resulted in an increase in the quantity demanded. If so, what caused the lower price? In economic analysis, the answer would have to be an increase in supply, either new supplies from new discoveries and new mines or mining technology advances that lower the cost of producing bullion.

There are no reports of any such supply increasing developments. To the contrary, the lower prices of bullion have been causing reductions in mining output as falling prices make existing operations unprofitable.

There are abundant other signs of high demand for bullion, yet the prices continue their four-year decline on the Comex. Even as massive uncovered shorts (sales of gold contracts that are not covered by physical bullion) on the bullion futures market are driving down price, strong demand for physical bullion has been depleting the holdings of GLD, the largest exchange traded gold fund. Since February 27, 2015, the authorized bullion banks (principally JPMorganChase, HSBC, and Scotia) have removed 10 percent of GLD's gold holdings. Similarly, strong demand in China and India has resulted in a 19% increase of purchases from the Shanghai Gold Exchange, a physical bullion market, during the first quarter of 2015. Through the week ending July 10, 2015, purchases from the Shanghai Gold Exchange alone are occurring at an annualized rate approximately equal to the annual supply of global mining output.

India's silver imports for the first four months of 2015 are 30% higher than 2014. In the first quarter of 2015 Canadian Silver Maple Leaf sales increased 8.5% compared to sales for the same period of 2014. Sales of Gold Eagles in June, 2015, were more than triple the sales for May. During the first 10 days of July, Gold Eagles sales were 2.5 times greater than during the first 10 days of June.

Clearly the demand for physical metal is very high, and the ability to meet this demand is constrained. Yet, the prices of bullion in the futures market have consistently fallen during this entire period. The only possible explanation is manipulation.

Precious metal prices are determined in the futures market, where paper contracts representing bullion are settled in cash, not in markets where the actual metals are bought and sold. As the Comex is predominantly a cash settlement market, there is little risk in uncovered contracts (an uncovered contract is a promise to deliver gold that the seller of the contract does not possess). This means that it is easy to increase the supply of gold in the futures market where price is established simply by printing uncovered (naked) contracts. Selling naked shorts is a way to artificially increase the supply of bullion in the futures market where price is determined. The supply of paper contracts representing gold increases, but not the supply of physical bullion.

As we have documented on a number of occasions, the prices of bullion are being systematically driven down by the sudden appearance and sale during thinly traded times of day and night of uncovered future contracts representing massive amounts of bullion. In the space of a few minutes or less massive amounts of gold and silver shorts are dumped into the Comex market, dramatically increasing the supply of paper claims to bullion. If purchasers of these shorts stood for delivery, the Comex would fail. Comex bullion futures are used for speculation and by hedge funds to manage the risk/return characteristics of metrics like the Sharpe Ratio. The hedge funds are concerned with indexing the price of gold and silver and not with the rate of return performance of their bullion contracts.

A rational speculator faced with strong demand for bullion and constrained supply would not short the market. Moreover, no rational actor who wished to unwind a large gold position would dump the entirety of his position on the market all at once. What then explains the massive naked shorts that are hurled into the market during thinly traded times?

The bullion banks are the primary market-makers in bullion futures. They are also clearing members of the Comex, which gives them access to data such as the positions of the hedge funds and the prices at which stop-loss orders are triggered. They time their sales of uncovered shorts to trigger stop-loss sales and then cover their short sales by purchasing contracts at the price that they have forced down, pocketing the profits from the manipulation

The manipulation is obvious. The question is why do the authorities tolerate it?

Perhaps the answer is that a free gold market serves both to protect against the loss of a fiat currency's purchasing power from exchange rate decline and inflation and as a warning that destabilizing systemic events are on the horizon. The current round of on-going massive short sales compressed into a few minutes during thinly traded periods began after gold hit $1,900 per ounce in response to the build-up of troubled debt and the Federal Reserve's policy of Quantitative Easing. Washington's power is heavily dependent on the role of the dollar as world reserve currency. The rising dollar price of gold indicated rising discomfort with the dollar. Whereas the dollar's exchange value is carefully managed with help from the Japanese and European central banks, the supply of such help is not unlimited. If gold kept moving up, exchange rate weakness was likely to show up in the dollar, thus forcing the Fed off its policy of using QE to rescue the "banks too big to fail."

The bullion banks' attack on gold is being augmented with a spate of stories in the financial media denying any usefulness of gold. On July 17 the Wall Street Journal declared that honesty about gold requires recognition that gold is nothing but a pet rock. Other commentators declare gold to be in a bear market despite the strong demand for physical metal and supply constraints, and some influential party is determined that gold not be regarded as money.

Why a sudden spate of claims that gold is not money? Gold is considered a part of the United States' official monetary reserves, which is also the case for central banks and the IMF. The IMF accepts gold as repayment for credit extended. The US Treasury's Office of the Comptroller of the Currency classifies gold as a currency, as can be seen in the OCC's latest quarterly report on bank derivatives activities in which the OCC places gold futures in the foreign exchange derivatives classification.

The manipulation of the gold price by injecting large quantities of freshly printed uncovered contracts into the Comex market is an empirical fact. The sudden debunking of gold in the financial press is circumstantial evidence that a full-scale attack on gold's function as a systemic warning signal is underway.

It is unlikely that regulatory authorities are unaware of the fraudulent manipulation of bullion prices. The fact that nothing is done about it is an indication of the lawlessness that prevails in US financial markets.

First published on July 27, 2015.

Central Banks Have Become A Corrupting Force

Paul Craig Roberts and Dave Kranzler

Are we witnessing the corruption of central banks? Are we observing the money-creating powers of central banks being used to drive up prices in the stock market for the benefit of the mega-rich?

These questions came to mind when we learned that the central bank of Switzerland, the Swiss National Bank, purchased 3,300,000 shares of Apple stock in the first quarter of this year, adding 500,000 shares in the second quarter. Smart money would have been selling, not buying.

It turns out that the Swiss central bank, in addition to its Apple stock, holds very large equity positions, ranging from $250,000,000 to $637,000,000, in numerous US corporations – Exxon Mobil, Microsoft, Google, Johnson & Johnson, General Electric, Procter & Gamble, Verizon, AT&T, Pfizer, Chevron, Merck, Facebook, Pepsico, Coca Cola, Disney, Valeant, IBM, Gilead, Amazon.

Among this list of the Swiss central bank's holdings are stocks which are responsible for more than 100% of the year-to-date rise in the S&P 500 prior to the latest sell-off.

What is going on here?

The purpose of central banks was to serve as a "lender of last resort" to commercial banks faced with a run on the bank by depositors demanding cash withdrawals of their deposits.

Banks would call in loans in an effort to raise cash to pay off depositors. Businesses would fail, and the banks would fail from their inability to pay depositors their money on demand.

As time passed, this rationale for a central bank was made redundant by government deposit insurance for bank depositors, and central banks found additional functions for their existence. The Federal Reserve, for example, under the Humphrey-Hawkins Act, is responsible for maintaining full employment and low inflation. By the time this legislation was passed, the worsening "Phillips Curve tradeoffs" between inflation and employment had made the goals inconsistent. The result was the introduction by the Reagan administration of the supply-side economic policy that cured the simultaneously rising inflation and unemployment.

Neither the Federal Reserve's charter nor the Humphrey-Hawkins Act says that the Federal Reserve is supposed to stabilize the stock market by purchasing stocks. The Federal Reserve is supposed to buy and sell bonds in open market operations in order to encourage employment with lower interest rates or to restrict inflation with higher interest rates.

If central banks purchase stocks in order to support equity prices, what is the point of having a stock market? The central bank's ability to create money to support stock prices negates the price discovery function of the stock market.

The problem with central banks is that humans are fallible, including the chairman of the Federal Reserve Board and all the board members and staff. Nobel prize-winner Milton Friedman and Anna Schwartz established that the Great Depression was the consequence of the failure of the Federal Reserve to expand monetary policy sufficiently to offset the restriction of the money supply due to bank failure. When a bank failed in the pre-deposit insurance era, the money supply would shrink by the amount of the bank's deposits. During the Great Depression, thousands of banks failed, wiping out the purchasing power of millions of Americans and the credit creating power of thousands of banks.

The Fed is prohibited from buying equities by the Federal Reserve Act. But an amendment in 2010 – Section 13(3) – was enacted to permit the Fed to buy AIG's insolvent Maiden Lane assets. This amendment also created a loophole which enables the Fed to lend money to entities that can use the funds to buy stocks. Thus, the Swiss central bank could be operating as an agent of the Federal Reserve.

If central banks cannot properly conduct monetary policy, how can they conduct an equity policy? Some astute observers believe that the Swiss National Bank is acting as an agent for the Federal Reserve and purchases large blocks of US equities at critical times to arrest stock market declines that would puncture the propagandized belief that all is fine here in the US economy.

We know that the US government has a "plunge protection team" consisting of the US Treasury and Federal Reserve. The purpose of this team is to prevent unwanted stock market crashes.

Is the stock market decline of August 20-21 welcome or unwelcome?

At this point we do not know. In order to keep the dollar up, the basis of US power, the Federal Reserve has promised to raise interest rates, but always in the future. The latest future is next month. The belief that a hike in interest rates is in the cards keeps the US dollar from losing exchange value in relation to other currencies, thus preventing a flight from the dollar that would reduce the Uni-power to Third World status.

The Federal Reserve can say that the stock market decline indicates that the recovery is in doubt and requires more stimulus. The prospect of more liquidity could drive the stock market back up. As asset bubbles are in the way of the Fed's policy, a decline in stock prices removes the equity market bubble and enables the Fed to print more money and start the process up again.

On the other hand, the stock market decline last Thursday and Friday could indicate that the players in the market have comprehended that the stock market is an artificially inflated bubble that has no real basis. Once the psychology is destroyed, flight sets in.

If flight turns out to be the case, it will be interesting to see if central bank liquidity and purchases of stocks can stop the rout.

First published on August 23, 2015.

Our House of Cards

As John Williams (shadowstats.com) has observed, the payroll jobs reports no longer make any logical or statistical sense. Ask yourself, do you believe that retailers responded to the very disappointing Christmas season by rushing out in January to hire 46,000 more retail clerks?

Perhaps those 46,000 retail jobs is the BLS telling us that they have to come up with new jobs to report whether or not there are any.

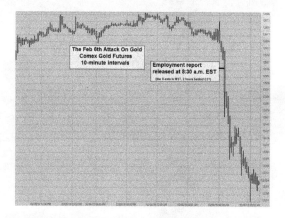

As we have reported on a number of occasions, whenever the price of gold in the futures market starts to rise, massive uncovered shorts are suddenly dumped on the market. As the shorts dramatically increase the supply of future contracts all at once, the supply overwhelms demand, and the price of gold is driven down despite the fact that the demand for gold in the physical market is strong. (Remember, the price of gold is determined in the futures market in which contracts are largely settled in cash and seldom in gold. The physical market is where gold bullion is purchased, not paper claims on gold for speculation.)

Last Friday the attack on gold was coordinated with the announcement of the suspicious jobs report. The price of gold was hit hard with an avalanche of uncovered gold futures contracts dumped at the same time that the U.S. Government's Bureau of Labor Statistics (BLS) released what can only be described as an incorrect employment report. The avalanche of paper contracts that were dumped onto the Comex (both the trading floor and electronic trading computer system) took the price of gold down $39 in three hours, with most of the price hit occurring in the first 40 minutes after the jobs report was released.

The volume of contracts that traded after 8:00 a.m. on the Comex was unusually high for a Friday, running about 60% above Thursday's volume for the same time period. Such departures without cause from normal trading patterns are indicative of market manipulation, and Friday's price smash capped a week in which the price of gold was taken lower every day at 8:30 a.m. after the release of economic reports, most of which reflected a deteriorating condition of the U.S. economy.

Gold is a refuge in times of uncertainty. With yen, dollars, and euros all being created at a faster rate than goods and services are being produced, with both stock and bond prices at bubble levels, gold is definitely an attractive refuge. Confidence in gold would pull money out of the rigged markets for financial instruments and make it more difficult to maintain the appearance that all is well. To attack gold simultaneously with issuing a happy jobs report doubles the encouragement to remain invested in financial paper and to continue to hold the over-printed currencies.

The expectation is that more money will be printed. The prices of troubled sovereign debt have been bid unrealistically high because of expectations that quantitative easing by the European Central Bank will result in central bank purchases of the troubled sovereign debt. In the US the 100 percent and more than 100 percent auto loans have been securitized and sold as investments. Borrowers whose trade-in value is less than their remaining loan can borrow more than the purchase price of the new car in order to pay off the old car loan.

The lenders made their money on loan fees, but as defaults rise the securitized loans and associated derivatives will likely require a bailout like the securitized mortgages.

Anyone looking at these prospects is tempted by gold, but a rising gold price could bring down the fiat currencies and, thus, must be prevented.

In other words, those who have rigged the system know that it is a house of cards.

First published on February 10, 2015.

How Long Can The Federal Reserve Stave Off the Inevitable?

When are America's global corporations and Wall Street going to sit down with President Trump and explain to him that his trade war is not with China but with them? The biggest chunk of America's trade deficit with China is the offshored production of America's global corporations. When the corporations bring the products that they produce in China to the US consumer market, the products are classified as imports from China.

Six years ago when I was writing The Failure of Laissez Faire Capitalism, I concluded on the evidence that half of US imports from China consist of the offshored production of US corporations. Offshoring is a substantial benefit to US corporations because of much lower labor and compliance costs. Profits, executive bonuses, and shareholders' capital gains receive a large boost from offshoring. The costs of these benefits for a few fall on the many – the former American employees who formerly had a middle class income and expectations for their children.

In my book, I cited evidence that during the first decade of the 21st century "the US lost 54,621 factories, and manufacturing employment fell by 5 million employees. Over the decade, the number of larger factories (those employing 1,000 or more employees) declined by 40 percent. US factories employing 500-1,000 workers declined by 44 percent; those employing between 250-500 workers declined by 37 percent, and those employing between 100-250 workers shrunk by 30 percent. These losses are net of new start-ups. Not all the losses are due to offshoring. Some are the result of business failures" (p. 100).

In other words, to put it in the most simple and clear terms, millions of Americans lost their middle class jobs not because China played unfairly, but because American corporations betrayed the American people and exported their jobs. "Making America great again" means dealing with these corporations, not with China. When Trump learns this, assuming anyone will tell him, will he back off China and take on the American global corporations?

The loss of middle class jobs has had a dire effect on the hopes and expectations of Americans, on the American economy, on the finances of cities and states and, thereby, on their ability to meet pension obligations and provide public services, and on the tax base for Social Security and Medicare, thus threatening these important elements of the American consensus. In short, the greedy corporate elite have benefitted themselves at enormous cost to the American people and to the economic and social stability of the United States.

The job loss from offshoring also has had a huge and dire impact on Federal Reserve policy. With the decline in income growth, the US economy stalled. The Federal Reserve under Alan Greenspan substituted an expansion in consumer credit for the missing growth in consumer income in order to maintain aggregate consumer demand. Instead of wage increases, Greenspan relied on an increase in consumer debt to fuel the economy.

The credit expansion and consequent rise in real estate prices, together with the deregulation of the banking system, especially the repeal of the Glass-Steagall Act, produced the real estate bubble and the fraud and mortgage-backed derivatives that gave us the 2007-08 financial crash.

The Federal Reserve responded to the crash not by bailing out consumer debt but by bailing out the debt of its only constituency – the big banks. The Federal Reserve let little banks fail and be bought up by the big ones, thus further increasing financial concentration. The multi-trillion dollar increase in the Federal Reserve's balance sheet was entirely for the benefit of a handful of large banks. Never before in history had an agency of the US government acted so decisively in behalf only of the ownership class.

118

The way the Federal Reserve saved the irresponsible large banks, which should have failed and have been broken up, was to raise the prices of troubled assets on the banks' books by lowering interest rates. To be clear, interest rates and bond prices move in opposite directions. When interest rates are lowered by the Federal Reserve, which it achieves by purchasing debt instruments, the prices of bonds rise. As the various debt risks move together, lower interest rates raise the prices of all debt instruments, even troubled ones. Raising the prices of debt instruments produced solvent balance sheets for the big banks.

To achieve its aim, the Federal Reserve had to lower the interest rates to zero, which even the low reported inflation reduced to negative interest rates. These low rates had disastrous consequences. On the one hand low interest rates caused all sorts of speculations. On the other low interest rates deprived retirees of interest income on their retirement savings, forcing them to draw down capital, thus reducing accumulated wealth among the 90 percent. The under-reported inflation rate also denied retirees Social Security cost-of-living adjustments, forcing them to spend retirement capital.

The low interest rates also encouraged corporate boards to borrow money in order to buy back the corporation's stock, thus raising its price and, thereby, the bonuses and stock options of executives and board members and the capital gains of shareholders. In other words, corporations indebted themselves for the short-term benefit of executives and owners. Companies that refused to participate in this scam were threatened by Wall Street with takeovers.

Consequently today the combination of offshoring and Federal Reserve policy has left us a situation in which every aspect of the economy is indebted – consumers, government at all levels, and businesses. A recent Federal Reserve study concluded that Americans are so indebted and so poor that 41 percent of the American population cannot raise $400 without borrowing from family and friends or selling personal possessions.

A country whose population is this indebted has no consumer market. Without a consumer market there is no economic growth, other than the false orchestrated figures produced by the US government by under counting the inflation rate and the unemployment rate.

Without economic growth, consumers, businesses, state, local, and federal governments cannot service their debts and meet their obligations.

The Federal Reserve has learned that it can keep afloat the Ponzi scheme that is the US economy by printing money with which to support financial asset prices. The alleged rises in interest rates by the Federal Reserve are not real interest rates rises. Even the under-reported inflation rate is higher than the interest rate increases, with the result that the real interest rate falls.

It is no secret that the Federal Reserve controls the price of bonds by openly buying and selling US Treasuries. Since 1987 the Federal Reserve can also support the price of US equities. If the stock market tries to sell off, before much damage can be done the Federal Reserve steps in and purchases S&P futures, thus driving up stock prices. In recent years, when corrections begin they are quickly interrupted and the fall is arrested.

As a member of the Plunge Protection Team known officially as the Working Group on Financial Markets, the Federal Reserve has an open mandate to prevent another 1987 "Black Monday." In my opinion, the Federal Reserve would interpret this mandate as authority to directly intervene. However, just as the Fed can use the big banks as agents for its control over the price of gold, it can use the Wall Street banks dark pools to manipulate the equity markets. In this way the manipulation can be disguised as banks making trades for clients. The Plunge Protection Team consists of the Federal Reserve, the Treasury, the SEC, and the Commodity Futures Trading Corporation. As

Washington's international power comes from the US dollar as world reserve currency, protecting the value of the dollar is essential to American power. Foreign inflows into US equities are part of the dollar's strength. Thus, the Plunge Protection Team seeks to prevent a market crash that would cause flight from US dollar assets.

Normally so much money creation by the Federal Reserve, especially in conjunction with such a high debt level of the US government and also state and local governments, consumers, and businesses, would cause a falling US dollar exchange rate. Why hasn't this happened?

For three reasons. One is that the central banks of the other three reserve currencies – the Japanese central bank, the European central bank, and the Bank of England – also print money. Their Quantitative Easing, which still continues, offsets the dollars created by the Federal Reserve and keeps the US dollar from depreciating.

A second reason is that when suspicion of the dollar's worth sends up the gold price, the Federal Reserve or its bullion banks short gold futures with naked contracts. This drives down the gold price. There are numerous columns on my website by myself and Dave Kranzler proving this to be the case. There is no doubt about it.

The third reason is that money managers, individuals, pension funds, everyone and all the rest had rather make money than not. Therefore, they go along with the Ponzi scheme. The people who did not benefit from the Ponzi scheme of the past decade are those who understood it was a Ponzi scheme but did not realize the corruption that has beset the Federal Reserve and the central bank's ability and willingness to continue to feed the Ponzi scheme.

As I have explained previously, the Ponzi scheme falls apart when it becomes impossible to continue to support the dollar as burdened as the dollar is by debt levels and abundance of dollars that could be dumped on the exchange markets.

This is why Washington is determined to retain its hegemony. It is Washington's hegemony over Japan, Europe, and the UK that protects the American Ponzi scheme. The moment one of these central banks ceases to support the dollar, the others would follow, and the Ponzi scheme would unravel. If the prices of US debt and stocks were reduced to their real values, the United States would no longer have a place in the ranks of world powers.

The implication is that war, and not economic reform, is America's most likely future.

In a subsequent column I hope to explain why neither US political party has the awareness and capability to deal with real problems.

First published on June 26, 2018.

The State of the Economy

The story line is going out that the economic boom is weakening and the Federal Reserve has to get the printing press running again. The Fed uses the money to purchase bonds, which drives up the prices of bonds and lowers the interest rate. The theory is that the lower interest rate encourages consumer spending and business investment and that this increase in consumer and business spending results in more output and employment.

The Federal Reserve, European Central Bank, and Bank of England have been wedded to this policy for a decade, and the Japanese for longer, without stimulating business investment. Rather than borrowing at low interest rates in order to invest more, corporations borrowed in order to buy back their stock. In other words, some corporations after using all their profits to buy back their own stock went into debt in order to further reduce their market capitalization!

Far from stimulating business investment, the liquidity supplied by the Federal Reserve drove up stock and bond prices and spilled over into real estate. The fact that corporations used their profits to buy back their shares rather than to invest in new capacity means that the corporations did not experience a booming economy with good investment opportunities. It is a poor economy when the best investment for a company is to repurchase its own shares.

Consumers, devoid of real income growth, maintained their living standards by going deeper into debt. This process was aided, for example, by stretching out car payments from three years to six and seven years, with the result that loan balances exceed the value of the vehicles. Many households live on credit cards by paying the minimum amount, with the result that their indebtedness grows by the month. The Federal Reserve's low interest rates are not reciprocated by the high credit card interest rate on outstanding balances.

Some European countries now have negative interest rates, which means that the bank does not pay you interest on your deposit, but charges you a fee for holding your money. In other words, you are charged an interest rate for having money in a bank. One reason for this is the belief of neoliberal economists that consumers would prefer to spend their money than to watch it gradually wither away and that the spending will drive the economy to higher growth.

What is the growth rate of the economy? It is difficult to know, because the measures of inflation have been tampered with in order to avoid cost-of-living adjustments for Social Security recipients and the payment of COLA adjustments in contracts. The consumer price index is a basket of goods that represents an average household's expenditures. The weights of the items in the index are estimates of the percentage of the household budget that is spent on those items. A rise in the prices of items in the index would raise the index by the weight of those items, and this was the measure of inflation.

Changes were made that reduced the inflation that the index measured. One change was to substitute a lower price alternative when an item in the index rose in price. Another was to designate a rise in price of an item as a quality improvement and not count it as inflation.

Something similar was done to the producer price index which is used to deflate nominal GDP in order to measure real economic growth. GDP is measured in terms of money, and some of the growth in the measure is due to price increases rather than to more output of goods and services. In order to have a good estimate of how much real output has increased, it is necessary to deflate the nominal measure of GDP by taking out the price rises. If inflation is underestimated, then real GDP will be overestimated. When John Williams of Shadowstats adjusts the real GDP measure for what he calculates is a two-percentage point understatement of annual inflation, there has been very little economic growth since 2009 when a recovery allegedly began, and the economy remains far below its pre-recession level in 2008.

In other words, the belief that the US has had a decade long economic recovery is likely to be an illusion produced by underestimating inflation. Indeed, every day experience with the prices of food, clothing, household goods, and services indicates a higher rate of inflation than is officially reported.

The low unemployment rate that is reported is also an illusion. The government achieves the low rate by not counting the unemployed. The economic and psychological cost of searching for a job are high. There are the economic costs of a presentable appearance and transport to the interview. For a person without a pay check, these costs rapidly mount. The psychological costs of failure to find a job time after time also mount. People become discouraged and cease looking. The government treats discouraged workers who cannot find jobs as no longer being in the work force and omits them from the measure of unemployment. John Williams estimates that the real rate of US unemployment is 20%, not 3.5%

The decline in the labor force participation rate supports Williams' conclusion. Normally, a booming economy, which is what 3.5% unemployment represents, would have a rising labor force participation rate as people enter the work force to take advantage of the employment opportunities. However, during the alleged ten year boom, the participation rate has fallen, an indication of poor job opportunities.

The government measures jobs in two ways: the payroll jobs report that seeks to measure the new jobs created each month (which is not a measure of employment as a person may hold two or more jobs) and the household survey that seeks to measure employment. The results are usually at odds and cannot be reconciled. What does seem to emerge is that the new jobs reported are for the most part low productivity, low value-added, lowly paid jobs. Another conclusion is that the number of full time jobs with benefits are declining and the number of part-time jobs are rising.

A case could be made that US living standards have declined since the 1950s when one income was sufficient to support a family. The husband took the slings and arrows of the work experience, and the wife provided household services such as home cooked nutritious meals, child care, clean clothes, and an orderly existence. Today most households require two earners to make ends meet and then only barely. Saving is a declining option. A Federal Reserve report a couple of years ago concluded that about half of American households could not produce $400 cash unless personal possessions were sold.

As the Federal Reserve's low interest rate policy has not served ordinary Americans or spurred investment in new plant and equipment, who has it served? The answer is corporate executives and shareholders. As the liquidity supplied by the Federal Reserve has gone mainly into the prices of financial assets, it is the owners of these assets who have benefited from the Federal Reserve's policy. Years ago Congress in its unwisdom capped the amount of executive pay that could be deducted as a business expense at one million dollars unless performance related. What "performance related" means is a rise in profits and share price. Corporate boards and executives achieved "performance" by reducing labor costs by moving jobs offshore and by using profits and borrowing in order to buy back the company's shares, thus driving up the price.

In other words, corporate leaders and owners benefited by harming the US economy, the careers and livelihoods of the American work force, and their own companies.

This is the reason for the extraordinary worsening of the income and wealth distribution in the United States that is polarizing the US into a handful of mega-rich and a multitude of have-nots.

The America I grew up in was an opportunity society. There were ladders of upward mobility that could be climbed on merit alone without requiring family status or social and political connections.

Instate college tuition was low. Most families could manage it, and the students of those families that could not afford the cost worked their way through university with part time jobs. Student loans were unknown.

That America is gone.

The few economists capable of thought wonder about the high price/earnings ratios of US stocks and the 26,000 Dow Jones when stock buy-backs indicate that US corporations see no investment opportunities. How can stock prices be so high when corporations see no growth in US consumer income that would justify investment in the US?

When President Reagan's supply-side economic policy got the Dow Jones up to 1,000 the US still had a real economy. How can it be that today with America's economy hollowed out the Dow Jones is 25 or 26 times higher? Manipulation plays a role in the answer. In Reagan's last year in office, the George H.W. Bush forces created the Working Group on Financial Markets, otherwise known as the "plunge protection team," the purpose of which was to prevent a stock market fall that would deny Bush the Republican nomination and the presidency as Reagan's successor. The Bush people did not want any replay of October 1987.

The plunge protection team brought together the Federal Reserve, Treasury, and Securities and Exchange Commission in a format that could intervene in the stock market to prevent a fall. The easiest way to do this is, when faced with falling stock prices, to step in and purchase S&P futures. Hedge funds follow the leader and the market decline is arrested.

The Federal Reserve now has the ability to intervene in any financial market. Dave Kranzler and I have shown repeatedly how the Federal Reserve or its proxies intervene in the gold market to support the value of the excessively-supplied US dollar by printing naked gold contracts to drop on the gold futures market in order to knock down the price of gold. A rising gold price would show that the dollar support arrangements that the Federal Reserve has with other central banks to maintain the illusion of a strong dollar is a contrived arrangement rejected by the gold market.

What few, if any, economists and financial market commentators understand is that today all markets are rigged by the plunge protection team. For at least a decade it has not been possible to evaluate the financial situation by relying on traditional thinking and methods. Rigged markets do not respond in the way that competitive markets respond. This is the explanation why companies that see no investment opportunities for their profits better than the repurchase of their own shares can have high price/earnings ratios. This is the explanation why the market's effort to bring stock prices in line with realistic price/earnings ratios is unsuccessful.

As far as I can surmise, the Federal Reserve and plunge protection team can continue to rig the financial markets for the mega-rich until the US dollar loses its role as world reserve currency.

First published on June 6, 2019.

What Globalism Did Was To Transfer The US Economy To China

The main problem with the US economy is that globalism has been deconstructing it. The offshoring of US jobs has reduced US manufacturing and industrial capability and associated innovation, research, development, supply chains, consumer purchasing power, and tax base of state and local governments. Corporations have increased short-term profits at the expense of these long-term costs. In effect, the US economy is being moved out of the First World into the Third World.

Tariffs are not a solution. The Trump administration says that the tariffs are paid by China, but unless Apple, Nike, Levi, and all of the offshoring companies got an exemption from the tariffs, the tariffs fall on the offshored production of US firms that are sold to US consumers. The tariffs will either reduce the profits of the US firms or be paid by US purchasers of the products in higher prices. The tariffs will hurt China only by reducing Chinese employment in the production of US goods for US markets.

The financial media is full of dire predictions of the consequences of a US/China "trade war." There is no trade war. A trade war is when countries try to protect their industries by placing tariff barriers on the import of cheaper products from foreign countries. But half or more of the imports from China are imports from US companies. Trump's tariffs, or a large part of them, fall on US corporations or US consumers.

One has to wonder that there is not a single economist anywhere in the Trump administration, the Federal Reserve, or anywhere else in Washington capable of comprehending the situation and conveying an understanding to President Trump.

One consequence of Washington's universal economic ignorance is that the financial media has concocted the story that "Trump's tariffs" are not only driving Americans into recession but also the entire world. Somehow tariffs on Apple computers and iPhones, Nike footwear, and Levi jeans are sending the world into recession or worse. This is an extraordinary economic conclusion, but the capacity for thought has pretty much disappeared in the United States.

In the financial media the question is: Will the Trump tariffs cause a US/world recession that costs Trump his reelection? This is a very stupid question. The US has been in a recession for two or more decades as its manufacturing/industrial/engineering capability has been transferred abroad. The US recession has been very good for the Asian part of the world. Indeed, China owes its faster than expected rise as a world power to the transfer of American jobs, capital, technology, and business know-how to China simply in order that US shareholders could receive capital gains and US executives could receive bonus pay for producing them by lowering labor costs.

Apparently, neoliberal economists, an oxymoron, cannot comprehend that if US corporations produce the goods and services that they market to Americans offshore, it is the offshore locations that benefit from the economic activity.

Offshore production started in earnest with the Soviet collapse as India and China opened their economies to the West. Globalism means that US corporations can make more money by abandoning their American work force. But what is true for the individual company is not true for the aggregate. Why? The answer is that when many corporations move their production for US markets offshore, Americans, unemployed or employed in lower paying jobs, lose the power to purchase the offshored goods.

I have reported for years that US jobs are no longer middle class jobs. The jobs have been declining for years in terms of value-added and pay. With this decline, aggregate demand declines. We have proof of this in the fact that for years US corporations have been using their profits not for investment in new plant and equipment, but to buy back their own shares. Any economist worthy of the name should instantly recognize that when corporations repurchase their shares rather than invest, they see no demand for increased output. Therefore, they loot their corporations for bonuses, decapitalizing the companies in the process. There is perfect knowledge that this is what is going on, and it is totally inconsistent with a growing economy.

As is the labor force participation rate. Normally, economic growth results in a rising labor force participation rate as people enter the work force to take advantage of the jobs. But throughout the alleged economic boom, the participation rate has been falling, because there are no jobs to be had.

In the 21st century the US has been decapitalized and living standards have declined. For a while the process was kept going by the expansion of debt, but consumer income has not kept pace and consumer debt expansion has reached its limits.

The Fed/Treasury "plunge protection team" can keep the stock market up by purchasing S&P futures. The Fed can pump out more money to drive up financial asset prices. But the money doesn't drive up production, because the jobs and the economic activity that jobs represent have been sent abroad. What globalism did was to transfer the US economy to China.

Real statistical analysis, as contrasted with the official propaganda, shows that the happy picture of a booming economy is an illusion created by statistical deception. Inflation is undermeasured, so when nominal GDP is deflated, the result is to count higher prices as an increase in real output, that is, inflation becomes real economic growth. Unemployment is not counted. If you have not searched for a job in the past 4 weeks, you are officially not a part of the work force and your unemployment is not counted. The way the government counts unemployment is so extraordinary that I am surprised the US does not have a zero rate of unemployment.

How does a country recover when it has given its economy away to a foreign country that it now demonizes as an enemy? What better example is there of a ruling class that is totally incompetent than one that gives its economy bound and gagged to an enemy so that its corporate friends can pocket short-term riches?

We can't blame this on Trump. He inherited the problem, and he has no advisers who can help him understand the problem and find a solution. No such advisers exist among neoliberal economists. I can only think of four economists who could help Trump, and one of them is a Russian.

The conclusion is that the United States is locked on a path that leads directly to the Third World of 60 years ago. President Trump is helpless to do anything about it.

First published on August 21, 2019.

Are Gold and Silver Money?

Former Federal Reserve Chairman Bernanke answers no.
And so do America's youth. Awhile back I posted videos of a podcaster who would offer Americans a one-ounce gold coin worth approximately $1,800 for one piece of chewing gum, only to be refused. The youth, who pay with credit cards, not with cash, think money is digital. Consequently a bitcoin is worth many times the value of a gold coin despite the fact that a bitcoin's value is nebulous and can decline thousands of dollars in a day.

And, apparently, gold and silver are not money for people worried about inflation that is allegedly so serious that the Federal Reserve is engineering a recession and pension fund and Big Bank wipeout to stop.

With inflation high and financial investments paying so little, why haven't people sought to protect their purchasing power by going into gold and silver? Gold and silver prices have fallen while inflation has risen. This is nonsensical.

Part of the answer is that the US dollar is high despite high inflation. This normally nonsensical relationship is because the UK pound, euro, and yen are adversely impacted by economy shutdowns due to Covid lockdowns and energy shortages created by Washington's Russian sanctions, and these countries are experiencing their own inflations from the sanctions and from the Covid lockdowns that reduced supply and cut them off from global deliveries. Supply reductions can result in higher prices just as effectively as excessive consumer demand.

Another part of the answer is that the supply of gold and silver in the futures market where price is determined can be increased by printing uncovered contracts and, thereby can be increased in supply like fiat paper money. As I explained many times on this website, often in collaboration with Dave Kranzler, the prices of gold and silver are set

133

in futures markets, not in the physical market where gold and silver are purchased. The futures market in gold and silver permits "naked shorts." This means that unlike the stock market, where the person shorting the market has to have the actual stock to sell, which is usually borrowed, gold and silver can be sold short without the seller owning any gold or silver.

What this means is that gold and silver that trade in future markets can be created by printing contracts that are not covered by gold and silver. In other words, today gold and silver can be increased in supply by printing contracts in the futures market where price is determined just as fiat paper money can be printed.

The printing of contracts and then dumping them into the futures market suddenly increases the supply of paper gold. A sudden increase in shorts in the futures market drives down the gold price. The Federal Reserve and the Big Banks have used naked shorting to prevent rising gold and silver prices that would show the true depreciation in the dollar's value.

The futures market clears in cash. The holders of contracts do not demand payment in gold, that is, they do not take delivery. They settle in cash. If those holding delivery contracts actually demanded delivery, it is unlikely the Comex would have the gold to deliver. Comex would simply refuse delivery and settle the contract in cash at a price determined by the manipulation of gold's and silver's values by naked shorting.

Gold investors believe that eventually this way of holding down the price of gold and silver will be overwhelmed by flight from excessively printed paper currencies.

There is reason to believe that they are correct. Unless the Federal Reserve has become involved with the World Economic Forum's plan to force with crises a worldwide "Great Reset" in which we all become serfs owning nothing, in which case a different agenda is being served, the Federal Reserve's current policy will cause problems for Big Banks, such as Credit Suisse's current problems, pension funds, insurers, and for stock and bond prices and the many speculative deals based on former interest rates, and part of the resulting flight from financial assets will find its way into gold and silver

Gold and silver were the original money, because they are rare and can serve as a store of value as well as a means of exchange. A gold and silver money supply can nevertheless be inflated. Gold coins can be shaved – thus the ridges placed on the edges of the coins to reveal the diminution of the gold content. And the coins can be debased by the addition of non-precious metals, as was the silver denarius with which the Roman army was paid. I have a "silver denarius" that is 90% lead.

As economist Milton Friedman demonstrated, even when operating under a gold system, a central bank can essentially cancel it by interventions that offset the currency effects of the import and export of gold to bring the balance of payments into balance.

Nevertheless, gold and silver coins that are not debased hold their real value in inflation times, that is they rise in value with inflation while fiat money declines in value unless the central bank suppresses the rise in precious metals prices with naked shorts.

The conclusion is that only gold and silver are real money.

Paper money came in as a stand-in for real money as gold and silver are heavy and their presence in significant amounts is obvious and requires the expense of protection. In previous times, gold and silver were deposited in vaults, and the depositor was provided a receipt, which traded as the first paper money.

In later periods when paper currency, such as Bank of England notes, entered circulation, they were backed by and convertible into gold. The same was true in the US until the Franklin D. Roosevelt era in the 1930s when Roosevelt confiscated gold from Americans and then raised its price.

US Senator Jesse Helms returned to Americans the right to own gold four decades later in the 1970s.

In the 1930s President Roosevelt called in the gold and then raised the official price from $20 an ounce to $35, where it stood until the official price became $42.22. In the 1970s Senator Helms got a law passed permitting Americans to again own gold in the form of coins and bars and not merely jewelry. In the 1980s the price of gold rose to $800 per ounce despite the large rise in the value of the US dollar due to the success of President Reagan's supply-side economic policy. Wall St had, of course, incorrectly predicted high inflation and dollar collapse from Reagan's policy, and some investors acted on the basis of this incorrect prediction.

In 2022 the price of gold per ounce peaked at $2,043.30 and currently stands at $1,655. Over my lifetime the price of one ounce of gold at today's price, has risen by 47 times – from $35 to $1,650.

The question is what has inflation done to the paper dollar? Is the dollar worth 47 times less than in my youth? How much has gold outperformed the paper dollar despite Washington's methods of suppressing the values of gold and silver?

I haven't enough confidence in the inflation data to compute this, but would be pleased to publish anyone's computation that is adequately explained.

What Americans born and raised after my generation do not understand is that at World War II's close, the United States stood at the top of the world. America emerged as the only industrial economy intact and expanded in productive power after the disastrous war. All other industrial economies were in ruins, and the plans were to convert Germany to a permanent non-industrial agricultural economy. This plan was abandoned only because of the rise of the "Soviet threat."

As MIT Professor Paul Samuelson, the doyen of American economics in the second half of the 20th century, emphasized, the United States was a self-sufficient economy. Its work force was employed producing products for domestic use and therefore Americans produced the goods and services that they consumed. This meant strong tax bases for numerous cities and states that were later ruined by the offshoring of American manufacturing forced by Wall Street in pursuit of lower labor costs and higher profits, a pursuit that cost America her ladders for upper mobility into the middle class and much of the middle class itself. Foreign trade or "Globalism" was an insignificant and unneeded component of American GDP. US debt, despite the accumulated war debt, was insignificant and of no consequent to the US economy as we owed it all to ourselves.

America's prosperity was destroyed by the Soviet Collapse in 1991. The reason is that the Soviet Collapse convinced China and India, with their massive underemployed work forces, that capitalism, not socialism, was the future, and they opened their economies to foreign capital.

Wall St forced American corporations under threat of takeovers to move their manufacturing abroad. This occurred and collapsed the growth of US consumer income and the tax bases of former manufacturing cities and states, many of which, like Detroit, became highly publicized ruins (see, for example, Paul Craig Roberts, The Failure of Laissez Faire Capitalism).

It was not competition from abroad, from China, India, Russia, that stopped the growth of American real incomes. It was the short-sighted, self-serving policies imposed by narrow economic interests, such as Wall St, that knocked America off its perch.

Today the American economy is a marketer of goods made by American firms abroad with foreign labor. Americans do not receive the income from the manufacture of the goods that they consume. Billionaires, such as Sir James Goldsmith and Roger Milliken, and a few economists, such as myself, made this completely clear for years to no effect. In America Greed, not facts, rules.

Greed prevailed over the public interest and what was good for America.

Now we have a country that cannot even produce its latest jet fighters without Chinese parts and whose consumer goods have Chinese labor costs and not American.

A country that has destroyed itself in this way is so poorly led that a revolution is long overdue.

Trump tried to show us what was happening to us, but so far Americans have proven too stupid to save themselves.

The incompetence of America is perhaps the reason Putin does not concern himself with the American interference in his Ukrainian operation.

As Putin faces a totally incompetent West, Putin, despite his own shortcomings, will prevail. And so will China.

First published on October 19, 2022.

How America's Economy Was Destroyed

In 1945 the United States emerged from a world war with the only intact industrial economy in the world. The British, European, Soviet, and Japanese economies were in ruins. China and the rest of Asia, Africa, and South America had undeveloped economies, later renamed third world economies. Additionally, the US held most of the world's gold reserves. President Franklin D. Roosevelt had used WWII to destroy Britain's control of international trade and the British pound as the world reserve currency. The US forced breakup of the British system of trade preferences and the coerced Bretton Woods Agreement gave those roles to the United States.

Four years of war production gave the US a large, disciplined, and skilled work force, and war time consumer shortages provided enormous pent-up consumer demand to drive the postwar economy's growth. Jobs were plentiful, and US real income rose strongly in the 1950s and into the 1960s.

But then things started to go wrong. President Johnson's program of "guns and butter" (the Vietnam War and "Great Society" welfare spending) resulted in a proliferation of US dollars that eventually forced President Nixon to close the gold window and terminate the right of foreign central banks to redeem their holdings of US dollars for gold. Additionally, the Keynesian demand management macroeconomic policy began breaking down. High marginal income tax rates resulted in weaker supply increases to increases in aggregate demand. Expansionary monetary policy pushed up consumer demand, but high tax rates curtailed supply response, culminating in the "stagflation" of President Carter's administration.

President Reagan's supply-side economic policy cured stagflation and the worsening "Phillips curve" trade-off between inflation and unemployment, and real economic growth resumed throughout the

1980s and into the Clinton years, an administration that piggy-backed on Reagan's success.

But in the last decade of the 20th century things turned for the worse. The success of Reagan's and Margaret Thatcher's economic policies created excessive confidence in unregulated free market economies. In the US the Glass-Steagall Act, which separated commercial from investment banking and had served the country well since 1933 was repealed. Federal Reserve Chairman Alan Greenspan and the Clinton Treasury claimed that "markets are self-regulating." The repeal set in motion the 2008 financial crisis that launched the largest and longest money printing activity in the US in history. The Federal Reserve's balance sheet increased by $8.2 trillion as the Fed printed money with which to buy up the troubled investments of the large banks in order to keep the banks solvent. The massive increase in the money supply went mainly into the prices of stocks, bonds, and real estate, thus dramatically worsening the income and wealth distribution in the US and creating the One Percent. Years of pumping up financial asset and real estate values with money creation has left the Federal Reserve today in a precarious position now that Covid lockdowns and economic sanctions against Russia have broken supply chains and caused shortages that are raising prices. The Fed is trying to overcome supply problems by nonsensically raising interest rates, which threatens the financial wealth created by years of Quantitative Easing. Simultaneously, the sanctions policy is driving countries away from the dollar which will eventually reduce its value, thereby forcing the Fed to choose between the stock market and the dollar.

Soviet collapse in 1991 compared to American success was an even worse development. It convinced China and India that capitalist markets, not socialist planning, was the way to economic success. Both countries with their large under-utilized labor forces opened themselves to foreign investment. This sped the era of "globalism" or jobs offshoring. American manufacturing corporations, under pressure from Wall Street of takeovers if they did not increase their profits by moving their manufacturing operations abroad where labor was cheaper, abandoned their work forces and their communities and began making abroad the products they marketed in the US. This separated Americans' incomes from the production of the goods and services that they consumed and dismantled the ladders of upward mobility in the US that had been erected by a vibrant manufacturing economy.

American economists with grants from Wall St and the offshoring corporations produced "studies" allegedly showing that it was good for America to lose its high productivity, high value-added jobs and for American communities to lose their tax base. Manufacturing jobs were denigrated as "dirty fingernail jobs," and the work force was promised better, higher paying, high-tech jobs. These studies and promises comprise the worse kind of junk economics.

One study by a Dartmouth academic, Matthew J Slaughter, concluded that offshoring American jobs, that is, by giving them to foreigners, created twice as many US domestic jobs as jobs for foreigners. He did not arrive at this conclusion by consulting the BLS payroll jobs data or the BLS Occupational Employment Statistics. Instead, he measured the growth of US multinational employment and failed to take into account the reasons for the increase in multinational employment. US multinationals acquired many existing smaller US domestic firms, thus raising multinational employment but not overall employment, and many US firms established foreign operations for the first time and thereby became multinationals, thus adding their existing US employment to multinational employment.

In 2006 Michael Porter, a Harvard professor, used a press conference to hype the benefits of globalism, that is, the offshoring of American jobs. His report for the Council on Competitiveness showed falsely that Americans were benefitting from giving their jobs to Asians and Mexicans. He did this by stressing US economic performance over a 20-year period. As jobs offshoring was relatively new, the 20 year period went all the way back to the Reagan 1980s. Thus Porter used the strong performance of the Reagan years to soften the economic deterioration from globalism.

I could go on at length presenting the fake claims used to block opposition to America's loss of its pre-eminent manufacturing status. Today 16 years after Porter's promise of better jobs, former well-paid US manufacturing workers have lowly paid retail jobs at Walmart and Home Depot. Their health insurance and pension benefits disappeared with their manufacturing jobs. The fact of the matter is that today American economists are either engaged in writing propaganda for their benefactors or they are playing games in their professional journals modeling scenarios that do not exist in the real world.

Another disastrous consequence of the repeal of Glass-Steagall is the acceleration it gave to the financialization of the economy that had been creeping up on us for decades. A financialized economy is one in which the financial sector has succeeded in getting most consumer income committed to paying interest and fees on debt – mortgage payments, car payments, credit card payments, student loans – leaving little to drive economic growth with expenditures on new goods and services. Many people live on their credit card, paying only the minimum payment as the balance grows with compound interest.

According to a Federal Reserve study of a few years ago, 40% of US households cannot raise $400 in cash without selling personal assets such as TVs, cell phones, clothes, or pawning tools.

The full extent of the over-indebted US economy, and here I do not include the government debt, can be understood by going back to 1945 where this essay began.

Michael Hudson reports that in 1945 homeowners' equity in the properties on which they were mortgaged was 85%. Today homeowners' equity in their properties has fallen to 33%.

Additionally, American home ownership has declined from 70% to 63% as the result of President Obama's policy of bailing out the financial fraudsters responsible for the 2008 crash, while foreclosing on their victims.

Once upon a time long ago the Democrat Party was honest. The party tried to protect the American South from invasion for its refusal to finance at the South's expense the cost of Northern industrialization. As the North saw it, it was the South's responsibility to pay the tariff that would protect Northern industry from Britain's better made and less costly products.

Until 1965 the Democrats continued to try to protect the working class. But in 1965 the Democrats betrayed Americans on two fronts. They passed an immigration bill that has flooded America with third world immigrants who are alien to our culture and whose numbers suppress wages. Simultaneously, the Democrats passed a Civil Rights Act that itself did not permit preference to "preferred minorities," but was used for that purpose by Alfred W. Blumrosen, compliance chief of the EEOC. Blumrosen reasoned that he could stand the Civil Rights Act on its head and require the prohibited racial quotas, because the federal courts traditionally since the 1930s "deferred to the regulatory authority."

Racial preferences for "preferred minorities" have developed into the aristocratic rights of an otherwise bygone era. Today in the Western World "preferred" peoples such as blacks and sexual perverts have special protections that do not extend to white heterosexual persons. A white person who objects to verbal or physical aggression by a black is declared a racist. A white woman who accuses a black of rape is in danger of being arrested for a hate crime in the Scandinavian countries and Germany. In what was once upon a time Great Britain, a white British citizen has been arrested by white British police for reposting a meme that shows disapproval of the ever growing collection of sexual perverts.

Today in the Western World the situation is this. The ethnic composition of the Western countries is under fierce attack by the liberal-left elements of their own ethnicity. The rights of the ethnic base of the population are ceasing to exist in the areas of free speech and due process of law. People are fired for using gender pronouns. Scientists are terminated for challenging a fake explanation. People are coerced into accepting violations of the Nuremberg Laws. Wherever a person turns for information, the media lies.

This is a hopeless situation for the Western World. As awareness spreads slowly but gradually among the ethnic populations of the West that their governments are against them, the ethnic majorities begin to realize that they are targeted for dispossession. Some of the French have realized this, and also farmers in Holland and Italy. Once the ethnic composition of a country realizes that the government does not represent them but represents their enemies, a revolutionary situation develops. All that can possibly save Western Civilization is revolution across the entire front. The entirety of governments and the vested interests they represent must be overthrown. Otherwise we face institutionalized tyranny and economies run for the benefit of the One Percent.

First published on August 3, 2022.

The Inflation Hoax

Yes, prices are rising, but not for the reasons the Federal Reserve says. When I say inflation is a hoax, I mean the purported cause is a hoax. The Fed is fighting a consumer inflation, a "demand-pull" inflation. But what we are experiencing is a supply-side inflation caused by the Covid lockdowns and economic sanctions that closed businesses, disrupted supply chains, and broke business relationships while reducing energy supplies to the UK and European countries, thus forcing up costs in a globalized economy. One of the many neglected problems of globalism is that inflations and recessions are no long simply a national problem. Interconnectedness sends adversity globally, although in varying degrees.

The Fed thinks that the inflation is the result of the trillions of dollars of Covid payments that were dumped into the economy. To the extent that this money was simply replacing the lost wages, salaries, and business earnings from the lockdowns, there would be no net addition of money, just a replacement. I don't have the data on the lost earnings from the lockdowns, but it is obvious that there was a large supply disruption.

Monetarists think that the inflation was caused by 12 years of Quantitative Easing during which the Fed's balance sheet expanded five-fold. But it is not supposed to take 12 years for monetary expansion to result in inflation. All the while the Fed, still believing in the Phillips Curve that President Reagan's supply-side policy had eliminated, said it was trying to get inflation up to 2% annually, which neoliberal economists, junk economics in Michael Hudson's view with which I agree, say is the inflation needed to spur economic growth.

Demand side inflations appear gradually and rise with a booming economy. They don't suddenly appear overnight as the present inflation has. It is sudden supply shortages that produce instantly higher prices.

The Fed fights a demand-pull inflation by reducing the growth of money and credit, thereby reducing sales and employment. But this and the higher interest rates reduce supply. If sales fall off, so does production. Higher interest rates raise costs and adversely impact supply. Thus, the Fed's interest rate policy can raise, rather than lower, inflation.

The way inflation is measured today adds to the problem. Inflation is no longer measured in terms of weighted prices in a constant basket of goods. The goods in the basket change as items with smaller price rises are substituted for those with larger rises. There is a subjective element in this substitution. Also, some price rises are attributed to quality improvements, and this decision also has a subjective element. If the agenda is to have a lower inflation rate, there can be more substitution and more quality improvements. If the agenda needs a higher inflation rate, minimize the substitutions and quality improvements.

If inflation is coming down, and it is not just a product of manipulating subjective elements, how do we know it is not from increased supply from reopened businesses and repaired supply chains? If there is reliable data, this could be studied. But neoliberal economists are locked into explaining everything in terms of demand. I have spent 40 years trying to teach them supply-side economics, but they are incapable of learning.

Just as inflation was redefined by changing its measurement, now recession is being redefined. Whether or not 3 down quarters mean a recession, the view is that the second half of next year will be bad and that the Fed will stop raising interest rates and begin lowering them. At that point or earlier if sufficiently anticipated, the stock and bond markets will begin another rise. Recession means that the Fed injects liquidity and the financial markets rise with liquidity.

This is the way it has been, but the landscape has changed, and we are faced with a new development. Gradually over the years government through the many welfare programs, which in the Biden regime includes handing money to illegal immigrant-invaders, has accumulated a constituency that is paid but does not work. These people have money to spend on goods and services, but do not contribute to the supply of goods and services. This constituency introduces an inflationary bias and this constituency is rapidly growing with the millions of immigrant-invaders who are allowed to enter the country each year. If a substantial part of the population is supported with purchasing power but does not work, whether because welfare exceeds their prospective wages or it is illegal to employ them or they prefer sustainable leisure to work and higher income, consumer demand grows relative to output. This gives us demand-pull inflation with a vengeance. Military spending is similar to welfare. The associated wages and salaries pump money into consumer demand, but there are no corresponding goods and services to absorb it. Consumers do not purchase tanks, missiles, fighter aircraft, and warships. The size of the US military budget makes it inflationary.

What can the Fed do? Throwing people out of work reduces demand from the productive part of the population, not from the subsidized part. Throwing productive people out of work also reduces supply, which acts on prices in a counter direction to reduced demand. Which force prevails?

Large cities tend to accumulate subsidized populations that boost consumer demand but not supply. Even rich cities can find themselves with budget outlays that exceed their revenues. I will use New York to illustrate it, with thanks to Nicole Gelinas writing in the Autumn 2022 issue of City Journal. New York City, the home of Wall Street and the largest banks, is a high income city. But only in part and less and less as the city fills up with welfare dependent people. New York City and its host state today have to rely on vice to bring in the revenues to keep afloat. NYC has gone from a lottery, to a planned casino in Manhattan, to sports gambling, to legalizing cannabis, all of which can be taxed, and now the city is talking about legalizing prostitution in order to benefit from taxing the revenues. What is the future if New York has to turn into Sodom and Gomorrah in order to survive?

The Democrat vote is forcing the richest city in the US to go into the business of marketing vice industries that its police formerly arrested the Mafia for operating. To me this shows desperation. If NYC cannot cope without creating and marketing vice industries for revenue purposes, what can, for example, St. Louis, once one of America's great cities, do?

St. Louis was one of America's cities devastated by the offshoring of manufacturing jobs. Its population has shrunk. The city is 45% black, and its government is in black hands.

What is the black mayor doing? She has created a commission to decide on reparations paid by white St. Louis residents to black residents. In other words, white residents of St. Louis, none of whom ever owned a slave and only a minuscule number descended from plantation owners who did, are targeted to have some portion of their income or wealth confiscated and given to black beneficiaries of St. Louis' reparations scheme.

Here we see the inability of St. Louis' mayor to think. Why live in St. Louis if you have to pay a tax to blacks to live there?

Like every other tax, once institutionalized the tax will rise. It is the United States of America that is resurrecting the feudal order in which there are class rights and whites are the underclass paying tribute to black aristocrats like serfs paid to lords. You can pretend this is not the case. But it is.

What incentive does this give whites to be productive, or to stay in areas under black political control?

The United States is already merely a name as the states are clearly disunited. Will the country devolve into separate political entities on a racial basis and even into city states?

The Democrat Party has turned its back on white Americans, labeling them "Trump deplorables," "white supremacists," and "threats to democracy." The Rino Republican Party will not defend white Americans or stand by any politician, such as Trump, who does. What stake do Trump Americans have in a country in which they are labeled as undesirables?

The white liberals, indoctrinated into their racial guilt, will simply submit, but the "Trump deplorables" will organize into separate communities. They will be aided by US over-reach abroad and the subsequent demise of the dollar and empire as the rising power of a reinvigorated China and Russia take the lead from the culturally exhausted Western world.

Meanwhile the Fed yesterday raised interest rates another half a percentage point in the face of expectations of a bad recession in the coming year. This is the high level of incompetence that today rules Americans.

Personally, I am suspicious of this inflation. If it is, as I believe, the result of supply disruptions, the resumption of productive activity following the disastrous lockdowns would itself have brought prices down without need of Fed action. I also suspect that the inflation resulted in part from announcements of its arrival, in which announcements executives and boards saw opportunity to boost profits and obtain their bonus rewards by raising prices. A lot goes on that passes unnoticed by economists and pundits.

First published on December 15, 2022.

Washington's Power Will Decline With the Dollar

Saudi Arabia's recent announcement that the government is open to accepting payment for oil in currencies other than the dollar is a major announcement ignored by the presstitutes. The end of the petrodollar would have severe adverse effects on the value of the dollar and on US inflation and interest rates.

For a half century the petrodollar has supported the value of the US dollar and ensured financing for America's large budget and trade deficits. By billing for oil in dollars, the Saudis guaranteed a worldwide demand for US dollars. Without this demand for dollars, the constant increase in the US money supply would have eroded the dollar's exchange value in terms of other currencies. As the US has offshored so much of its production for home use, the US is import-dependent, and the widening trade deficit would have eroded the dollar's exchange value and resulted in high inflation.

Similarly, as the world needed dollars for oil payments, countries held dollars in the form of interest bearing US Treasuries rather than currency, and this made financing easy for large US budget deficits.

The petrodollar supported the continuing role of the dollar as world currency after President Nixon closed the gold window in 1971, in effect ending the Bretton Woods system following WWII that gave the US dollar the reserve currency role. Under Bretton Woods, foreign central banks had the right to demand US gold for their dollar holdings. When France made this demand, Nixon abrogated the Bretton Woods agreement. To save the dollar's value and its reserve currency role, the petrodollar system was created.

In recent years Washington has so abused the dollar's reserve currency role with sanctions and asset seizes that many countries desire to settle their trade imbalances in their own currencies in order to escape

Washington's ability to threaten and punish them for serving their own interests rather than Washington's. If Saudi Arabia abandons the petrodollar, the demand for dollars and the dollar's value will fall.

This is a major threat to Washington's power and to the financial power of American banks.

It is possible that the Saudis are sending a signal to Washington that Washington's failure to comply with some Saudi concerns or interests can have undesirable consequences for the US. In other words, the Saudis might be using their leverage to get what they want from Washington.

Time will tell. If the Saudis do drop the petrodollar, Americans will face stiff inflation and high interest rates necessary to finance US budget deficits, unless the Fed itself finances the deficits by printing money, in which case monetary inflation would be added to inflation caused by the drop in the dollar's foreign exchange value resulting from declining foreign demand for the US dollar.

Should this come to pass the implication for the US is massive austerity.

First published January 30, 2023.

CHAPTER 3
THE UKRAINE
DECEPTION

Defeated By The Taliban, Washington Decides To Take On Russia And China

The several days of organized protests in Ukraine are notable for the relative lack of police violence. Unlike in the US, Canada, Thailand, Greece, and Spain, peaceful protesters have not been beaten, tear gassed, water cannoned, and tasered by Ukrainian police. Unlike in Egypt, Palestine, and Bahrain, Ukrainian protesters have not been fired upon with live ammunition. The restraint of the Ukrainian government and police in the face of provocations has been remarkable. Apparently, Ukrainian police have not been militarized by US Homeland Security.

What are the Ukrainian protests about? On the surface, the protests don't make sense. The Ukrainian government made the correct decision to stay out of the EU. Ukraine's economic interests lie with Russia, not with the EU. This is completely obvious.

The EU wants Ukraine to join so that Ukraine can be looted, like Latvia, Greece, Spain, Italy, Ireland, and Portugal. The situation is so bad in Greece, for example, that the World Health Organization reports that some Greeks are infecting themselves with HIV in order to receive the 700 euro monthly benefit for the HIV-infected.

The US wants Ukraine to join so it can become a location for more of Washington's missile bases against Russia.

Why would Ukrainians want to be looted?

Why would Ukrainians want to become targets for Russia's Iskander Missiles as a host country for Washington's aggression against Russia?

Why would Ukrainians having gained their sovereignty from Russia want to lose it to the EU?

Obviously, an intelligent, aware, Ukrainian population would not accept these costs of joining the EU.

So, why the protests?

Part of the answer is Ukrainian nationalists' hatred of Russia. With the Soviet collapse, Ukraine became a country independent of Russia. When empires break up, other interests can seize power. Various secessions occurred producing a collection of small states such as Georgia, Azerbaijan, the former central Asian Soviet Republics, Ukraine, the Baltics, and the pieces into which Czechoslovakia and Yugoslavia were broken by "nationalism." The governments of these weak states were easy for Washington to purchase. The governments of these powerless states are more responsive to Washington than to their own people. Much of the former Soviet Empire is now part of Washington's Empire. Georgia, the birthplace of Joseph Stalin, now sends its sons to die for Washington in Afghanistan, just as Georgia did for the Soviet Union,

These former constituent elements of the Russian/Soviet Empire are being incorporated into Washington's Empire. The gullible nationalists, naïfs really, in these American colonies might think that they are free, but they simply have exchanged one master for another.

They are blind to their subservience, because they remember their subservience to Russia/Soviet Union and have not yet realized their subservience to Washington, which they see as a liberator with a checkbook. When these weak and powerless new countries, which have no protector, realize that their fate is not in their own hands, but in Washington's hands, it will be too late for them.

With the collapse of the Soviet Union, Washington quickly stepped into the place of Russia. The new countries were all broke, as was Russia at the time and, thus, helpless. Washington used NGOs funded by Washington and its EU puppets to create anti-Russian, pro-

American, pro-EU movements in the former constituent parts of Soviet Russia. The gullible peoples were so happy to have escaped the Soviet thumb that they did not realize that they now had new masters.

It is a good bet that the Ukrainian protests are a CIA organized event, using the Washington and EU funded NGOs and manipulating the hatred of Ukrainian nationalists for Russia. The protests are directed against Russia. If Ukraine can be realigned and brought into the fold of Washington's Empire, Russia is further diminished as a world power.

To this effect NATO conducted war games against Russia last month in operation Steadfast Jazz 2013. Finland, Ukraine, Georgia, and neutral Sweden have offered their military participation in the next iteration of NATO war games close to Russia's borders despite the fact that they are not NATO members.

The diminishment of Russia as a powerful state is critical to Washington's agenda for world hegemony. If Russia can be rendered impotent, Washington's only concern is China.

The Obama regime's "Pivot to Asia" announced Washington's plan to surround China with naval and air bases and to interject Washington into every dispute that China has with Asian neighbors. China has responded to Washington's provocation by expanding its air space, an action that Washington calls destabilizing when in fact it is Washington that is destabilizing the region.

China is unlikely to be intimidated, but could undermine itself if its economic reform opens China's economy to western manipulation. Once China frees its currency and embraces "free markets," Washington can manipulate China's currency and drive China's currency into volatility that discourages its use as a rival to the dollar. China is disadvantaged by having so many university graduates from US universities, where they have been indoctrinated with Washington's view of the world. When these American-programmed graduates return to China, some tend to become a fifth column whose influence will ally with Washington's war on China.

So where does this leave us? Washington will prevail until the US dollar collapses.

Many support mechanisms are in place for the dollar. The Federal Reserve and its dependent bullion banks have driven down the price of gold and silver by short-selling in the paper futures market, allowing bullion to flow into Asia at bargain prices, but removing the pressure of a rising gold price on the exchange value of the US dollar.

Washington has prevailed on Japan and, apparently, the European Central Bank, to print money in order to prevent the rise of the yen and euro to the dollar.

The Trans-Pacific and Trans-Atlantic Partnerships are designed to keep countries in the US dollar payments system, thus supporting the dollar's value in currency markets.

Eastern European members of the EU that still have their own currencies have been told that they must print their own currencies in order to prevent a rise in their currency's value relative to the US dollar that would curtail their exports.

The financial world is under Washington's thumb. And Washington is printing money for the sake of 4 or 5 mega-banks.

That should tell the protestors in Ukraine all they need to know.

First published on December 4, 2013.

Washington Drives the World Toward War

Washington has had the US at war for 12 years: Afghanistan, Iraq, Somalia, Libya, Pakistan, Yemen, and almost Syria, which could still happen, with Iran waiting in the wings. These wars have been expensive in terms of money, prestige, and deaths and injuries of both US soldiers and the attacked civilian populations. None of these wars appears to have any compelling reason or justifiable explanation. The wars have been important to the profits of the military/security complex. The wars have provided cover for the construction of a Stasi police state in America, and the wars have served Israel's interest by removing obstacles to Israel's annexation of the entire West Bank and southern Lebanon.

As costly and destructive as these wars have been, they are far below the level of a world war, much less a world war against nuclear armed opponents.

The fatal war for humanity is the war with Russia and China toward which Washington is driving the US and Washington's NATO and Asian puppet states. There are a number of factors contributing to Washington's drive toward the final war, but the overarching one is the doctrine of American exceptionalism.

According to this self-righteous doctrine, America is the indispensable country. What this means is that the US has been chosen by history to establish the hegemony of secular "democratic capitalism" over the world. The primacy of this goal places the US government above traditional morality and above all law, both its own and international.

Thus, no one in the US government has been held accountable for unprovoked aggression against other countries and for attacking civilian populations, unambiguous war crimes under international law and the Nuremberg standard. Neither has anyone in the US government been held accountable for torture, a prohibited crime under US law and the Geneva Conventions. Neither has anyone been held accountable for numerous violations of constitutional rights – spying without warrants, warrantless searches, violations of habeas corpus, murder of citizens without due process, denial of legal representation, conviction on secret evidence. The list is long.

A person might wonder what is exceptional and indispensable about a government that is a reincarnation of Nazi Germany in every respect. People propagandized into the belief that they are the world's special people inevitably lose their humanity. Thus, as the US military video released by Bradley Manning reveals, US troops get their jollies by mowing down innocent people as they walk along a city street.

With the exception of the ACLU, constitutional rights groups and independent Internet voices, the American people including the Christian churches have accepted their government's criminality and immorality with scant protest.

The absence of moral denunciation emboldens Washington which is now pushing hard against Russia and China, the current governments of which stand in the way of Washington's world hegemony.

Washington has been working against Russia for 22 years ever since the collapse of the Soviet Union in 1991. In violation of the Reagan-Gorbachev agreement, Washington expanded NATO into Eastern Europe and the Baltic states and established military bases on Russia's borders. Washington is also seeking to extend NATO into former constituent parts of Russia itself such as Georgia and Ukraine.

The only reason for Washington to establish military and missile bases on Russia's frontiers is to negate Russia's ability to resist Washington's hegemony. Russia has made no threatening gestures toward its neighbors, and with the sole exception of Russia's response to Georgia's invasion of South Ossetia, has been extremely passive in the face of US provocations.

This is now changing. Faced with the George W. Bush regime's alteration of US war doctrine, which elevated nuclear weapons from a defensive, retaliatory use to pre-emptive first strike, together with the construction on Russia's borders of US anti-ballistic missile bases and Washington's weaponization of new technologies, has made it clear to the Russian government that Washington is setting up Russia for a decapitating first strike.

In his presidential address to the Russian National Assembly (both chambers of parliament) on December 12, Vladimir Putin addressed the offensive military threat that Washington poses to Russia. Putin said that Washington calls its anti-ballistic missile system defensive, but "in fact it is a significant part of the strategic offensive potential" and designed to tip the balance of power in Washington's favor. Having acknowledged the threat, Putin replied to the threat: "Let no one have illusions that he can achieve military superiority over Russia. We will never allow it."

Faced with the Obama regime's murder of the nuclear weapons reduction treaty, Putin said: "We realize all this and know what we need to do."

If anyone remains to write a history, the Obama regime will be known as the regime that resurrected the cold war, which President Reagan worked so hard to end, and drove it into a hot war.

Not content to make Russia an enemy, the Obama regime has also made an enemy of China. The Obama regime declared the South China Sea to be an area of "US national security interest." This is akin to China declaring the Gulf of Mexico to be an area of Chinese national security interest.

To make clear that the claim to the South China Sea was not rhetorical, the Obama regime announced its "Pivot to Asia," which calls for the redeployment of 60% of the US fleet to China's zone of influence. Washington is busy at work securing naval and air bases from the Philippines, South Korea, Vietnam, Australia, and Thailand. Washington has increased the provocation by aligning itself with China's neighbors who are disputing China's claims to various islands and an expanded air space.

China has not been intimidated. China has called for "de-americanizing the world." Last month the Chinese government announced that it now possesses sufficient nuclear weapons and delivery systems to wipe the US off of the face of the earth. A couple of days ago, China aggressively harassed a US missile cruiser in the South China Sea.

The militarily aggressive stance that Washington has taken toward Russia and China is indicative of the extreme self-assuredness that usually ends in war. Washington is told that US technological prowess can prevent or intercept the launch of Russian and Chinese missiles, thus elevating a US pre-emptive attack to slam-dunk status. Yet the potential danger from Iran acquiring nuclear weapons is said to be so great that a pre-emptive war is necessary right now, and a massive Department of Homeland Security is justified on the grounds that the US remains vulnerable to a few stateless Muslims who might acquire a nuclear weapon. It is an anomalous situation that the Russian and Chinese retaliatory response to US attack is considered to be inconsequential, but not nuclear threats from Iran and stateless Muslims.

Not content with sending war signals to Russia and China, Washington has apparently also decided to torpedo the Iranian settlement by announcing new sanctions against companies doing business with Iran. The Iranians understood Washington's monkey wrench as Washington probably intended, as a lack of Washington's commitment to the agreement, left Geneva and returned to Iran. It remains to be seen

160

whether the agreement can be resurrected or whether the Israel Lobby has succeeded in derailing the agreement that promised to end the threat of war with Iran.

American citizens seem to have little, if any, influence on their government or even awareness of its intentions. Moreover, there is no organized opposition behind which Americans could rally to stop Washington's drive toward world war. Hope, if there is any, would seem to lie with Washington's European and Asian puppets. What interests do these governments have in putting the existence of their countries at risk for no other purpose than to help Washington acquire hegemony over the world? Cannot they realize that Washington's game is a death-dealing one for them?

Germany alone could save the world from war while simultaneously serving its own interests. All Germany has to do is to exit the EU and NATO. The alliance would collapse, and its fall would terminate Washington's hegemonic ambition.

First published on December 14, 2013.

Russia Under Attack

In a number of my articles I have explained that the Soviet Union served as a constraint on US power. The Soviet collapse unleashed the neoconservative drive for US world hegemony. Russia under Putin, China, and Iran are the only constraints on the neoconservative agenda.

Russia's nuclear missiles and military technology make Russia the strongest military obstacle to US hegemony. To neutralize Russia, Washington broke the Reagan-Gorbachev agreements and expanded NATO into former constituent parts of the Soviet Empire and now intends to bring former constituent parts of Russia herself – Georgia and Ukraine – into NATO. Washington withdrew from the treaty that banned anti-ballistic missiles and has established anti-ballistic missile bases on Russia's frontier. Washington changed its nuclear war doctrine to permit nuclear first strike.

All of this is aimed at degrading Russia's deterrent, thereby reducing the ability of Russia to resist Washington's will.

The Russian government (and also the government of Ukraine) foolishly permitted large numbers of US funded NGOs to operate as Washington's agents under cover of "human rights organizations," "building democracy," etc. The "pussy riot" event was an operation designed to put Putin and Russia in a bad light. (The women were useful dupes.) The Western media attacks on the Sochi Olympics are part of the ridiculing and demonizing of Putin and Russia. Washington is determined that Putin and Russia will not be permitted any appearance of success in any area, whether diplomacy, sports, or human rights.

The American media is a Ministry of Propaganda for the government and the corporations and helps Washington paint Russia in bad colors. Stephen F. Cohen accurately describes US media coverage of Russia as a "tsunami of shamefully unprofessional and politically inflammatory articles."

As a holdover from the Cold War, the US media retains the image of a free press that can be trusted. In truth, there is no free press in America (except for Internet sites). During the later years of the Clinton regime, the US government permitted 5 large conglomerates to concentrate the varied, dispersed and somewhat independent media. The value of these large mega-companies depends on their federal broadcast licenses. Therefore, the media dares not go against the government on any important issue. In addition, the media conglomerates are no longer run by journalists but by corporate advertising executives and former government officials, with an eye not on facts but on advertising revenues and access to government "sources."

Washington is using the media to prepare the American people for confrontation with Russia and to influence Russians and other peoples in the world against Putin. Washington would love to see a weaker or more pliable Russian leader than Putin.

Many Russians are gullible. Having experienced communist rule and the chaos from collapse, they naively believe that America is the best place, the example for the world, the "white hat" that can be trusted and believed. This idiotic belief, which we see manifested in western Ukraine as the US destabilizes the country in preparation for taking it over, is an important weapon that the US uses to destabilize Russia.

Some Russians make apologies for Washington by explaining the anti-Russian rhetoric as simply a carryover from old stereotypes from the Cold War. "Old stereotypes" is a red herring, a misleading distraction. Washington is gunning for Russia. Russia is under attack, and if Russians do not realize this, they are history.

Many Russians are asleep at the switch, but the Izborsk Club is trying to wake them up. In an article (February 12) in the Russian weekly

Zavtra, strategic and military experts warned that the Western use of protests to overturn the decision of the Ukraine government not to join the European Union had produced a situation in which a coup by fascist elements was a possibly. Such a coup would result in a fratricidal war in Ukraine and would constitute a serious "strategic threat to the Russian Federation."

The experts concluded that should such a coup succeed, the consequences for Russia would be:

– Loss of Sevastopol as the base of the Russian Federation's Black Sea Fleet;

– Purges of Russians in eastern and southern Ukraine, producing a flood of refugees;

– Loss of manufacturing capacities in Kiev, Dnepropetrovsk, Kharkov where
contract work is done for the Russian military;

– Suppression of the Russian speaking population by forcible Ukrainianization;

– The establishment of US and NATO military bases in Ukraine, including in Crimea and the establishment of training centers for terrorists who would be set upon the Caucasus, the Volga Basin, and perhaps Siberia.

– Spread of the orchestrated Kiev protests into non-Russian ethnicities in cities of the Russian Federation.

The Russian strategists conclude that they "consider the situation taking shape in Ukraine to be catastrophic for the future of Russia."

What is to be done? Here the strategic experts, who have correctly analyzed the situation, fall down. They call for a national media campaign to expose the nature of the takeover that is underway and for the government of the Russian Federation to invoke the Budapest Memorandum of 1994 in order to convene a conference of representatives of the governments of Russia, Ukraine, the USA, and Great Britain to deal with the threats to the Ukraine. In the event that the Budapest Memorandum governing the sovereignty of Ukraine is set aside by one or more of the parties, the experts propose that the Russian government, using the precedent of the Kennedy-Khrushchev negotiations that settled the 1962 Cuban Missile Crisis, negotiate directly with Washington a settlement of the developing crisis in Ukraine.

This is a pipe dream. The experts are indulging in self-deception. Washington is the perpetrator of the crisis in Ukraine and intends to take over Ukraine for the precise reasons that the experts list. It is a perfect plan for destabilizing Russia and for negating Putin's successful diplomacy in preventing US military attack on Syria and Iran.

Essentially, if Washington succeeds in Ukraine, Russia would be eliminated as a constraint on US world hegemony, Only China would remain.

I suspected that Ukraine would come to a boiling point when Putin and Russia were preoccupied with the Sochi Olympics, leaving Russia unprepared. There is little doubt that Russia is faced with a major strategic threat. What are Russia's real options? Certainly the options do not include any good will from Washington.

Possibly, Russia could operate from the American script. If Russia has drones, Russia could use drones like Washington does and use them to assassinate the leaders of the Washington-sponsored protests. Or Russia could send in Special Forces teams to eliminate the agents who are operating against Russia. If the EU continues to support the destabilization of Ukraine, Russia could cut off oil and gas supplies to Washington's European puppet states.

Alternatively, the Russian Army could occupy western Ukraine while arrangements are made to partition Ukraine, which until recently was part of Russia for 200 years. It is certain that the majority of residents in eastern Ukraine prefer Russia to the EU. It is even possible that the brainwashed elements in the western half might stop foaming at the mouth long enough to comprehend that being in US/EU hands means being looted as per Latvia and Greece.

I am outlining the least dangerous outcomes of the crisis that Washington and its stupid European puppet states have created, not making recommendations to Russia. The worst outcome is a dangerous war. If the Russians sit on their hands, the situation will become unbearable for them. As Ukraine moves toward NATO membership and suppression of the Russian population, the Russian government will have to attack Ukraine and overthrow the foreign regime or surrender to the Americans. The likely outcome of the audacious strategic threat with which Washington is confronting Russia would be nuclear war.

The neoconservative Victoria Nuland sits in her State Department office happily choosing the members of the next Ukrainian government. Is this US official oblivious to the risk that Washington's meddling in the internal affairs of Ukraine and Russia could be triggering nuclear war? Are President Obama and Congress aware that there is an Assistant Secretary of State who is provoking Armageddon?

Insouciant Americans are paying no attention and have no idea that a handful of neoconservative ideologues are pushing the world toward destruction.

First published on February 14, 2014.

Is Ukraine Drifting Toward Civil War And Great Power Confrontation?

People ask for solutions, but no solutions are possible in a disinformed world. Populations almost everywhere are dissatisfied, but few have any comprehension of the real situation. Before there can be solutions, people must know the truth about the problems. For those few inclined to be messengers, it is largely a thankless task.

The assumption that man is a rational animal is incorrect. He and she are emotional creatures, not Mr. Spock of Star Trek. Humans are brainwashed by enculturation and indoctrination. Patriots respond with hostility toward criticisms of their governments, their countries, their hopes and their delusions. Their emotions throttle facts, should any reach them. Aspirations and delusions prevail over truth. Most people want to be told what they want to hear. Consequently, they are always gullible and their illusions and self-delusions make them easy victims of propaganda. This is true of all levels of societies and of the leaders themselves.

We are witnessing this today in western Ukraine where a mixture of witless university students, pawns in Washington's drive for world hegemony, together with paid protesters and fascistic elements among ultra-nationalists are bringing great troubles upon Ukraine and perhaps a deadly war upon the world.

Many of the protesters are just the unemployed collecting easy money. It is the witless idealistic types that are destroying the independence of their country. Victoria Nuland, the American neoconservative Assistant Secretary of State, whose agenda is US world hegemony, told the Ukrainians what was in store for them last December 13, but the protesters were too delusional to hear.

In an eight minute, 46 second speech at the National Press Club sponsored by the US-Ukraine Foundation, Chevron, and Ukraine-in-

Washington Lobby Group, Nuland boasted that Washington has spent $5 billion to foment agitation to bring Ukraine into the EU. Once captured by the EU, Ukraine will be "helped" by the West acting through the IMF. Nuland, of course, presented the IMF as Ukraine's rescuer, not as the iron hand of the West that will squeeze all life out of Ukraine's struggling economy.

Nuland's audience consisted of all the people who will be enriched by the looting and by connections to a Washington-appointed Ukrainian government. Just look at the large Chevron sign next to which Nuland speaks, and you will know what it is all about.

Nuland's speech failed to alert the Ukraine protesters, who are determined to destroy the independence of Ukraine and to place their country in the hands of the IMF so that it can be looted like Latvia, Greece and every country that ever had an IMF structural adjustment program. All the monies that protesters are paid by the US and EU will soon be given back manyfold as Ukraine is "adjusted" by Western looting.

In her short speech the neoconservative agitator Nuland alleged that the protesters whom Washington has spent $5 billion cultivating were protesting "peacefully with enormous restraint" against a brutal government.

According to RT, which has much more credibility than the US State Department (remember Secretary of State Colin Powell's address to the UN setting up the US invasion of Iraq with his "evidence" of Iraqi weapons of mass destruction, a speech Powell later disavowed as Bush regime disinformation), Ukrainian rioters have seized 1,500 guns, 100,000 rounds of ammunition, 3 machine guns, and grenades from military armories.

The human-rights trained Ukrainian police have permitted the violence to get out of hand. A number of police have been burned by Molotov cocktails. The latest report is that 108 police have been shot. A number are dead and 63 are in critical condition. These casualties are the products of Nuland's "peacefully protesting protesters acting with enormous restraint." On February 20, the elected, independent Ukraine government responded to the rioters use of firearms by allowing police to use firearms in self-defense.

Perhaps the Russophobic western Ukrainians deserve the IMF, and perhaps the EU deserves the extreme nationalists who are trying to topple the Ukraine government. Once Ukrainians experience being looted by the West, they will be on their knees begging Russia to rescue them. The only certain thing is that it is unlikely that the Russian part of Ukraine will remain part of Ukraine.

During the Soviet era, parts of Russia herself, such as the Crimea, were placed into the Ukrainian Soviet Socialist Republic, perhaps in order to increase the Russian population in Ukraine. In other words, a large part of today's Ukraine – eastern and southern provinces – are traditional Russian territory, not part of historical Ukraine.

Until Russia granted Ukraine independence in the early 1990s, Ukraine had experienced scant independence since the 14th century and had been a part of Russia for 200 years. The problem with the grant of independence is that much of Ukraine is not Ukrainian. It is Russian.

As I have reported previously, Russia regards the prospect of Ukraine as a member of the EU with NATO with US bases on Russia's frontier as a "strategic threat." It is unlikely that the Russian government and the Russian territories in Ukraine will accept Washington's plan for Ukraine. Whatever their intention, Secretary of State John Kerry's provocative statements are raising tensions and fomenting war. The vast bulk of the American and Western populations have no idea of what the real situation is, because all they hear from the "free press" is the neoconservative propaganda line.

Washington's lies are destroying not only civil liberties at home and countries abroad, but are raising dangerous alarms in Russia about the country's security. If Washington succeeds in overthrowing the Ukrainian government, the eastern and southern provinces are likely to secede. If secession becomes a civil war instead of a peaceful divorce, Russia would not be able to sit on the sidelines. As the Washington warmongers would be backing western Ukraine, the two nuclear powers would be thrown into military conflict.

The Ukrainian and Russian governments allowed this dangerous situation to develop, because they naively permitted for many years billions of US dollars to flow into their countries where the money was used to create fifth columns under the guise of educational and human rights organizations, the real purpose of which is to destabilize both countries. The consequence of the trust Ukrainians and Russians placed in the West is the prospect of civil and wider war.

Reading the collection of foreign news dispatches provided by Richard Rozoff about the situation in Ukraine, reminded me of histories about how the pointless and destructive First World War began. In their blind desire to overthrow the democratically elected government of Ukraine and impose an EU puppet state in its place, the American, British, and French governments are lying through their teeth and provoking a situation that is headed toward armed conflict.

Unless the Russian government and people are willing to accept Washington's hegemony over Russia, Russia cannot tolerate the coup that the West is preparing in Ukraine. As it is unlikely that Western forces would be a match for the Russian army in its own backyard, or that self-righteous, hubristic Washington could accept defeat, the conflict toward which the corrupt Western governments are driving is likely to turn nuclear.

As worldwide polls consistently show, Washington is regarded as the greatest threat to world peace. As I have often written, Washington is not merely a threat to peace. Washington and its despicable European puppet states are a threat to the existence of life on the planet. Essentially, Washington is insane, and European "leaders" are paid to provide cover for Washington's insanity.

The world could end before the unpayable Western debts come due.

First published on February 20, 2014.

Ukrainian Neo-Nazis Declare that Power Comes Out of the Barrels of their Guns

Reality on the ground in Ukraine contradicts the incompetent and immoral Obama regime's portrait of Ukrainian democracy on the march.

To the extent that government exists in post-coup Ukraine, it is laws dictated by gun and threat wielding thugs of the neo-Nazi, Russophobic, ultra-nationalist, right-wing parties. Watch the video of the armed thug, Aleksandr Muzychko, who boosts of killing Russian soldiers in Chechnya, dictating to the Rovno regional parliament a grant of apartments to families of protesters.

Read about the neo-Nazis intimidating the Central Election Commission in order to secure rule and personnel changes in order to favor the ultra-right in the forthcoming elections. Thug Aleksandr Shevchenko informed the CEC that armed activists will remain in CEC offices in order to make certain that the election is not rigged against the neo-Nazis. What he means, of course, is the armed thugs will make sure the neo-Nazis win. If the neo-Nazis don't win, the chances are high that they will take power regardless.

Members of President Yanukovich's ruling party, the Party of Regions, have been shot, had arrest warrants issued for them, have experienced home invasions and physical threats, and are resigning in droves in hopes of saving the lives of themselves and their families. The prosecutor's office in the Volyn region (western Ukraine) has been ordered by ultra-nationalists to resign en masse .

Jewish synagogues and Eastern Orthodox Christian churches are being attacked.

To toot my own horn, I might have been the first and only to predict that Washington's organization of pro-EU Ukrainian politicians into a coup against the elected government of Ukraine would destroy democracy and establish the precedent that force prevails over elections, thereby empowering the organized and armed extreme right-wing.

This is precisely what has happened. Note that there was no one in the Obama regime who had enough sense to see the obvious result of their smug, self-satisfied interference in the internal affairs of Ukraine.

If a democratically elected president and ruling party are so easily driven from power by armed neo-Nazis, what chance do Washington's paid stooges among the so-called "moderates" have of forming a government? These are the corrupt people who wanted President Yanukovich out of office so that they could take the money instead. The corruption charge against Yanukovich was cover for the disloyal, undemocratic "moderate" schemers to seize power and be paid millions of dollars by Washington for taking Ukraine into the EU and NATO.

The Washington-paid schemers are now reaping their just reward as they sit in craven silence while neo-Nazi Muzychko wielding an Ak-47 challenges government officials to their face: "I dare you take my gun!"

Only Obama, Susan Rice, Victoria Nuland, Washington's European puppets, and the Western prostitute media can describe the brutal reality of post-coup Ukraine as "the forward march of democracy."

The West now faces a real mess, and so does Russia. The presstitutes will keep the American public from ever knowing what has happened, and the Obama regime will never admit it. It is not always clear that even the Russians want to admit it. The intelligent, reasonable, and humane Russian Foreign Minister, a person 100 cuts above the despicable John Kerry, keeps speaking as if this is all a mistake and appealing to the Western governments to stand behind the agreement that they pressured President Yanukovich to sign.

Yanukovich is history, as are Washington's "moderates." The moderates are not only corrupt; they are stupid. The fools even disbanded the Riot Police, leaving themselves at the mercy of the armed right-wing Nazi-thugs.

Ukraine is out of control. This is what happens when an arrogant, but stupid, Assistant Secretary of State (Victoria Nuland) plots with an equally arrogant and stupid US ambassador (Pyatt) to put their candidates in power once their coup against the elected president succeeds. The ignorant and deluded who deny any such plotting occurred can listen to the conversation between Nuland and Pyatt here [1].

The situation will almost certainly lead to war. Only Putin's diplomatic skills could prevent it. However, Putin has been demonized by Washington and the whores who comprise the US print and TV media. European and British politicians would have their Washington paychecks cut off if they aligned with Putin.

War is unavoidable, because the Western public is out to lunch. The more facts and information I provide, the more emails I receive defending the "sincere [and well paid] protesters' honest protests against corruption," as if corruption were the issue. I hear from Ukrainians and from those of Ukrainian ethnicity in Canada and the US that it is natural for Ukrainians to hate Russians because Ukrainians suffered under communism, as if suffering under communism, which disappeared in 1991, is unique to Ukrainians and has anything to do with the US coup that has fallen into neo-Nazi hands,

No doubt. Many suffered under communism, including Russians. But was the suffering greater than the suffering of Japanese civilians twice nuked by the "Indispensable people," or the suffering by German civilians whose cities were firebombed, like Tokyo, by the "exceptional people"?

Today Japan and Germany are Washington's puppet states. In contrast, Ukraine was an independent country with a working relationship with Russia. It was this relationship that Washington wished to destroy.

Now that a reckless and incompetent Washington has opened Pandora's Box, more evil has been released upon the world. The suffering will not be confined to Ukraine.

There are a number of reasons why the situation is likely to develop in a very bad way. One is that most people are unable to deal with reality even when reality directly confronts them. When I provide the facts as they are known, here are some of the responses I receive: "You are a Putin agent;" "you hate Ukrainians;" "you are defending corruption;" "you must not know how Ukrainians suffered at the hands of Stalin."

Of course, having done Russian studies in graduate school, having been a member of the US-USSR student exchange program in 1961, having traveled in Russia, Georgia, Ukraine, and Uzbekistan, having published in scholarly journals of Slavic and Russian studies, having twice addressed the Soviet Academy of Sciences, having been invited to explain to the CIA why the Soviet economic collapse occurred despite the CIA's predictions to the contrary, I wouldn't know anything about how people suffered under communism. The willingness of readers to display to me their utter ignorance and stupidity is astonishing. There is a large number of people who think reality consists of their delusions.

Reality is simply too much for mentally and emotionally weak people who are capable of holding on to their delusions in the face of all evidence to the contrary. The masses of deluded people and the total inability of Washington, wallowing it its hubris, to admit a mistake, mean that Washington's destabilization of Ukraine is a problem for us all.

RT reports that "Russian President Vladimir Putin has ordered an urgent military drill to test combat readiness of the armed forces across western and central Russia." According to Russia's Defense Minister, the surprise drill tested ground troops, Air Force, airborne troops and aerospace defense [2]. The Defense Minister said: "The drills are not connected with events in Ukraine at all."

Yes, of course. The Defense Minister says this, because Putin still hopes that the EU will come to its senses. In my opinion, and I hope I am wrong, the European "leaders" are too corrupted by Washington's money to have any sense. They are bought-and-paid-for. Nothing is important to them but money.

Ask yourself, why does Russia need at this time an urgent readiness test unrelated to Ukraine? Anyone familiar with geography knows that western and central Russia sit atop Ukraine.

Let us all cross our fingers that another war is not the consequence of the insouciant American public, the craven cowardice of the presstitute media, Washington's corrupt European puppets, and the utter mendacity of the criminals who rule in Washington.

First published on February 20, 2014.

[1]. "Марионетки Майдана"
https://www.youtube.com/watch?v=MSxaa-67yGM
[2]. "Putin orders 'combat readiness' tests for western, central Russian troops" https://www.rt.com/news/putin-drill-combat-army-864/

Western Looting Of Ukraine Has Begun

It is now apparent that the "Maiden protests" in Kiev were in actuality a Washington organized coup against the elected democratic government. The purpose of the coup is to put NATO military bases on Ukraine's border with Russia and to impose an IMF austerity program that serves as cover for Western financial interests to loot the country. The sincere idealistic protesters who took to the streets without being paid were the gullible dupes of the plot to destroy their country.

Politically Ukraine is an untenable aggregation of Ukrainian and Russian territory, because traditional Russian territories were stuck into the borders of the Ukraine Soviet Republic by Lenin and Khrushchev. The Crimea, stuck into Ukraine by Khrushchev, has already departed and rejoined Russia. Unless some autonomy is granted to them, Russian areas in eastern and southern Ukraine might also depart and return to Russia. If the animosity displayed toward the Russian speaking population by the stooge government in Kiev continues, more defections to Russia are likely.

The Washington-imposed coup faces other possible difficulties from what seems to be a growing conflict between the well-organized Right Sector and the Washington-imposed stooges. If armed conflict between these two groups were to occur, Washington might conclude that it needs to send help to its stooges. The appearance of US/NATO troops in Ukraine would create pressure on Putin to occupy the remaining Russian speaking parts of Ukraine.

Before the political and geographical issues are settled, the Western looting of Ukraine has already begun. The Western media, doesn't tell any more truth about IMF "rescue packages" than it does about anything else. The media reports, and many Ukrainians believe, that the IMF is going to rescue Ukraine financially by giving the country billions of dollars.

Ukraine will never see one dollar of the IMF money. What the IMF is going to do is to substitute Ukrainian indebtedness to the IMF for Ukrainian indebtedness to Western banks. The IMF will hand over the money to the Western banks, and the Western banks will reduce Ukraine's indebtedness by the amount of IMF money. Instead of being indebted to the banks, Ukraine will now be indebted to the IMF.

Now the looting can begin. The IMF loan brings new conditions and imposes austerity on the Ukrainian people so that the Ukraine government can gather up the money with which to repay the IMF. The IMF conditions that will be imposed on the struggling Ukraine population will consist of severe reductions in old-age pensions, in government services, in government employment, and in subsidies for basic consumer purchases such as natural gas. Already low living standards will plummet. In addition, Ukrainian public assets and Ukrainian owned private industries will have to be sold off to Western purchasers.

Additionally, Ukraine will have to float its currency. In a futile effort to protect its currency's value from being driven very low (and consequently import prices very high) by speculators ganging up on the currency and short-selling it, Ukraine will borrow more money with which to support its currency in the foreign exchange market. Of course, the currency speculators will end up with the borrowed money, leaving Ukraine much deeper in debt than currently.

The corruption involved is legendary, so the direct result of the gullible Maiden protesters will be lower Ukrainian living standards, more corruption, loss of sovereignty over the country's economic policy, and the transfer of Ukrainian public and private property to Western interests.

If Ukraine also falls into NATO's clutches, Ukraine will also find itself in a military alliance against Russia and find itself targeted by Russian missiles. This will be a tragedy for Ukraine and Russia as Ukrainians have relatives in Russia and Russians have relatives in Ukraine. The two countries have essentially been one for 200 years. To have them torn apart by Western looting and Washington's drive for world hegemony is a terrible shame and a great crime.

The gullible dupes who participated in the orchestrated Maiden protests will rue it for the rest of their lives.

When the protests began, I described what the consequences would be and said that I would explain the looting process. It is not necessary for me to do so. Professor Michel Chossudovsky has explained the IMF looting process along with much history [1].

One final word. Despite unequivocal evidence of one country after another being looted by the West, governments of indebted countries continue to sign up for IMF programs. Why do governments of countries continue to agree to the foreign looting of their populations? The only answer is that they are paid. The corruption that is descending upon Ukraine will make the former regime look honest.

First published on March 29, 2014.

[1]. "Regime Change in Ukraine and the IMF's Bitter 'Economic Medicine'" http://www.globalresearch.ca/regime-change-in-ukraine-and-the-imfs-bitter-economic-medicine/5374877

"Putin Has Misread the West And if He Doesn't Wake Up Soon, Armageddon Is Upon Us"

Mike Whitney Interviews Paul Craig Roberts

Question 1 – You think that Putin should have acted more forcefully from the beginning in order to end the war quickly. Is that an accurate assessment of your view on the war? And – if it is – then what do you think is the downside of allowing the conflict to drag on with no end in sight?

Paul Craig Roberts – Yes, you have correctly stated my position. But as my position can seem "unAmerican" to the indoctrinated and brainwashed many, those who watch CNN, listen to NPR, and read the New York Times, I am going to provide some of my background before going on with my answer.

I was involved in the 20th century Cold War in many ways: As a Wall Street Journal editor; as an appointee to an endowed chair in the Center for Strategic and International Studies, part of Georgetown University at the time of my appointment, where my colleagues were Henry Kissinger, National Security Advisor and Secretary of State, Zbigniew Brzezinski, National Security Advisor, and James Schlesinger, a Secretary of Defense and CIA director who was one of my professors in graduate school at the University of Virginia; as a member of the Cold War Committee on the Present Danger; and as a member of a secret presidential committee with power to investigate the CIA's opposition to President Reagan's plan to end the Cold War.

With a history such as mine, I was surprised when I took an objective position on Russian President Putin's disavowal of US hegemony, and found myself labeled a "Russian dupe/agent" on a website, "PropOrNot," which may have been financed by the US Department of

State, the National Endowment for Democracy, or the CIA itself, still harboring old resentments against me for helping President Reagan end the Cold War, which had the potential of reducing the CIA's budget and power. I still wonder what the CIA might do to me, despite the agency inviting me to address the agency, which I did, and explain why they went wrong in their reasoning.

I will also say that in my articles I am defending truth, not Putin, although Putin is, in my considered opinion, the most honest player, and perhaps the most naive, in the current game that could end in nuclear Armageddon. My purpose is to prevent nuclear Armageddon, not to take sides. I remember well President Reagan's hatred of "those godawful nuclear weapons" and his directive that the purpose was not to win the Cold War but to end it.

Now to Mike's question, which is to the point. Perhaps to understand Putin we need to remember life, or how it was presented by the West to the Soviet Union and the American broadcasts into the Soviet Union of the freedom of life in the West where streets were paved with gold and food markets had every conceivable delicacy. Possibly this created in the minds of many Soviets, not all, that life in the Western world was heavenly compared to the hell in which Russians existed. I still remember being on a bus in Uzbekistan in 1961 when a meat delivery truck appeared on the street. All traffic followed the truck to the delivery store where a several block long line already waited. When you compare this life with a visit to an American supermarket, Western superiority stands out. Russian hankerings toward the West have little doubt constrained Putin, but Putin himself has been affected by the differences in life between the US in those times and the Soviet Union.

Putin is a good leader, a human person, perhaps too human for the evil he faces. One way to look at my position that Putin does too little instead of too much is to remember the World War II era when British Prime Minister Chamberlin was accused of encouraging Hitler by accepting provocation after provocation. My own view of this history is that it is false, but it remains widely believed. Putin accepts provocations despite having declared red lines that he does not enforce. Consequently, his red lines are not believed. Here is one report:

RT reported on December 10 that "The US has quietly given Ukraine the go-ahead to launch long-range strikes against targets inside Russian territory, the Times reported on Friday, citing sources. The Pentagon has apparently changed its stance on the matter as it has become less concerned that such attacks could escalate the conflict."

In other words, by his inaction Putin has convinced Washington and its European puppet states that he doesn't mean what he says and will endlessly accept ever worsening provocations, which have gone from sanctions to Western financial help to Ukraine, weapons supply, training and targeting information, provision of missiles capable of attacking internal Russia, attack on the Crimea bridge, destruction of the Nord Stream pipelines, torture of Russian POWs, attacks on Russian parts of Ukraine reincorporated into the Russian Federation, and attacks on internal Russia.

At some point there will be a provocation that is too much. That's when the SHTF.

Putin's goal has been to avoid war. Thus, his limited military objective in Ukraine to throw the Ukrainian forces out of Donbas meant a limited operation that left Ukrainian war infrastructure intact, able to receive and deploy advanced weapons from the West, and to force Russian withdrawals to lines more defensible with the very limited forces Putin committed to the conflict. The Ukrainian offensives convinced the West that Russia could be defeated, thus making the war a primary way of undermining Russia as an obstacle to Washington's hegemony. The British press proclaimed that the Ukrainian Army would be in Crimea by Christmas.

What Putin needed was a quick victory that made it completely clear that Russia had enforceable red lines that Ukraine had violated. A show of Russian military force would have stopped all provocations. The decadent West would have learned that it must leave the bear alone. Instead the Kremlin, misreading the West, wasted eight years on the Minsk Agreement that former German Chancellor Merkel said was a deception to keep Russia from acting when Russia could have easily succeeded. Putin now agrees with me that it was his mistake not to have intervened in Donbas before the US created a Ukrainian army.

My last word to Mike's question is that Putin has misread the West. He still thinks the West has in its "leadership" reasonable people, who no doubt act the role for Putin's benefit, with whom he can have negotiations. Putin should go read the Wolfowitz Doctrine. If Putin doesn't soon wake up, Armageddon is upon us, unless Russia surrenders.

Question 2 – I agree with much of what you say here, particularly this: "Putin's inaction has convinced Washington… that he doesn't mean what he says and will endlessly accept ever worsening provocations."

You're right, this is a problem. But I'm not sure what Putin can do about it. Take, for example, the drone attacks on airfields on Russian territory. Should Putin have responded tit-for-tat by bombing supply lines in Poland? That seems like a fair response but it also risks NATO retaliation and a broader war which is definitely not in Russia's interests.

Now, perhaps, Putin would not have faced these flashpoints had he deployed 500,000 combat troops to begin and leveled a number of cities on his way to Kiev, but keep in mind, Russian public opinion about the war was mixed at the beginning, and only grew more supportive as it became apparent that Washington was determined to defeat Russia, topple its government, and weaken it to the point where it could not project power beyond its borders. The vast majority of the

Russian people now understand what the US is up-to which explains why Putin's public approval ratings are presently at 79.4% while support for the war is nearly universal. In my opinion, Putin needs this level of support to sustain the war effort; so, postponing the mobilization of additional troops has actually worked to his benefit.

More importantly, Putin must be perceived to be the rational player in this conflict. This is absolutely essential. He must be seen as a cautious and reasonable actor who operates with restraint and within the confines of international law. This is the only way he will be able to win the continued support of China, India etc. We must not forget that the effort to build a multipolar world order requires coalition building which is undermined by impulsive, violent behavior. In short, I think Putin's "go-slow" approach (your words) is actually the correct course of action. I think if he had run roughshod across Ukraine like Sherman on his way to the sea, he would have lost critical allies that will help him establish the institutions and economic infrastructure he needs to create a new order.

So, my question to you is this: What does a Russian victory look like? Is it just a matter of pushing the Ukrainian army out of the Donbas or should Russian forces clear the entire region east of the Dnieper River? And what about the west of Ukraine? What if the western region is reduced to rubble but the US and NATO continue to use it as a launching pad for their war against Russia?

I can imagine many scenarios in which the fighting continues for years to come, but hardly any that end in either a diplomatic settlement or an armistice. Your thoughts?

Paul Craig Roberts – I think, Mike, that you have identified the reasoning that explains Putin's approach to the conflict in Ukraine. But I think Putin is losing confidence in his approach. Caution about approaching war is imperative. But when war begins it must be won quickly, especially if the enemy has prospects of gaining allies and their support. Putin's caution delayed Russia's rescue of Donbas for eight years, during which Washington created and equipped an Ukrainian army that turned what would have been an easy rescue in 2014 like Crimea into the current war approaching a year in duration. Putin's caution in waging the war has given Washington and the Western media plenty of time to create and control the narrative, which is unfavorable to Putin, and to widen the war with US and NATO direct participation, now admitted by Foreign Minister Lavrov. The war has widened into direct attacks on Russia herself.

These attacks on Russia might bring the pro-Western Russian liberals into alignment with Putin, but the ability of a corrupt third world US puppet state to attack Russia is anathema to Russian patriots. The Russians who will do the fighting see in the ability of Ukraine to attack Mother Russia the failure of the Putin government.

As for China and India, the two countries with the largest populations, they have witnessed Washington's indiscriminate use of force without domestic or international consequence to Washington. They don't want to ally with a week-kneed Russia.

I will also say that as Washington and NATO were not constrained by public opinion in their two decades of wars in the Middle East and North Africa, based entirely on lies and secret agendas, what reason does Putin have to fear a lack of Russian public support for rescuing Donbas, formerly a part of Russia, from neo-Nazi persecution? If Putin must fear this, it shows his mistake in tolerating US-financed NGOs at work in Russia brainwashing Russians.

No, Putin should not engage in tit-for-tat. There is no need for him to send missiles into Poland, Germany, the UK, or the US. All Putin needs to do is to close down Ukrainian infrastructure so that Ukraine, despite Western help, cannot carry on the war. Putin is starting to do this, but not on a total basis.

The fact of the matter is that Putin never needed to send any troops to the rescue of Donbas. All he needed to do was to send the American puppet, Zelensky, a one hour ultimatum and if surrender was not forthcoming shut down with conventional precision missiles, and air attacks if necessary, the entirety of the power, water, and transportation infrastructure of Ukraine, and send special forces into Kiev to make a public hanging of Zelensky and the US puppet government.

The effect on the degenerate Woke West, which teaches in its own universities and public schools hatred of itself, would have been electric. The cost of messing with Russia would have been clear to all the morons who talk about Ukraine being in Crimea by Christmas. NATO would have dissolved. Washington would have removed all sanctions and shut up the stupid, war-crazy neoconservatives. The world would be at peace.

The question you have asked is, after all of Putin's mistakes, what does a Russian victory look like? First of all, we don't know if there is going to be a Russian victory. The cautious way that Putin reasons and acts, as you explained, is likely to deny Russia a victory. Instead, there could be a negotiated demilitarized zone and the conflict will be set on simmer, like the unresolved conflict in Korea.

On the other hand, if Putin is waiting the full deployment of Russia's hypersonic nuclear missiles that no defense system can intercept and, following Washington, moves to first use of nuclear weapons, Putin will have the power to put the West on notice and be able to use the power of Russian military force to instantly end the conflict.

Question 3 – You make some very good points, but I still think that Putin's slower approach has helped to build public support at home and abroad. But, of course, I could be wrong. I do disagree strongly with your assertion that China and India "don't want to ally with weak-kneed Russia". In my opinion, both leaders see Putin as a bright and reliable statesman who is perhaps the greatest defender of sovereign rights in the last century. Both India and China are all-too-familiar with Washington's coercive diplomacy and I'm sure they appreciate the efforts of a leader who has become the world's biggest proponent of self-determination and independence. I'm sure the last thing they want, is to become cowering houseboys like the leaders in Europe who are, apparently, unable to decide anything without a 'nod' from Washington. (Note: Earlier today Putin said that EU leaders were allowing themselves to be treated like a doormat. Putin: "Today, the EU's main partner, the US, is pursuing policies leading directly to the de-industrialization of Europe. They even try to complain about that to their American overlord. Sometimes even with resentment they ask 'Why are you doing this to us?' I want to ask: 'What did you expect?' What else happens to those who allow feet to be wiped on them?")

Paul Craig Roberts – Mike, I agree that Russia for the reasons you provide is the choice partner of China and India. What I meant is that China and India want to see a powerful Russia that shields them from Washington's interference. China and India are not reassured by what at times seems to be Putin's irresolution and hesitancy. The rules that Putin plays by are no longer respected in the West.

Putin is correct that all European, and the Canadian, Australian, Japanese, and New Zealand governments, are doormats for Washington. What escapes Putin is that Washington's puppets are comfortable in this role. Therefore, how much chance does he have in scolding them for their subservience and promising them independence? A reader recently reminded me about the Asch experiment in the 1950s, which found that people tended to conform to the prevalent narratives, and of the use to which Edward Bernays' analysis of propaganda is put. And there is the information given me in the 1970s by a high government official that European governments do what we want because we "give the leaders bags of money. We own them. They report to us."

In other words, our puppets live in a comfort zone. Putin will have a hard time breaking into this with merely exemplary behavior.

Question 4 – For my final question, I'd like to tap into your broader knowledge of the US economy and how economic weakness might be a factor in Washington's decision to provoke Russia. Over the last 10 months, we've heard numerous pundits say that NATO's expansion to Ukraine creates an "existential crisis" for Russia. I just wonder if the same could be said about the United States? It seems like everyone from Jamie Diamond to Nouriel Roubini has been predicting a bigger financial cataclysm than the full-system meltdown of 2008. In your opinion, is this the reason why the media and virtually the entire political establishment are pushing so hard for a confrontation with Russia? Do they see war as the only way the US can preserve its exalted position in the global order?

Paul Craig Roberts – The idea that governments turn to war to focus attention away from a failing economy is popular, but my answer to your question is that the operating motive is US hegemony. The Wolfowitz Doctrine states it clearly. The doctrine says the principal goal of US foreign policy is to prevent the rise of any country that could serve as a constraint on US unilateralism. At the 2007 Munich security conference Putin made it clear that Russia will not subordinate its interest to the interest of the US.

There are some crazed neoconservatives in Washington who believe nuclear war can be won and who have shaped US nuclear weapons policy into a pre-emptive attack mode focused on reducing the ability of the recipient of a first strike to retaliate. The US is not seeking a war with Russia, but might blunder into one. The operative neoconservative policy is to cause problems for Russia that can cause internal problems, distract the Kremlin from Washington's power moves, isolate Russia with propaganda, and even possibly pull off a color revolution inside Russia or in a former Russian province, such as Belarus, as was done in Georgia and Ukraine. People have forgot the US-instigated invasion of South Ossetia by the Georgian army that Putin sent in Russian forces to stop, and they have forgot the recent disturbances in Kazakhstan that were calmed by the arrival of Russian troops. The plan is to keep picking away at the Kremlin. Even if Washington doesn't meet in every case with the success enjoyed in the Maidan Revolution in Ukraine, the incidents succeed as distractions that use up Kremlin time and energy, result in dissenting opinions within the government, and that require military contingency planning. As Washington controls the narratives, the incidents also serve to blacken Russia as an aggressor and portray Putin as "the new Hitler." The propaganda successes are considerable – the exclusion of Russian athletes from competitions, refusals of orchestras to play music of Russian composers, exclusion of Russian literature, and a general refusal to cooperate with Russia in any way. This has a humiliating effect on Russians and might be corrosive of public support for the government. It has to be highly frustrating for Russian athletes, ice skaters, entertainers, and their fans.

Nevertheless, the conflict in Ukraine can turn into a general war intended or not. This is my concern and is the reason I think the Kremlin's limited go-slow operation is a mistake. It offers too many opportunities for Washington's provocations to go too far.

There is an economic element. Washington is determined to prevent its European empire from being drawn into closer relations with Russia from energy dependence and business relationships. Indeed, some explain the economic sanctions as de-industrializing Europe in behalf of Washington's economic and financial hegemony [1].

First published on December 19, 2022.

[1]. "German Interview" https://www.unz.com/mhudson/german-interview

Washington Has Resurrected the Threat of Nuclear Armageddon

As a participant in the 20th century Cold War, I can tell you that the Cuban Missile Crisis had the effect of convincing the leaders of the US and the USSR that trust had to be created between the two nuclear superpowers in order resolve differences and prevent a reoccurrence of tensions at the level of the Cuban Missile Crisis.

President John F. Kennedy and Soviet leader Nikita Khrushchev worked together independently of their military/security bureaucracies to resolve the issue. Both paid a price. President Kennedy was murdered by the CIA and Joint Chiefs of Staff who were determined not to lose the Soviet enemy that justified their power and budgets. Khrushchev was removed from power by Communist Party hardliners suspicious of accommodation to the capitalist enemy.

After President Johnson destroyed himself in the military/security complex's Vietnam War, President Nixon renewed the tension reducing policy of President Kennedy. The Strategic Arms Limitations Talks (SALT) and arms limitations agreements followed. President Nixon topped them off by opening to China and replacing that tense relationship with the "one China" policy. This was again too much for the US military/security complex, and they orchestrated with the Washington Post the "Watergate" scandal to remove him from office.

President Carter tried to continue building bridges. He signed the SALT II agreement that Nixon had initiated, but Carter had his hands full with Israel and Palestine. The situation awaited President Reagan to bring about the end of the Cold War.

President Reagan was a cold warrior who wanted to end it. He hated what he called "those godawful nuclear weapons." He thought it was terrible that the world continued to live under the threat that they might be used.

President Reagan was convinced that the Soviet economy was broken and could not be fixed, whereas the right policy could fix the US economy. Once the US economy was fixed, he could put pressure on the Soviet leadership to come to the negotiating table by threatening an arms race that the broken Soviet economy could not meet.

The problem was stagflation, and the fix was the Kemp-Roth bill which I had drafted and explained to the House and Senate. The Republican minority on the House Budget Committee supported it. Democrat Senator Russell Long, Chairman of the Senate Finance Committee supported it as did Democrat Chairman of the Joint Economic Committee Lloyd Bentsen and Democrat Senator on the Senate Armed Services Committee Sam Nunn. Energetic new Republican senators such as Orrin Hatch and S.I. Hayakawa supported it. Reagan accepted it, campaigned on it, and appointed me to the US Treasury to get the bill out of his administration so that Congress could vote on it.

Faced with yet another president determined to wind down the Cold War, the CIA told President Reagan that he must not renew the arms race, because the Soviets would win. The agency's reasoning was that the Soviet economy was planned, and thereby the Soviet leadership could put a far greater percentage of the society's resources into the military than could Reagan.

To deal with the CIA, Reagan established a secret committee to examine the CIA's case. He put me on it. The committee's conclusion was that the CIA's position was based on its power and stratus that a continuation of the Cold War ensured.

The Reagan/Gorbachev rapprochement held together in the George H.W. Bush administration. President Bush (senior) and Secretary of State James Baker promised Gorbachev that there would be no movement of NATO east if he agreed to the reunification of Germany.

Some American conservatives misinterpret President Reagan's policy as a hostile one against Russia designed to win the Cold War. Reagan told us the goal was not to win the Cold War but to end it. The Soviet collapse was the result of hardline Communist Party members, disturbed at Gorbachev's rapid release of Eastern Europe, placing him under house arrest, thus setting in motion the events that led to the collapse of the Soviet government. This was as much a surprise to Washington as it was to Moscow.

The point of this brief history is to contrast the efforts of American presidents to reduce tensions during the 20th century Cold War with Washington's efforts in the 21st century to undo this accomplishment and to elevate tensions to their current high peak.

We owe this disaster to the neoconservatives. The neoconservatives were responsible for Iran-Contra and were fired and prosecuted by President Reagan. They were pardoned by Reagan's successor, President George H.W. Bush and wormed their way into conservative ranks and into policy positions in government. When the Soviet Union collapsed, they came up with the Wolfowitz Doctrine, a declaration of US hegemony over the world as the principal goal of US foreign policy.

An early manifestation of neoconservative treachery was on March 12, 1999 when the Clinton regime expanded NATO eastward to incorporate the Czech Republic, Hungary, and Poland in NATO in violation of the promise giving to Gorbachev by President George H.W. Bush and Secretary of State James Baker. This was the fledgling Russian state's first indication that the word of the US government means nothing.

A false argument was made that no such pledge had been made or if it had, it didn't count because it wasn't in writing. I know for a fact that the promise was made, and not only by Washington but also by NATO itself [1]. The 1999 NATO enlargement was followed in 2004 by

Bulgaria, Estonia, Latvia, Lithuania, Romania, Slovakia, and Slovenia. In 2009 Albania and Croatia were added, and in 2017 Montenegro and in 2020 North Macedonia.

Readers need to understand what this means. The US government took what was formerly the Soviet Empire and transformed it into Washington's empire. Washington proved that the Soviet Communist hardliners were correct that it is a mistake to trust the West.

Twelve days after putting the Czechs, Hungarians, and Poles in NATO, without UN approval NATO began a three month bombing campaign against the Federal Republic of Yugoslavia, leading to the breakup of the country.

In 2001 the neoconservative regime of President George W. Bush pulled the US out of the ABM Treaty, the cornerstone of the arms control and reduction agreements achieved in the 20th century. Washington's withdrawal also had the effect of cancelling START II, because Russia's agreement to START II was conditional on the US remaining in the ABM treaty.

This was followed by the further additions to NATO described above.

In 2007 the US government announced that nuclear capable missiles would be placed in Poland on Russia's borders. The blatantly false claim was made that these were a defense system against an Iranian attack on Europe. Such a claim must have amused the Kremlin in addition to worrying them.

In 2008 a US trained and equipped Georgian army (a province of the former Soviet Union) invaded South Ossetia and killed Russian peacekeepers. The Russian Army entered the conflict, quickly defeated the Georgian Army and withdrew, disproving the claim that Putin intended to restore the Soviet empire. Washington and its whore media misrepresented the conflict, as they have done the Ukrainian one, as a Russian invasion of Georgia.

In 2014 Washington overthrew the government of Ukraine and established a puppet regime. The regime began attacking the Russian population of Donbas. For the next 8 years thousands of Russians were murdered by neo-Nazi militias and Ukrainian armed forces while President Putin tried to obtain to no avail Western compliance with the Minsk Agreement. The French and German leaders who signed the Minsk Agreement have recently acknowledged that it was a trick to deceive Putin while the US and NATO built and equipped a large Ukrainian army. In February, 2022, this army was poised to invade the Donbas region and to do away with the two independent republics, thus provoking the Russian intervention.

2014 also brought the shooting down of Malaysia Airlines flight 17 which, falsely blamed on Russia, served to initiate a propaganda campaign against Russia and justify the initiation of economic sanctions against Russia.

In 2018 President Trump, beat up by the false "Russiagate" narrative, withdrew the US from the INF treaty to prove he was tough on Russia and not a Russian agent.

Also in 2018 there was the concocted case of alleged poisoning of Sergei and Yulia Skripal in the UK with Russian nerve gas which they somehow survived. The alleged event was blamed on Putin. The Skripals mysteriously disappeared and have not been seen or heard from since.

In 2020 Washington withdrew from the Open Skies Treaty.

In December 2021 and January 2022 the Kremlin made strenuous efforts to reach a mutual security treaty with the US and NATO and was coldly rebuffed by the US Secretary of State and the NATO

Secretary General. Instead, a large Ukrainian army was poised on the Donbas border and heavy shelling began, bringing in the Russians in February 2022.

In 2022 more sanctions were applied to Russia, and Russia's foreign reserves were seized. Massive arms shipments from the US and NATO began arriving in Ukraine. In September 2022 the US and UK blew up the Nordstream gas pipelines. Washington accused Russia of sabotaging its own pipelines.

The efforts of 20th century American presidents to end the Cold War, restrain armaments, and reduce the possibility of nuclear war have been completely overturned by neoconservative-dominated governments in the 21st century. The tensions today are far greater than at any time during the 20th century Cold War. Today the Kremlin openly states that the Russian government has zero trust in the West and believes that the West intends to destroy Russia. This is extremely dangerous. During the Cold War there were numerous incidences of false alarms of incoming ICBMs, but neither side believed them because the ongoing negotiations had created a framework of mutual trust. This achievement has been squandered by America's 21st century leadership which in pursuit of the neoconservative goal of US hegemony has left the door wide open to Nuclear Armageddon.

The situation is even worse than the Atomic Scientists' Doomsday Clock indicates. The correct time is one nano-second to Midnight.

And there is no one in the West to take this into account. There are no more Presidents such as Kennedy, Nixon, Reagan or experts such as Steven Cohen. America's foreign policy "experts" are a collection of whores on military/security grants and consultancies, and the presstitutes support rather than investigate official narratives. As I have previously reported, David Johnson at George Washington University provides a daily list of media and academic comment on US/Russia relations. The unreality of almost all of it is beyond belief. It is difficult to believe that the foreign policy community that got us through the Cold War has been replaced by Russophobic emotions incapable of objective reasoning and unaware of the dangerous situation that they have created.

Instead we have neoconservatives blabbering about how we can win a nuclear war.

Here we are a superpower made dangerous to ourselves and to the entire world by the total absence of any awareness and any leadership whatsoever.

First published on January 19, 2023.

[1]. "US, UK, France Promised USSR Not to Expand NATO East of Germany, Newly Discovered Document Proves" https://www.globalresearch.ca/us-uk-france-promised-ussr-not-expand-nato-east-germany-newly-discovered-document-proves/5772441

CHAPTER 4
THE LIES OF
HISTORY

Empires Then and Now

Great empires, such as the Roman and British, were extractive. The empires succeeded, because the value of the resources and wealth extracted from conquered lands exceeded the value of conquest and governance. The reason Rome did not extend its empire east into Germany was not the military prowess of Germanic tribes but Rome's calculation that the cost of conquest exceeded the value of extractable resources.

The Roman empire failed, because Romans exhausted manpower and resources in civil wars fighting amongst themselves for power. The British empire failed, because the British exhausted themselves fighting Germany in two world wars.

In his book, The Rule of Empires (2010), Timothy H. Parsons replaces the myth of the civilizing empire with the truth of the extractive empire. He describes the successes of the Romans, the Umayyad Caliphate, the Spanish in Peru, Napoleon in Italy, and the British in India and Kenya in extracting resources. To lower the cost of governing Kenya, the British instigated tribal consciousness and invented tribal customs that worked to British advantage.

Parsons does not examine the American empire, but in his introduction to the book he wonders whether America's empire is really an empire as the Americans don't seem to get any extractive benefits from it. After eight years of war and attempted occupation of Iraq, all Washington has for its efforts is several trillion dollars of additional debt and no Iraqi oil. After ten years of trillion dollar struggle against the Taliban in Afghanistan, Washington has nothing to show for it except possibly some part of the drug trade that can be used to fund covert CIA operations.

America's wars are very expensive. Bush and Obama have doubled the national debt, and the American people have no benefits from it. No riches, no bread and circuses flow to Americans from Washington's wars. So what is it all about?

The answer is that Washington's empire extracts resources from the American people for the benefit of the few powerful interest groups that rule America. The military-security complex, Wall Street, agribusiness and the Israel Lobby use the government to extract resources from Americans to serve their profits and power. The US Constitution has been extracted in the interests of the Security State, and Americans' incomes have been redirected to the pockets of the 1 percent. That is how the American Empire functions.

The New Empire is different. It happens without achieving conquest. The American military did not conquer Iraq and has been forced out politically by the puppet government that Washington established. There is no victory in Afghanistan, and after a decade the American military does not control the country.

In the New Empire success at war no longer matters. The extraction takes place by being at war. Huge sums of American taxpayers' money have flowed into the American armaments industries and huge amounts of power into Homeland Security. The American empire works by stripping Americans of wealth and liberty.

This is why the wars cannot end, or if one does end another starts. Remember when Obama came into office and was asked what the US mission was in Afghanistan? He replied that he did not know what the mission was and that the mission needed to be defined.

Obama never defined the mission. He renewed the Afghan war without telling us its purpose. Obama cannot tell Americans that the purpose of the war is to build the power and profit of the military/security complex at the expense of American citizens.

This truth doesn't mean that the objects of American military aggression have escaped without cost. Large numbers of Muslims have been bombed and murdered and their economies and infrastructure ruined, but not in order to extract resources from them.

It is ironic that under the New Empire the citizens of the empire are extracted of their wealth and liberty in order to extract lives from the targeted foreign populations. Just like the bombed and murdered Muslims, the American people are victims of the American empire.

First published on March 26, 2012.

How Liberty Was Lost

When did things begin going wrong in America?

"From the beginning," answer some. English colonists, themselves under the thumb of a king, exterminated American Indians and stole their lands, as did late 18th and 19th century Americans. Over the course of three centuries the native inhabitants of America were dispossessed, just as Israelis have been driving Palestinians off their lands since 1948.

Demonization always plays a role. The Indians were savages and the Palestinians are terrorists. Any country that can control the explanation can get away with evil.

I agree that there is a lot of evil in every country and civilization. In the struggle between good and evil, religion has at times been on the side of evil. However, the notion of moral progress cannot so easily be thrown out.

Consider, for example, slavery. In the 1800s, slavery still existed in countries that proclaimed equal rights. Even free women did not have equal rights. Today no Western country would openly tolerate the ownership of humans or the transfer of a woman's property upon her marriage to her husband.

It is true that Western governments have ownership rights in the labor of their citizens through the income tax. This remains as a mitigated form of serfdom. So far, however, no government has claimed the right of ownership over the person himself.

Sometimes I hear from readers that my efforts are pointless, that elites are always dominant and that the only solution is to find one's way into the small, connected clique of elites either through marriage or service to their interests.

This might sound like cynical advice, but it is not devoid of some truth. Indeed, it is the way Washington and New York work, and increasingly the way the entire country operates.

Washington serves powerful private interests, not the public interest. University faculties in their research increasingly serve private interests and decreasingly serve truth. In the US the media is no longer a voice and protection for the people. It is becoming increasingly impossible in America to get a good job without being connected to the system that serves the elites.

The problem I have with this "give up" attitude is that over the course of my life, and more broadly over the course of the 20th century, many positive changes occurred through reforms. It is impossible to have reforms without good will, so even the elites who accepted reforms that limited their powers were part of the moral progress.

Labor unions became a countervailing power to corporate management and Wall Street.

Working conditions were reformed. Civil rights were extended. People excluded by the system were brought into it. Anyone who grew up in the 20th century can add his own examples.

Progress was slow – unduly so from a reformer's standpoint – and mistakes were made. Nevertheless, whether done properly or improperly there was a commitment to the expansion of civil liberty.

This commitment ended suddenly on September 11, 2001. In eleven years the Bush/Obama Regime repealed 800 years of human achievements that established law as a shield of the people and, instead, converted law into a weapon in the hands of the government. Today Americans and citizens of other countries can, on the will of the US executive branch alone, be confined to torture dungeons for the duration of their lives with no due process or evidence presented to any court, or they can be shot down in the streets or exterminated by drone missiles.

The power that the US government asserts over its subjects and also over the citizens of other countries is unlimited. Lenin described unlimited power as power "resting directly on force, not limited by anything, not restricted by any laws, nor any absolute rules."

Washington claims that it is the indispensable government representing the exceptional people and thereby has the right to impose its will and "justice" on the rest of the world and that resistance to Washington constitutes terrorism to be exterminated by any possible means.

Thus, the American neoconservatives speak of nuking Iran for insisting on its independence from American hegemony and exercising its rights to nuclear energy under the non-proliferation treaty to which Iran is a signatory.

In other words, Washington's will prevails over international treaties that have the force of law, treaties which Washington itself imposed on the world. According to the neoconservatives and Washington, Iran is not protected by the legal contract that Iran made with Washington when Iran signed the non-proliferation treaty.

Iran finds itself as just another 17th or 18th century American Indian tribe to be deprived of its rights and to be exterminated by the forces of evil that dominate Washington, D.C.

The vast majority of "superpower" Americans plugged into the Matrix, where they are happy with the disinformation pumped into their brains by Washington and its presstitute media, would demur rather than face my facts.

This raises the question: how does one become unplugged and unplug others from the Matrix? Readers have asked, and I do not have a complete answer.

It seems to happen in a number of ways. Being fired and forced to train your H-1B foreign replacement who works for lower pay, being convicted of a crime that you did not commit, having your children stolen from you by Child Protective Services because bruises from sports activities were alleged to be signs of child abuse, your home stolen from you because a mortgage based on fraud was given the force of law, laid off by "free market capitalism" as your age advanced and the premium of your employer-provided medical insurance increased, being harassed by Homeland Security on your re-entry to the US because you are a non-embedded journalist who reports truthfully on US behavior abroad. There are many instances of Americans being jolted into reality by the "freedom and democracy" scales falling away from their eyes.

It is possible that becoming unplugged from the Matrix is a gradual lifelong experience for the few who pay attention. The longer they live, the more they notice that reality contradicts the government's and media's explanations. The few who can remember important stuff after watching reality shows and their favorite sports teams and fantasy movies gradually realize that there is no "new economy" to take the place of the manufacturing economy that was given away to foreign countries. Once unemployed from their "dirty fingernail jobs," they learn that there is no "new economy" to employ them.

Still seething from the loss of the Vietnam War and anger at war protesters, some flag-waving patriots are slowly realizing the consequences of criminalizing dissent and the exercise of First Amendment rights. "You are with us or against us" is taking on threatening instead of reassuring connotations, implying that anyone who opens his or her mouth in any dissent is thereby transformed into an "enemy of the state."

More Americans, but far from enough, are coming to the realization that the extermination of the Branch Davidians at Waco in 1993 was a test run to confirm that the public and Congress would accept the murder of civilians who had been demonized with false charges of child abuse and gun-running.

The next test was the Oklahoma City Bombing in 1995. Whose explanation would prevail: the government's or that of experts? Air Force General Partin, a top expert on explosives, proved conclusively in a heavily documented report given to every member of Congress that the Murruh Federal Office Building blew up from the inside out, not from the outside in from the fertilizer car bomb. But General Partin's facts lost out to the government's propaganda and to Congress' avoidance of cognitive dissonance.

Once the "national security" government learned that its pronouncements and those of the presstitute media carried more weight than the facts presented by experts, conspiracies such as Operation Northwoods could be put into play. A 9/11 became possible.

The Pentagon, CIA, and military/security complex were desperate for a new enemy to replace the "Soviet threat," which had ceased to exist. The military/security complex and its servants in Congress were determined to replace the profits made from the cold war and to preserve and increase the powers accumulated in the Pentagon and CIA. The only possible replacement for the Soviet threat was "Muslim terrorists." Thus, the creation of the "al Qaeda threat" and the conflation of this new threat with secular Arab governments, such as Iraq's and Syria's, which were the real targets of Islamists.

Despite the evidence provided by experts that secular Arab governments, such as Saddam Hussein's, were allies against Islamic extremism, the US government used propaganda to link the secular Iraq government with Iraq's enemies among Islamic revolutionaries.

Once Washington confirmed that the American public was both too ignorant and too inattentive to pay any attention to events that would alter their lives and jeopardize their existence, everything else followed: the PATRIOT Act, the suspension of the Constitution and destruction of civil liberty, Homeland Security which has quickly extended its Gestapo reach from airports to train stations, bus terminals and highway road blocks, the criminalization of dissent, the equating of critics of the government with supporters of terrorism, the home invasions of antiwar protesters and their arraignment before a grand jury, the prosecution of whistleblowers who reveal government crimes, the equating of journalism organizations such as WikiLeaks with spies. The list goes on.

The collapse of truth in the US and in its puppet states is a major challenge to my view that truth and good will are powers that can prevail over evil. It is possible that my perception that moral progress has occurred in various periods of Western civilization reflects a progressive unplugging from the Matrix. What I remember as reforms might be events experienced through the rose colored glasses of the Matrix.

But I think not. Reason is an important part of human existence. Some are capable of it. Imagination and creativity can escape chains. Good can withstand evil. The extraordinary film, The Matrix, affirmed that people could be unplugged. I believe that even Americans can be unplugged. If I give up this belief, I will cease writing.

First published on April 23, 2012.

The Power of Lies

It is one of history's ironies that the Lincoln Memorial is a sacred space for the Civil Rights Movement and the site of Martin Luther King's "I Have a Dream" speech.

Lincoln did not think blacks were the equals of whites. Lincoln's plan was to send the blacks in America back to Africa, and if he had not been assassinated, returning blacks to Africa would likely have been his post-war policy.

As Thomas DiLorenzo and a number of non-court historians have conclusively established, Lincoln did not invade the Confederacy in order to free the slaves. The Emancipation Proclamation did not occur until 1863 when opposition in the North to the war was rising despite Lincoln's police state measures to silence opponents and newspapers. The Emancipation Proclamation was a war measure issued under Lincoln's war powers. The proclamation provided for the emancipated slaves to be enrolled in the Union army replenishing its losses. It was also hoped that the proclamation would spread slave revolts in the South while southern white men were away at war and draw soldiers away from the fronts in order to protect their women and children. The intent was to hasten the defeat of the South before political opposition to Lincoln in the North grew stronger.

The Lincoln Memorial was built not because Lincoln "freed the slaves," but because Lincoln saved the empire. As the Savior of the Empire, had Lincoln not been assassinated, he could have become emperor for life.

As Professor Thomas DiLorenzo writes: "Lincoln spent his entire political career attempting to use the powers of the state for the benefit of the moneyed corporate elite (the 'one-percenters' of his day), first in Illinois, and then in the North in general, through protectionist tariffs, corporate welfare for road, canal, and railroad corporations, and a national bank controlled by politicians like himself to fund it all."

Lincoln was a man of empire. As soon as the South was conquered, ravaged, and looted, his collection of war criminal generals, such as Sherman and Sheridan, set about exterminating the Plains Indians in one of the worst acts of genocide in human history. Even today Israeli Zionists point to Washington's extermination of the Plains Indians as the model for Israel's theft of Palestine.

The War of Northern Aggression was about tariffs and northern economic imperialism. The North was protectionist. The South was free trade. The North wanted to finance its economic development by forcing the South to pay higher prices for manufactured goods. The North passed the Morrill Tariff which more than doubled the tariff rate to 32.6% and provided for a further hike to 47%. The tariff diverted the South's profits on its agricultural exports to the coffers of Northern industrialists and manufacturers. The tariff was designed to redirect the South's expenditures on manufactured goods from England to the higher cost goods produced in the North.

This is why the South left the union, a right of self-determination under the Constitution.

The purpose of Lincoln's war was to save the empire, not to abolish slavery. In his first inaugural address Lincoln "made an ironclad defense of slavery." His purpose was to keep the South in the Empire despite the Morrill Tariff. As for slavery, Lincoln said: "I have no purpose, directly or indirectly to interfere with the institution of slavery in the States where it exists. I believe I have no right to do so, and I have no inclination to do so." This position, Lincoln reminded his audience, was part of the 1860 Republican Party platform. Lincoln also offered his support for the strong enforcement of the Fugitive Slave Act, which required Northerners to hunt down and return runaway slaves, and he gave his support to the Corwin Amendment to the

Constitution, already passed by Northern votes in the House and Senate, that prohibited any federal interference with slavery. For Lincoln and his allies, the empire was far more important than slaves.

DiLorenzo explains what the deal was that Lincoln offered to the South. However, just as empire was more important to the North than slavery, for the South avoiding large taxes on manufactured goods, in effect a tax on Southern agricultural profits, was more important than northern guarantees for slavery.

If you want to dislodge your brainwashing about the War of Northern Aggression, read DiLorenzo's books, The Real Lincoln, and Lincoln Unmasked.

The so-called Civil War was not a civil war. In a civil war, both sides are fighting for control of the government. The South was not fighting for control of the federal government. The South seceded and the North refused to let the South go.

The reason I am writing about this is to illustrate how history is falsified on behalf of agendas. I am all for civil rights and participated in the movement while a college student. What makes me uncomfortable is the transformation of Lincoln, a tyrant who was an agent for the One Percent and was willing to destroy any and every thing in behalf of empire, into a civil rights hero. Who will be next? Hitler? Stalin? Mao? George W. Bush? Obama? John Yoo? If Lincoln can be a civil rights hero, so can be torturers. Those who murder in Washington's wars women and children can be turned into defenders of women's rights and child advocates. And probably they will be.

This is the twisted perverted world in which we live. Vladimir Putin, President of Russia, is confronted with Washington's overthrow of the elected government in Ukraine, a Russian ally and for centuries a part of Russia itself, while Putin is falsely accused of invading Ukraine. China is accused by Washington as a violator of human rights while

Washington murders more civilians in the 21st century than every other country combined.

Everywhere in the West monstrous lies stand unchallenged. The lies are institutionalized in history books, course curriculums, policy statements, movements and causes, and in historical memory.

America will be hard pressed to survive the lies that it lives.

First published on April 13, 2015.

Trump and American History Have Been Assassinated

When Trump was elected I wrote that it was unlikely that he would be successful in accomplishing the three objectives for which he was elected – peace with Russia, the return home of offshored US jobs, and effective limits on non-white immigration – because these objectives conflicted with the interests of those more powerful than the president.

I wrote that Trump was unfamiliar with Washington and would fail to appoint a government that would support his goals. I wrote that unless the ruling oligarchy could bring Trump under its control, Trump would be assassinated.

Trump has been brought under control by assassinating him with words rather than with a bullet. With Steve Bannon's dismissal, there is now no one in Trump's government who supports him. He is surrounded by Russophobic generals and Zionists.

But this is not enough for the liberal/progressive/left. They want Trump impeached and driven from office.

Marjorie Cohn, whom I have always admired for her defense of civil liberty, has disappointed me. She has written in Truthout, which sadly has become more like PropagandaOut, that the House must bring articles of impeachment against Trump for his abuse of power and before he launches a new civil war and/or nuclear war.

This is an extraordinary conclusion for a normally intelligent person to reach. What power does Trump have? How does he abuse his non-existent power? The ruling Establishment has cut his balls off. He is neutered. Powerless. He has been completely isolated within his own government by the oligarchy.

Even more astonishingly, Marjorie Cohn, together with 100% of the liberal/progressive/left are blind to the fact that they have helped the military/security complex destroy the only leader who advocated peace instead of conflict with the other major nuclear power. Cohn is so deranged by hatred of Trump that she thinks it is Trump who will bring nuclear war by normalizing relations with Russia.

Clearly, the American liberal/progressive/left is no longer capable of rational thought. Hate rules. There is nothing in their lexicon but hate.

The American liberal/progressive/left has degenerated into idiocy. They think that they are fighting "white nationalism" in the White House and that Trump is a champion or symbol of "white nationalism" and that there will be no victory until Trump and all symbols of "white nationalism" are obliterated.

Little do they understand. Ajamu Baraka spells it out for them in CounterPunch. White Supremacy, he writes, is inculcated into the cultural and educational institutions of the West. Liberal and leftist whites are also white supremacists, says Baraka, and Trump and the "alt-right" are nothing but a superficial useful platform on which the white supremacist American liberal/progressive/left can parade its self-righteousness. Ajamu Baraka's conclusion is "that in order for the world to live, the 525-year-old white supremacist Pan-European, colonial/capitalist patriarchy must die." It is not difficult to see in this statement that genocide is the solution for the white plague upon humanity. Little wonder the "alt-right" gets exercised by the anti-white propaganda of Identity Politics.

Non-white immigration will finish off the shards of remaining European civilization. All current demographics indicate that all of Europe and North America will sooner than you expect be occupied by non-white majorities.

The problem is not so much the immigrants themselves as it is that they are taught to hate whites by white liberal/progressive/leftists. The destruction of statues will not end with Robert E. Lee's. Thomas Jefferson and George Washington are next. They owned slaves, whereas the Lee family's slaves were freed by will three years prior to the Lincoln's invasion of the South. The Washington, Jefferson, and Lincoln memorials will have to be destroyed also as they, too, are monuments to racism. Indeed, according to the Identity Politics of the Liberal/progressive/left the Declaration of Independence and the US Constitution are White Supremacy documents written by racists. This doubles the indictment against Thomas Jefferson and adds all of the Founding Fathers to the indictment. All are guilty of institutionalizing White Supremacy in America.

The uninformed insouciant Average American may think that this is a joke. But no. It is the orthodoxy of the white American intellectual class. It is taught in all the universities.

In Atlanta they are talking about erasing the heads of the South's generals carved into Stone Mountain. Mount Rushmore in South Dakota will be next. It has carved into it the heads of Washington, Jefferson, Theodore Roosevelt, and Abraham Lincoln. All racists, and Roosevelt was a colonialist and imperialist to boot. Lincoln was the worst racist of all.

Economist/historian Thomas DiLorenzo reminds us that "to his dying day, Lincoln was busy plotting the deportation of all the black people in America, including the soon-to-be-freed slaves" [1].

The following statements are all statements that are in Abe Lincoln's Collected Works:

"I have said that the separation of the races is the only perfect preventive of amalgamation [of the white and black races] . . . Such separation . . . must be affected by colonization" [sending blacks to

Liberia or Central America]. (Collected Works of Abraham Lincoln vol. II, p. 409).

"Let us be brought to believe it is morally right, and . . . favorable to . . . our interest, to transfer the African to his native clime." (Collected Works, vol. II, p. 409).

"I am not nor ever have been in favor of bringing about in any way the social and political equality of the white and black races. I am not nor ever have been in favor of making voters or jurors of negroes, nor qualifying them to hold office, nor to intermarry with white people" (Collected Works, vol. III, pp. 145-146).

How did Lincoln in the face of his own words and deeds get to be the hero who liberated blacks from slavery? The Emancipation Proclamation did not free a single slave, as Lincoln's Secretary of State complained. It was a war measure that only applied to slaves under the jurisdiction of the Confederacy in hopes of fomenting a slave rebellion that would pull Southern soldiers off the front lines to rush to the protection of their wives and children. In 1861 the year the North invaded the South, President Lincoln said, "I have no purpose, directly or indirectly, to interfere with the institution of slavery in the States where it exists. I believe I have no lawful right to do so, and I have no inclination to do so" (First Inaugural Address). In 1862 during the war, Lincoln wrote to Horace Greeley: "If I could save the Union without freeing any slave I would do it."

Lincoln was elevated to the undeserved position of black liberator by the historical lies made up by white liberal/progressive/leftists who hate the South. They are so consumed by hate that they do not understand that the hate that they teach will also devour them. They should read Jean Raspail's book, The Camp of the Saints. People taught racial hate do not differentiate between good and bad members of the people they are taught to hate. All are equally guilty. As one Third Worlder wrote to me, "all whites are guilty," even those such as myself who speak out against the West's atrocities against the darker-skinned peoples.

The American liberal/progressive/left has long been engaged in demonizing white people exactly as Nazis demonized Jews and Communists demonized capitalists. One would think that the liberal/progressive/leftists would be aware of what happened to the Jews and to the Russian, Chinese and East European capitalists and bourgeois middle class. Why do the liberal/progressive/leftists think they will escape the consequences of teaching hate?

What has Charlottesville taught us other than that the hate expressed by the liberal/progressive/left exceeds the hate expressed by the white nationalists themselves. When it comes to hate, the White Supremacists are out-gunned by the liberal/progressive/left.

Hate is the hallmark of the American liberal/progressive/left, and hate always ends in violence.

The Northern ruling economic interests had no interest in devoting resources to a war to free slaves. They wanted the Union held together so that there would be no competition for the lands west of the Mississippi and so there would be an agrarian sector to which to market northern manufactured goods protected by tariffs against lower priced British goods.

The northern work force didn't want any freed slaves either. The large number of recent Irish immigrants driven out of Ireland by the British starvation policy called Lincoln's war "a rich man's war and a poor man's fight." What freed slaves meant for the northern working class was a larger labor supply and lower wages. In 1863 when the Republicans passed the draft, the Irish in Detroit and New York rioted. The rioters took out their anger and frustration on northern blacks, many of whom were lynched. It is not clear to me whether more backs were lynched in the North during the war or in the South during

Reconstruction. If there are any memorials to the Irish, those racist statues will have to be taken down also. Perhaps even the Statue of Liberty is racist.

And we haven't yet heard from Native Americans. In his excruciating history, The Long Death: The Last Days of the Plains Indians, Ralph K. Andrist describes the genocide of the Plains Indians by Lincoln's Civil War generals, William Tecumseh Sherman, Phillip Sheridan, Grenville Dodge and other of the first war criminals of the modern age who found it a lot easier to conduct warfare against Southern women and children than against armed troops. Against the Native Americans Lincoln's generals now conducted a policy of genocide that was even more horrible and barbaric than Sheridan's destruction of Virginia's Shenandoah Valley.

Lincoln historian Professor Thomas DiLorenzo provides a synopsis of the genocide of Native Americans here [2].

During the eight year presidency of General Ulysses S. Grant, 1868-76, the Union generals conducted a policy of extermination against the Native Americans. Entire villages, every man, woman, and child, were wiped out. The Union Army's scorched earth policy starved to death those Indians who escaped fire and sword.

Professor DiLorenzo writes:

"Sherman and Sheridan's troops conducted more than one thousand attacks on Indian villages, mostly in the winter months, when families were together. The U.S. Army's actions matched its leaders' rhetoric of extermination. As mentioned earlier, Sherman gave orders to kill everyone and everything, including dogs, and to burn everything that would burn so as to increase the likelihood that any survivors would starve or freeze to death. The soldiers also waged a war of extermination on the buffalo, which was the Indians' chief source of food, winter clothing, and other goods (the Indians even made fish hooks out of dried buffalo bones and bow strings out of sinews). By 1882, the buffalo were all but extinct."

Indian warriors who were captured were subjected to the type of trials and executions that the George W. Bush regime gave Saddam Hussein: "hundreds of Indians who had been taken prisoner were subjected to military 'trials' lasting about ten minutes each, according to Nichols (1978). Most of the adult male prisoners were found guilty and sentenced to death – not based on evidence of the commission of a crime, but on their mere presence at the end of the fighting." In other words, POWs were executed, for which the US executed German officers at Nuremberg.

The Union massacre of the Indians began before the Civil War was won. DiLorenzo reports:

"One of the most famous incidents of Indian extermination, known as the Sand Creek Massacre, took place on November 29, 1864. There was a Cheyenne and Arapaho village located on Sand Creek in southeastern Colorado. These Indians had been assured by the U.S. government that they would be safe in Colorado. The government instructed them to fly a U.S. flag over their village, which they did, to assure their safety. However, another Civil War 'luminary,' Colonel John Chivington, had other plans for them as he raided the village with 750 heavily armed soldiers. One account of what happened appears in the book Crimsoned Prairie: The Indian Wars (1972) by the renowned military historian S. L. A. Marshall, who held the title of chief historian of the European Theater in World War II and authored thirty books on American military history.

"Chivington's orders were: 'I want you to kill and scalp all, big and little.' (Marshall 1972, 37). Then, despite the display of the U.S. flag and white surrender flags by these peaceful Indians, Chivington's troops 'began a full day given over to blood-lust, orgiastic mutilation, rapine, and destruction – with Chivington looking on and approving'

(Marshall 1972, 38). Marshall notes that the most reliable estimate of the number of Indians killed is '163, of which 110 were women and children' (p. 39).

"Upon returning to his fort, Chivington 'and his raiders demonstrated around Denver, waving their trophies, more than one hundred drying scalps. They were acclaimed as conquering heroes, which was what they had sought mainly.' One Republican Party newspaper announced, 'Colorado soldiers have once again covered themselves with glory' (Marshall 1972, 39).

DiLorenzo reports: "The books by Brown and Marshall show that the kind of barbarism that occurred at Sand Creek, Colorado, was repeated many times during the next two decades."

General Sherman, a war criminal far in excess of anything the Nazis were able to produce, wrote to his wife early in the Civil War that his purpose was "extermination, not of soldiers alone, that is the least part of the trouble, but the [Southern] people."

His wife responded: Conduct a "war of extermination" and drive all Southerners "like the swine into the sea. May we carry fire and sword into their states till not one habitation is left standing" (Walters 1973, 61).

DiLorenzo observes that Sherman did his best to take his wife's advice.

The extreme hatred and barbarity to which the Northern war criminals had subjected Southern non-combatants broke like fury over the Plains Indians. Distinguished military historians have described the orders given to General Custer by Phillip Sheridan as "the most brutal orders ever published to American troops."

Clearly, if we are taking down statues, we can't stop with Robert E. Lee. We will have to take down the Statues of Lincoln, Grant, Sherman, Sheridan, and all the rest of the Union war criminals who implemented what they themselves called "the final solution to the Indian problem."

The designation of the northern invasion of the South as a civil war is itself a lie. The term "civil war" is used to cover up the fact that the North initiated a war of aggression, thus removing the sin of war from the North. A civil war is when two sides fight for control of the government. However, the South had no interest or intent to control the government in Washington. All the Southern states did is to use the constitutional right to end their voluntary association with other states in the United States. The South fought because the South was invaded. Southerners did not regard the War of Northern Aggression as a civil war. They clearly understood that the war was a war of Northern Aggression.

As brutal as Lincoln's war criminal armies were to Southern civilians, the inhumanity of the brutality toward Southern people escalated during the long period called Reconstruction. The Northern ruling Republicans did their best to subject the South to rule by the blacks while Northern "carpetbaggers" stole everything that they could. No white Southern woman was safe from rape. "Civil War" buffs have told me that there were southern towns in which all the women were hidden in the woods outside of town to protect them from the Republican Union soldiers and the former slaves that the Republican agents of Reconstruction encouraged. What happened to the South at the hands of the Republicans was no different from what the Russians and Americans did in Germany when the Wehrmacht surrendered. The demonized KKK was an organization that arose to protect what remained of the South's honor from unbearable humiliations.

Consequently, for decades no Southern person would vote Republican. The Democrats lost the "solid South" by aping the Reconstruction

Republicans and again bringing Reconstruction to the South, using federal force instead of persuasion.

No real facts are any longer taught in the US about the so-called "Civil War." In the place of the actual history stands only lies.

In an accompanying guest contribution, economist/historian Professor Thomas DiLorenzo explains the real reason that Lincoln invaded the South. He shows that Lincoln's success in conquering the South destroyed the political character of the United States that had been formed by the Founding Fathers. He also shows that the Union policy of conducting war against civilians created the precedents for the massive war crimes of the 20th and 21st centuries. Seldom does the opportunity arise to acquire an enlightening and accurate history lesson from one article. That is what Professor DiLorenzo has delivered [3].

First published on August 21, 2017.

[1]. "The Next Target of the Black Lives Matter Movement" https://www.lewrockwell.com/2015/11/thomas-dilorenzo/next-target-blacklivesmatter
[2]. "The Culture of Violence in the American West" http://www.independent.org/publications/tir/article.asp?a=803
[3]. "The Lincoln Myth: Ideological Cornerstone of the America Empire" https://www.paulcraigroberts.org/2017/08/21/lincoln-myth-ideological-cornerstone-america-empire/

How We Know The So-Called "Civil War" Was Not Over Slavery

When I read Professor Thomas DiLorenzo's, the question that kept to mind was, "How come the South is said to have fought for slavery when the North wasn't fighting against slavery?"

Two days before Lincoln's inauguration as the 16th President, Congress, consisting only of the Northern states, passed overwhelmingly on March 2, 1861, the Corwin Amendment that gave constitutional protection to slavery. Lincoln endorsed the amendment in his inaugural address, saying "I have no objection to its being made express and irrevocable."

Quite clearly, the North was not prepared to go to war in order to end slavery when on the very eve of war the US Congress and incoming president were in the process of making it unconstitutional to abolish slavery.

Here we have absolute total proof that the North wanted the South kept in the Union far more than the North wanted to abolish slavery.

If the South's real concern was maintaining slavery, the South would not have turned down the constitutional protection of slavery offered them on a silver platter by Congress and the President. Clearly, for the South also the issue was not slavery.

The real issue between North and South could not be reconciled on the basis of accommodating slavery. The real issue was economic as DiLorenzo, Charles Beard and other historians have documented. The North offered to preserve slavery irrevocably, but the North did not offer to give up the high tariffs and economic policies that the South saw as inimical to its interests.

Blaming the war on slavery was the way the northern court historians used morality to cover up Lincoln's naked aggression and the war crimes of his generals. Demonizing the enemy with moral language works for the victor. And it is still ongoing. We see in the destruction of statues the determination to shove remaining symbols of the Confederacy down the Memory Hole.

Today the ignorant morons, thoroughly brainwashed by Identity Politics, are demanding removal of memorials to Robert E. Lee, an alleged racist toward whom they express violent hatred. This presents a massive paradox. Robert E. Lee was the first person offered command of the Union armies. How can it be that a "Southern racist" was offered command of the Union Army if the Union was going to war to free black slaves?

Virginia did not secede until April 17, 1861, two days after Lincoln called up troops for the invasion of the South.

Surely there must be some hook somewhere that the dishonest court historians can use on which to hang an explanation that the war was about slavery. It is not an easy task. Only a small minority of southerners owned slaves. Slaves were brought to the New World by Europeans as a labor force long prior to the existence of the US and the Southern states in order that the abundant land could be exploited. For the South slavery was an inherited institution that pre-dated the South. Diaries and letters of soldiers fighting for the Confederacy and those fighting for the Union provide no evidence that the soldiers were fighting for or against slavery. Princeton historian, Pulitzer Prize winner, Lincoln Prize winner, president of the American Historical Association, and member of the editorial board of Encyclopedia Britannica, James M. McPherson, in his book based on the correspondence of one thousand soldiers from both sides, What They Fought For, 1861-1865, reports that they fought for two different understandings of the Constitution.

As for the Emancipation Proclamation, on the Union side, military officers were concerned that the Union troops would desert if the Emancipation Proclamation gave them the impression that they were being killed and maimed for the sake of blacks. That is why Lincoln stressed that the proclamation was a "war measure" to provoke an internal slave rebellion that would draw Southern troops off the front lines.

If we look carefully we can find a phony hook in the South Carolina Declaration of Causes of Secession (December 20, 1860) as long as we ignore the reasoning of the document. Lincoln's election caused South Carolina to secede. During his campaign for president Lincoln used rhetoric aimed at the abolitionist vote. (Abolitionists did want slavery abolished for moral reasons, though it is sometimes hard to see their morality through their hate, but they never controlled the government.)

South Carolina saw in Lincoln's election rhetoric intent to violate the US Constitution, which was a voluntary agreement, and which recognized each state as a free and independent state. After providing a history that supported South Carolina's position, the document says that to remove all doubt about the sovereignty of states "an amendment was added, which declared that the powers not delegated to the United States by the Constitution, nor prohibited by it to the States, are reserved to the States, respectively, or to the people."

South Carolina saw slavery as the issue being used by the North to violate the sovereignty of states and to further centralize power in Washington. The secession document makes the case that the North, which controlled the US government, had broken the compact on which the Union rested and, therefore, had made the Union null and void. For example, South Carolina pointed to Article 4 of the US Constitution, which reads: "No person held to service or labor in one State, under the laws thereof, escaping into another, shall, in consequence of any law or regulation therein, be discharged from such service or labor, but shall be delivered up, on claim of the party to whom such service or labor may be due." Northern states had passed laws that nullified federal laws that upheld this article of the compact. Thus, the northern states had deliberately broken the compact on which the union was formed.

The obvious implication was that every aspect of states' rights protected by the 10th Amendment could now be violated. And as time passed they were, so South Carolina's reading of the situation was correct.

The secession document reads as a defense of the powers of states and not as a defense of slavery. Here is the document [1]. Read it and see what you decide.

A court historian, who is determined to focus attention away from the North's destruction of the US Constitution and the war crimes that accompanied the Constitution's destruction, will seize on South Carolina's use of slavery as the example of the issue the North used to subvert the Constitution. The court historian's reasoning is that as South Carolina makes a to-do about slavery, slavery must have been the cause of the war.

As South Carolina was the first to secede, its secession document probably was the model for other states. If so, this is the avenue by which court historians, that is, those who replace real history with fake history, turn the war into a war over slavery.

Once people become brainwashed, especially if it is by propaganda that serves power, they are more or less lost forever. It is extremely difficult to bring them to truth. Just look at the pain and suffering inflicted on historian David Irving for documenting the truth about the war crimes committed by the allies against the Germans. There is no doubt that he is correct, but the truth is unacceptable.

The same is the case with the War of Northern Aggression. Lies masquerading as history have been institutionalized for 150 years. An institutionalized lie is highly resistant to truth.

Education has so deteriorated in the US that many people can no longer tell the difference between an explanation and an excuse or justification. In the US denunciation of an orchestrated hate object is a safer path for a writer than explanation. Truth is the casualty.

That truth is so rare everywhere in the Western World is why the West is doomed. The United States, for example, has an entire population that is completely ignorant of its own history.

As George Orwell said, the best way to destroy a people is to destroy their history.

Apparently Even Asians Can Be White Supremacists If They Are Named Robert Lee

ESPN has pulled an Asian-American named Robert Lee (Lee is a common name among Asians, for example, Bruce Lee) from announcing the University of Virginia/William & Mary football game in Charlottesville this Saturday because of his name.

First published on August 23, 2017.

[1]. "South Carolina's Declaration of the Causes of Secession" https://teachingamericanhistory.org/document/south-carolinas-declaration-of-the-causes-of-secession/

The Weaponization Of History And Journalism

In the United States, facts, an important element of truth, are not important. They are not important in the media, politics, universities, historical explanations, or the courtroom. Non-factual explanations of the collapse of three World Trade Center buildings are served up as the official explanation. Facts have been politicized, emotionalized, weaponized and simply ignored. As David Irving has shown, Anglo-American histories of World War 2 are, for the most part, feel-good histories, as are "civil war" histories as Thomas DiLorenzo and others have demonstrated. Of course, they are feel good only for the victors. Their emotional purpose means that inconvenient facts are unpalatable and ignored.

Writing the truth is no way to succeed as an author. Only a small percentage of readers are interested in the truth. Most want their biases or brainwashing vindicated. They want to read what they already believe. It is comforting, reassuring. When their ignorance is confronted, they become angry. The way to be successful as a writer is to pick a group and give them what they want. There is always a market for romance novels and for histories that uphold a country's myths. On the Internet successful sites are those that play to one ideology or another, to one emotion or the other, or to one interest group or another. The single rule for success is to confine truth to what the readership group you serve believes.

Keep this in mind when you receive shortly my September quarterly request for your support of this website. There are not many like it. This site does not represent an interest group, an ideology, a hate group, an ethnic group or any cause other than truth. This is not to say that this site is proof against error. It is only to say that truth is its purpose

Karl Marx said that there were only class truths. Today we have a large variety of truths: truths for feminists, truths for blacks, Muslims, Hispanics, homosexuals, transgendered, truths for the foreign policy community that serves the military/security complex, truths for the neocons, truths for the One Percent that control the economy and the economists who serve them, truths for "white supremacists," itself a truth term for their opponents. You can add to the list. The "truth" in these "truths" is that they are self-serving of the group that expresses them. Their actual relation to truth is of no consequence to those espousing the "truths."

Woe to you if you don't go along with someone's or some group's truth. Not even famous film-maker Oliver Stone is immune. Recently, Stone expressed his frustration with the "False Flag War Against Russia." Little doubt that Stone is frustrated with taunts and accusations from completely ignorant media talking heads in response to his documentary, Putin, based on many hours of interviews over two years. Stone came under fire, because instead of demonizing Putin and Russia, thus confirming the official story, he showed us glimpses of the truth.

The organization, Veteran Intelligence Professionals for Sanity, published a report that completely destroyed the false accusations about Trump/Russian hacking of the US presidential election. The Nation published an objective article about the report and was assaulted by writers, contributors, and readers for publishing information that weakens the case, which the liberal/progressive/left in conjunction with the military/security complex, is orchestrating against Trump. The magazine's audience felt that the magazine had an obligation not to truth but to getting Trump out of office. Reportedly, the editor is considering whether to recall the article.

So here we have left-leaning Oliver Stone and leftwing magazine, The Nation, under fire for making information available that is out of step with the self-serving "truth" to which the liberal/progressive/left and their ally, the military/security complex, are committed.

When a country has a population among whom there are no truths except group-specific truths, the country is so divided as to be over and done with. "A house divided against itself cannot stand." The white liberal/progressive/left leaders of divisive Identity Politics have little, if any, comprehension of where the movement they think they lead is headed. At the moment the hate is focused on the "alt-right," which has become "white nationalists," which has become "white supremacists." These "white supremacists" have become epitomized by statues of Confederate soldiers and generals. All over the South, if local governments are not removing the statues, violent crazed thugs consumed by hate attempt to destroy them. In New Orleans someone with money bused in thugs from outside flying banners that apparently are derived from a communist flag to confront locals protesting the departure of their history down the Orwellian Memory Hole.

What happens when all the monuments are gone? Where does the hate turn next? Once non-whites are taught to hate whites, not even self-hating whites are safe. How do those taught hate tell a good white from a bad white? They can't and they won't. By definition by Identity Politics, whites, for now white heterosexual males, are the victimizers and everyone else is their victim. The absurdity of this concept is apparent, yet the concept is unshaken by its absurdity. White heterosexual males are the only ones without the privilege of quotas. They and only they can be put at the back of the bus for university admissions, employment, promotion, and only their speech is regulated. They, and only they, can be fired for using "gender specific terms," for using race specific terms, for unknowingly offending some preferred group member by using a word that is no longer permissible. They can be called every name in the book, beginning with racist, misogynist, and escalating, and no one is punished for the offense.

Recently, a professor in the business school of a major university told me that he used the word, girls, in a marketing discussion. A young woman was offended. The result was he received a dressing down from the dean. Another professor told me that at his university there was a growing list of blacklisted words. It wasn't clear whether the list was official or unofficial, simply professors trying to stay up with Identity Politics and avoid words that could lead to their dismissal. Power, they tell me, is elsewhere than in the white male, the true victimized class.

For years commentators have recognized the shrinking arena of free speech in the United States. Any speech that offends anyone but a white male can be curtailed by punishment. Recently, John Whitehead, constitutional attorney who heads the Rutherford Institute, wrote that it is now dangerous just to defend free speech. Reference to the First Amendment suffices to bring denunciation and threats of violence. Ron Unz notes that any website that can be demonized as "controversial" can find itself disappeared by Internet companies and PayPal. They simply terminate free speech by cutting off service.

It must be difficult to teach some subjects, such as the "civil war" for example. How would it be possible to describe the actual facts? For example, for decades prior to the Union's invasion of the Confederacy North/South political conflict was over tariffs, not over slavery.

The fight over which new states created from former "Indian" territories would be "slave" and which "free" was a fight over keeping the protectionist (North) vs. free trade (South) balance in Congress equal so that the budding industrial north could not impose a tariff regime. Two days before Lincoln's inaugural address, a stiff tariff was signed into law. That same day in an effort to have the South accept the tariff and remain in or return to the Union – some southern states had seceded, some had not – Congress passed the Corwin amendment that provided constitutional protection to slavery. The amendment prohibited the federal government from abolishing slavery.

Two days later in his inaugural address, which seems to be aimed at the South, Lincoln said: "I have no purpose, directly or indirectly, to interfere with the institution of slavery in the States where it exists. I believe I have no lawful right to do so, and I have no inclination to do so."

Lincoln's beef with the South was not over slavery or the Fugitive Slave Act. Lincoln did not accept the secessions and still intended to collect the tariff that now was law. Under the Constitution slavery was up to the states, but the Constitution gave the federal government to right to levy a tariff. Lincoln said that "there needs to be no bloodshed or violence" over collecting the tariff. Lincoln said he will use the government's power only "to collect the duties and imposts," and that "there will be no invasion, no using of force against or among the people anywhere."

Here is Lincoln, "the Great Emancipator," telling the South that they can have slavery if they will pay the duties and imposts on imports. How many black students and whites brainwashed by Identity Politics are going to sit there and listen to such a tale and not strongly protest the racist professor justifying white supremacy and slavery?

So what happens to history when you can't tell it as it is, but instead have to refashion it to fit the preconceived beliefs formed by Identity Politics? The so-called "civil war," of course, is far from the only example.

In its document of secession, South Carolina made a case that the Constitutional contract had been broken by some of the northern states breaking faith with Article IV of the Constitution. This is true. However, it is also true that the Southern states had no inclination to abide by Section 8 of Article I, which says that "Congress shall have power to lay and collect taxes, duties, imposts and excises." So, also the South by not accepting the tariff was not constitutionally pure.

Before history became politicized, historians understood that the North intended for the South to bear costs of the North's development of industry and manufacturing. The agricultural South preferred the lower priced goods from England. The South understood that a tariff on British goods would push import prices above the high northern prices and lower the South's living standards in the interest of raising living standards in the North. The conflict was entirely economic and had nothing whatsoever to do with slavery, which also had existed in the North. Indeed, some northern states had "exclusion ordinances" and anti-immigration provisions in their state constitutions that prohibited the immigration of blacks into northern states.

If freeing slaves were important to the North and avoiding tariffs was important to the South, one can imagine some possible compromises. For example, the North could have committed to building factories in the South. As the South became industrialized, new centers of wealth would arise independently from the agricultural plantations that produced cotton exports. The labor force would adjust with the economy, and slavery would have evolved into free labor.

Unfortunately, there were too many hot heads. And so, too, today.

In America there is nothing on the horizon but hate. Everywhere you look in America you see nothing but hate. Putin is hated. Russia is hated. Muslims are hated. Venezuela is hated. Assad is hated. Iran is hated. Julian Assange is hated. Edward Snowden is hated. White heterosexual males are hated. Confederate monuments are hated. Truth-tellers are hated. "Conspiracy theorists" are hated. No one escapes being hated.

Hate groups are proliferating, especially on the liberal/progressive/left. For example, RootsAction has discovered a statue of Robert E. Lee in the U.S. Capitol and urges all good people to demand its removal. Whether the level of ignorance that RootsAction personifies is real or just a fund-raising ploy, I do not know. But clearly RootsAction is relying on public ignorance in order to get the response that they want. In former times when the US had an educated population, everyone understood that there was a great effort to reconcile the North and South and that reconciliation would not come from the kind of hate-mongering that now infects RootsAction and most of the action groups and websites of the liberal/progressive/left.

Today our country is far more divided that it was in 1860. Identity Politics has taught Americans to hate each other, but, nevertheless, the Zionist neoconservatives assure us that we are "the indispensable, exceptional people." We, a totally divided people, are said to have the right to rule the world and to bomb every country that doesn't accept our will into the stone age.

In turn the world hates America. Washington has told too many lies about other countries and used those lies to destroy them. Iraq, Libya, Yemen, Afghanistan, Somalia, and large chunks of Syria and Pakistan are in ruins. Washington intends yet more ruin with Venezuela currently in the cross hairs.

Eleven years ago Venezuelan President Hugo Chavez resonated with many peoples when he said in his UN speech: "Yesterday at this very podium stood Satan himself [Bush], speaking as if he owned the world; you can still smell the sulphur."

It is difficult to avoid the conclusion that America is a font for hatred both at home and abroad.

First published on August 28, 2017.

Whatever Happened to America?

Over the course of my lifetime America has become an infantile country.

When I was born America was a nation. Today it is a diversity country in which various segments divided by race, gender, and sexual preference, preach hate toward other segments. Currently white heterosexual males are losing in the hate game, but once hate is unleashed it can turn on any and every one. Working class white males understand that they are the new underclass in a diversity country in which everyone has privileges except them. Many of the university educated group of heterosexual white males are too brainwashed to understand what is happening to them. Indeed, some of them are so successfully brainwashed that they think it is their just punishment as a white male to be downtrodden.

Donald Trump's presidency has been wrecked by hate groups, i.e., the liberal/progressive/left who hate the "racist, misogynist, homophobic, gun nut working class" that elected Trump. For the liberal/progressive/left Trump is an illegitimate president because he was elected by illegitimate voters.

Today the American left hates the working class with such intensity that the left is comfortable with the left's alliance with the One Percent and the military/security complex against Trump.

America, the melting pot that produced a nation was destroyed by Identity Politics. Identity Politics divides a population into hate groups. This group hates that one and so on. In the US the most hated group is a southern white heterosexual male.

To rule America Identity Politics is competing with a more powerful group – the military/security complex supported by the neoconservative ideology of American world hegemony.

Currently, Identity Politics and the military/security complex are working hand-in-hand to destroy President Trump. Trump is hated by the powerful military/security complex because Trump wanted to "normalize relations with Russia," that is, remove the "Russian threat" that is essential to the power and budget of the military/security complex. Trump is hated by Identity Politics because the imbeciles think no one voted for him but racist, misogynists, homophobic gun-nuts.

The fact that Trump intended to unwind the dangerous tensions that the Obama regime has created with Russia became his hangman's noose. Designated as "Putin's agent," President Trump is possibly in the process of being framed by a Special Prosecutor, none other than member of the Shadow Government and former FBI director Robert Mueller. Mueller knows that whatever lie he tells will be accepted by the media presstitutes as the Holy Truth. However, as Trump, seeking self-preservation, moves into the war camp, it might not be necessary for the shadow government to eliminate him.

So the Great American Democracy, The Morally Pure Country, is actually a cover for the profits and power of the military/security complex. What is exceptional about America is the size of the corruption and evil in the government and in the private interest groups that control the government.

It wasn't always this way. In 1958 at the height of the Cold War a young Texan, Van Cliburn, 23 years of age, ventured to show up at the International Tchaikovsky Piano Competition in Moscow. Given the rivalry between the military powers, what chance did an American have of walking away with the prize? The cold warriors of the time would, if asked, had said none.

But Van Cliburn electrified the audience, the Moscow Symphony, and the famous conductor. His reception by the Soviet audience was extraordinary. The judges went to Khrushchev and asked, "Can we give the prize to the American?" Khrushchev asked, "Was he the best." The answer, "Yes." "Well, then give him the prize."

The Cold War should have ended right there, but the military/security complex would not allow it. In other words, the Soviet Union, unlike America today, did not need to prevail over the truth. The Soviets gave what has perhaps become the most famous of all prizes of musical competition to an American. The Soviets were able to see and recognize truth, something few Americans any longer can do.

The supporters of this website are supporters because, unlike their brainwashed fellows who are tightly locked within The Matrix, they can tell the difference between truth and propaganda. The supporters of this website comprise the few who, if it is possible, will save America and the world from the evil that prevails in Washington.

Van Cliburn came home to America a hero. He went on to a grand concert career. If Van Cliburn had been judged in his day, as Donald Trump is today for wanting to defuse the dangerously high level of tensions with Russia, Van Cliburn would have been greeted on his return with a Soviet prize as a traitor. The New York Times, the Washington Post, CNN, NPR and the rest of the presstitutes would have denounced him up one street and down another. How dare Van Cliburn legitimize the Soviet Union by participating in a music competition and accepting a Soviet prize!

Did you know that Van Cliburn, after his talented mother had provided all the music instruction she could, studied under a RUSSIAN woman? What more proof do you need that Van Cliburn was a traitor to America? Imagine, he studied under a RUSSIAN! I mean, really! Isn't this a RUSSIAN connection?!

How can we avoid the fact that all those music critics at the New York Times and Washington Post were also RUSSIAN agents. I mean, gosh, they actually praised Van Cliburn for playing RUSSIAN music in MOSCOW so well.

Makes a person wonder if Ronald Reagan wasn't also a RUSSIAN agent. Reagan, actually convinced Van Cliburn to come out of retirement and to play in the White House for Soviet leader Gorbachev, with whom Reagan was trying to end the Cold War.

I am making fun of what passes for reasoning today. Reason has been displaced by denunciation. If someone, anyone, says something, that can be misconstrued and denounced, it will be, the meaning of what was said notwithstanding. Consider the recent statement by the Deputy Prime Minister of Japan, Taro Aso, in an address to members of his ruling political party. He said: "I don't question your motives to be a politician. But the results are important. Hitler, who killed millions of people, was no good, even if his motives were right."

To anyone capable of reason, it is perfectly clear that Aso is saying that the ends don't justify the means. "Even if" is conditional. Aso is saying that even if Hitler acted in behalf of a just cause, his means were impermissible.

Aso, a man of principle, is instructing his party's politicians to be moral beings and not to sacrifice morality to a cause, much less an American cause of Japanese rearmament so as to amplify Washington's aggression toward China.

The response to a simple and straight forward statement that not even in politics do the ends justify the means was instant denunciation of the Deputy Prime Minister for "shameful" and "dangerous" remarks suggesting that Hitler "had the right motives."

Arrgh! screamed the Simon Wiesenthal Center which saw a new holocaust in the making. Reuters reported that Aso had put his foot in his mouth by making remarks that "could be interpreted as a defense of

236

Adolf Hitler's motive for genocide during World War Two." Even RT, to which we normally look for real as opposed to fake news, joined in the misreporting. The chairman of the Japanese opposition party joined in, terming Aso's statement that the ends don't justify the means "a serious gaffe."

Of course the South Koreans and the Chinese, who have WWII resentments against Japan, could not let the opportunity pass that the Western media created, and also unloaded on Japan, condemning the Deputy Prime Minister as a modern advocate of Hitlerism. The Chinese and South Koreans were too busy settling old scores to realize that by jumping on Aso they were undermining the Japanese opposition to the re-militarization of Japan, which will be at their expense.

Aso is astonished by the misrepresentation of his words. He said, "I used Hitler as an example of a bad politician. It is regrettable that my comment was misinterpreted and caused misunderstanding."

It seems that hardly anyone was capable of comprehending what Aso said. He clearly denounced Hitler, declaring Hitler "no good," but no one cared. He used the word, "Hitler," which was sufficient to set off the explosion of denunciation. Aso responded by withdrawing Hitler as his example of a "bad politician." And this is a victory?

The media, even RT alas, was quick to point out that Aso was already suspect. In 2013 Aso opposed the overturning of Japan's pacifist constitution that Washington was pushing in order to recruit Japan in a new war front against China. Aso, in the indirect way that the Japanese approach dissent, said "Germany's Weimar Constitution was changed [by the Nazis] before anyone knew. It was changed before anyone else noticed. Why don't we learn from the technique?" Aso's remarks were instantly misrepresented as his endorsement of surreptitiously changing Japan's constitution, which was Washington's aim, whereas Aso was defending its pacifist constraint, pointing out that Japan's pacifist Constitution was being changed without voters' consent.

An explanation of Aso's words, something that never would have needed doing prior to our illiterate times, has its own risks. Many Americans confuse an explanation with a defense. Thus, an explanation can bring denunciation for "defending a Japanese Nazi." Considering the number of intellectually-challenged Americans, I expect to read many such denunciations.

This is the problem with being a truthful writer in these times. More people want someone to denounce than want truth. Truth-tellers are persona non grata to the ruling establishment and to proponents of Identity Politics. It is unclear how much longer truth will be permitted to be expressed. Already it is much safer and more remunerative to tell the official lies than to tell the truth.

More people want their inculcated biases and beliefs affirmed by what they read than want to reconsider what they think, especially if changing their view puts them at odds with their peers. Most people believe what is convenient for them and what they want to believe. Facts are not important to them. Indeed, Americans deny the facts before their eyes each and every day. How can America be a superpower when the population for the most part is completely ignorant and brainwashed?

When truth-tellers are no more, it is unlikely they will be missed. No one will even know that they are gone. Already, gobs of people are unable to follow a reasoned argument based on undisputed facts.

Take something simple and clear, such as the conflict over several decades between North and South leading to the breakup of the union. The conflict was economic. It was over tariffs. The North wanted them in order to protect northern industry from lower priced British manufactures. Without tariffs, northern industry was hemmed in by British goods and could not develop.

The South did not want the tariffs because it meant higher prices for the South and likely retaliation against the South's export of cotton. The South saw the conflict in terms of lower income forced on southerners so that northern manufacturers could have higher incomes. The argument over the division of new states carved from former Indian territories was about keeping the voting balance equal in Congress so that a stiff tariff could not be passed. It is what the debates show. So many historians have written about these documented facts.

Slavery was not the issue, because as Lincoln said in his inaugural address, he had no inclination and no power to abolish slavery. Slavery was a states rights issue reserved to the states by the US Constitution.

The issue, Lincoln said in his inaugural address, was the collection of the tariff. There was no need, he said, for invasion or bloodshed. The South just needed to permit the federal government to collect the duties on imports. The northern states actually passed an amendment to the Constitution that prohibited slavery from ever being abolished by the federal government, and Lincoln gave his support.

For the South the problem was not slavery. The legality of slavery was clear and accepted by Lincoln in his inaugural address as a states right. However, a tariff was one of the powers given by the Constitution to the federal government. Under the Constitution the South was required to accept a tariff if it passed Congress and was signed by the President. A tariff had passed two days prior to Lincoln's inauguration.

The South couldn't point at the real reason it was leaving the union – the tariff – if the South wanted to blame the north for its secession. In order to blame the North for the breakup of the union (the British are leaving the European Union without a war), the South turned to the nullification by some northern states of the federal law and US

Constitutional provision (Article 4, Section 2) that required the return of runaway slaves. South Carolina's secession document said that some Northern states by not returning slaves had broken the contract on which the union was formed. South Carolina's argument became the basis for the secession documents of other states.

In other words, slavery became an issue in the secession because some Northern states – but not the federal government – refused to comply with the constitutional obligation to return property as required by the US Constitution.

South Carolina was correct, but the northern states were acting as individual states, not as the federal government. It wasn't Lincoln who nullified the Fugitive Slave Act, and states were not allowed to nullify constitutional provisions or federal law within the powers assigned to the federal government by the Constitution. Lincoln upheld the Fugitive Slave Act. In effect, what the South did was to nullify the power that the Constitution gives to the federal government to levy a tariff. Apologists for the South ignore this fact. The South had no more power under the Constitution to nullify a tariff than northern states had to nullify the Fugitive Slave Act.

Slavery was not, under the Constitution, a federal issue, but the tariff was. It was the South's refusal of the tariff that caused Lincoln to invade the Confederacy.

You need to understand that in those days people thought of themselves as citizens of the individual states, not as citizens of the United States, just as today people in Europe think of themselves as citizens of France, Germany, Italy, etc., and not as citizens of the European Union. In was in the states that most government power resided. Robert E. Lee refused the offer of the command of the Union Army on the grounds that it would be treasonous for him to attack his own country of Virginia.

Having explained history as it was understood prior to its rewrite by Identity Politics, which has thrown history down the Orwellian Memory Hole, I was accused of "lying about the motivations of the South" by a reason-impaired reader.

In this reader we see not only the uninformed modern American but also the rudeness of the uninformed modern American. I could understand a reader writing that perhaps I had misunderstood the secession documents, but "lying about the motivations of the South"? It is extraordinary to be called a liar by a reader incapable of understanding the issues. President Lincoln and the northern states gave the South complete and unequivocal assurances about slavery, but not about tariffs.

The reader sees a defense of slavery in the secession documents but is unable to grasp the wider picture that the South is making a states rights argument that some northern states, in the words of the South Carolina secession document, "have denied the rights of property . . . recognized by the Constitution." The reader saw that the documents mentioned slavery but not tariffs, and concluded that slavery was the reason that the South seceded.

It did not occur to the reason-impaired reader to wonder why the South would secede over slavery when the federal government was not threatening slavery. In his inaugural address Lincoln said that he had neither the power nor the inclination to forbid slavery. The North gave the South more assurances about slavery by passing the Corwin Amendment that added to the existing constitutional protection of slavery by putting in a special constitutional amendment upholding slavery. As slavery was under no threat, why would the South secede over slavery?

The tariff was a threat, and it was a tariff, not a bill outlawing slavery, that had just passed. Unlike slavery, which the Constitution left to the discretion of individual states, tariffs were a federal issue. Under the

Constitution states had no rights to nullify tariffs. Therefore, the South wanted out.

It also does not occur to the reason-impaired reader that if the war was over slavery why have historians, even court historians, been unable to find evidence of that in the letters and diaries of the soldiers on both sides?

In other words, we have a very full context here, and none of it supports that the war was fought over slavery. But the reader sees some words about slavery in the secession documents and his reasoning ability cannot get beyond those words.

This is the same absence of reasoning ability that led to the false conclusion that the Deputy Prime Minister of Japan was an admirer of Hitler.

Now for an example of an emotionally-impaired reader, one so emotional that he is unable to comprehend the meaning of his own words. This reader read Thomas DiLorenzo's article and my article, "The Weaponization Of History And Journalism," as an "absolution of the South" and as "whitewashing of the South." Of what he doesn't say. Slavery? Secession? All that I and DiLorenzo offer are explanations. DiLorenzo is a Pennsylvanian. I grew up in the South but lived my life outside it. Neither of us are trying to resurrect the Confederacy. As I understand DiLorenzo, his main point is that the so-called "civil war" destroyed the original US Constitution and centralized power in Washington in the interest of Empire. I am pointing out that ignorance has spawned a false history that is causing a lot of orchestrated hate. Neither of us thinks that the country needs the hate and the division hate causes. We need to be united against the centralized power in Washington that is turning on the people.

Carried away by emotion, the reader dashed off an article to refute us. My interest is not to ridicule the reader but to use him as an example of the emotionally-impaired American. Therefore, I am protecting him from personal ridicule by not naming him or linking to his nonsensical article. My only interest is to illustrate how for too many Americans emotion precludes reason.

First, the reader in his article calls DiLorenzo and I names and then projects his sin upon us, accusing us of "name-calling," which he says is "a poor substitute for proving points."

Here is his second mistake. DiLorenzo and I are not "proving points." We are stating long established known facts and asking how a new history has been created that is removed from the known facts.

So how does the emotionally-disturbed reader refute us in his article? He doesn't. He proves our point.

First he acknowledges "what American history textbooks for decades have acknowledged: The North did not go to War to stop slavery. Lincoln went to war to save the Union."

How does he get rid of the Corwin Amendment. He doesn't. He says everyone, even "the most ardent Lincoln-worshipping court historian," knows that the North and Lincoln gave the South assurances that the federal government would not involve itself in the slavery issue.

In other words, the reader says that there is nothing original in my article or DiLorenzo's and that it is just the standard history, so why is he taking exception to it?

The answer seems to be that after agreeing with us that Lincoln did not go to war over slavery and gave the South no reason to go to war over slavery, the reader says that the South did go to war over slavery. He says that the war was fought over the issue of expanding slavery into new states created from Indian territories.

This is an extremely problematic claim for two indisputable reasons.

First, the South went to war because Lincoln invaded the South.

Second, the South had seceded and no longer had any interest in the status of new territories.

As I reported in my article, it is established historical record that the conflict over the expansion of slavery as new states were added to the Union was a fight over the tariff vote in Congress. The South was trying to keep enough representation to block the passage of a tariff, and the North was trying to gain enough representation to enact protectionism over the free trade South.

It is so emotionally important to the reader that the war was over slavery that he alleges that the reason the South was not seduced by the Corwin Amendment is that it did not guarantee the expansion of slavery into new states, but only protected slavery in those states in which it existed. In other words, the reader asserts that the South fought for an hegemonic ideology of slavery in the Union. But the South had left the Union, so clearly it wasn't fighting to expand slavery outside its borders. Moreover, the North gave the South no assurances over the South's real concern – its economic exploitation by the North. The same day the North passed the Corwin Amendment the North passed the tariff. Clearly, it was not assurances over slavery that mattered to the South. Slavery was protected by states' rights. It was the tariff that was important to the South.

Whereas the tariff was the issue that brought the conflict to a head, correspondence between Lord Acton and Robert E. Lee shows that the deeper issue was liberty and its protection from centralized power. On November 4, 1866, Lord Acton wrote to Robert E. Lee: "I saw in State Rights the only availing check upon the absolutism of the sovereign will, and secession filled me with hope, not as the destruction but as the redemption of Democracy." Acton saw in the US Constitution defects that could lead to the rise of despotism. Acton regarded the

Confederate Constitution as "expressly and wisely calculated to remedy" the defects in the US Constitution. The Confederate Constitution, Acton said, was a "great Reform [that] would have blessed all the races of mankind by establishing true freedom purged of the native dangers and disorders of Republics" [1].

Lee replied: "I yet believe that the maintenance of the rights and authority reserved to the states and to the people, not only essential to the adjustment and balance of the general system, but the safeguard to the continuance of a free government. I consider it as the chief source of stability to our political system, whereas the consolidation of the states into one vast republic, sure to be aggressive abroad and despotic at home, will be the certain precursor of that ruin which has overwhelmed all those that have preceded it."

A present day American unfamiliar with the 18th and 19th century efforts to create a government that could not degenerate into despotism will see hypocrisy in this correspondence and misread it. How, the present day American will ask, could Acton and Lee be talking about establishing true freedom when slavery existed? The answer is that Acton and Lee, like George Washington and Thomas Jefferson, understood that there were more ways of being enslaved than being bought and sold. If the battle is lost over the character of government and power becomes centralized, then all are enslaved.

Lee's prediction of a government "aggressive abroad and despotic at home" has come true. What is despotism if not indefinite detention on suspicion alone without evidence or conviction, if not execution on suspicion alone without due process of law, if not universal spying and searches without warrants?

What I find extraordinary about today's concern with slavery in the 1800s is the lack of concern with our enslavement today. It is amazing that Americans do not realize that they were enslaved by the passage of the income tax in 1913. Consider the definition of a slave. It is a person who does not own his own labor or the products of his own labor. Of course, if the slave is to live to work another day some of his labor must go to his subsistence. How much depended on the technology and labor productivity. On 19th century southern plantations, the slave tax seems to have been limited short of the 50% rate.

When I entered the US Treasury as Assistant Secretary, the top tax rate on personal income was 50%. During the medieval era, serfs did not own all of their own labor. At the time I studied the era, the top tax rate on serfs was believed to have been limited to one-third of the serf's working time. Given labor productivity in those days, any higher tax would have prevented the reproduction of the labor force.

So what explains the concern about wage slavery in 1860 but not in 2017? The answer seems to be Diversity Politics. In 1860 blacks had the burden of wage slavery. In 2017 all have the burden except for the rich whose income is in the form of capital gains and those among the poor who don't work. Identity Politics cannot present today's wage slavery as the unique burder of a "preferred minority." Today those most subjected to wage slavery are the white professionals in the upper middle class. That is where the tax burden is highest. Americans living at public expense are exempted from wage slavery by lack of taxable income. Consequently, the liberal/progressive/left only objects to 19th century wage slavery. 20th Century wage slavery is perfectly acceptable to the liberal/progressive/left. Indeed, they want more of it.

People can no longer think or reason. There seems to be no rational component in their brain, just emotion set into action by fuse-lighting words.

Here is an example hot off the press. This month in Cobb County, Georgia, a car was pulled over for driving under the influence of alcohol. The white police lieutenant requested the ID of a white woman. She replied that she is afraid to reach into her purse for her license, because she has read many stories of people being shot because police officers conclude that they are reaching for a gun. Instead of tasering the woman for non-compliance, yanking her out of the car, and body slamming her, the lieutenant diffused the situation by making light of her concern. "We only shoot black people, you know." This is what a person would conclude from the news, because seldom is a big stink made when the police shoot a white person.

The upshot of the story is that the lieutenant's words were recorded on his recorder and when they were entered as part of the incident report, the chief of police announced that the lieutenant was guilty of "racial insensitivity" and would be fired for the offense.

Now think about this. A little reasoning is necessary. How are the words racially insensitive when no black persons were present? How are the words racially insensitive when the lieutenant said exactly what blacks themselves say? And now the clincher: Which is the real insensitivity, saying "we only shoot black people" or actually shooting black people? How is it possible that the officer who uses "racially insensitive" words to diffuse a situation is more worthy of punishment that an officer who actually shoots a black person? Seldom is an officer who has shot a black, white, Hispanic, Asian, child, grandmother, cripple, or the family dog ever fired. The usual "investigation" clears the officer on the grounds that he had grounds to fear his life was in danger – precisely the reason the woman didn't want to reach into her purse.

For a person who tries to tell the truth, writing is a frustrating and discouraging experience. What is the point of writing for people who cannot read, who cannot follow a logical argument because their limited mental capabilities are entirely based in emotion, who have no idea of the consequence of a population imbued with hate that destroys a nation in divisiveness?

I ask myself this question every time I write a column.

Indeed, given the policies of Google and PayPal it seems more or less certain that before much longer anyone who speaks outside The Matrix will be shut down.

Free speech is only allowed for propagandists. Megyn Kelly has free speech as long as her free speech lies for the ruling establishment. Her lies are protected by an entire media network backed by the Shadow Government and the Deep State.

First published on September 18, 2017.

[1]. The Acton-Lee Correspondence
https://www.lewrockwell.com/2017/09/no_author/famed-libertarian-writes-robert-e-lee/

The Prevalence of Myth over History

Today I heard a black historian on NPR say that the "civil war" was fought in order to establish a framework for human rights.

He also said that black civil rights achieved by the war were overturned by the rollback of Reconstruction, put back in place by the 1964 Civil Rights Act, and was now being overturned again by Trump's response to the caravan from Honduras.

As best as I could tell, this was an Identity Politics explanation of history with all of its contradictions and factual errors.

Identity Politics is based on the accusation that the white male is a racist and a misogynist. This is inconsistent with the belief that Washington, totally in the hands of white males, chose to fight a bloody civil war in order to bring human rights to black slaves. If white males are this idealistic and willing to make such a sacrifice for blacks, how is it that the white males are racists?

The black historian can't have it both ways.

Moreover, how would the black historian explain how it possibly can be that the same Union army that fought to bring human rights to black slaves immediately on war's end was sent under the same generals, Sherman and Sheridan, to slaughter the Plains Indians. Why did the Union army fight for human rights for blacks and against human rights for native American Indians?

As every competent historian knows, there was no "civil war." A civil war is when two sides fight for control of the government. The southern states had seceded and formed their own country. The Confederacy had no interest in controlling Washington. The war happened because Lincoln invaded the Confederacy. The Confederacy fought because they were invaded. The North fought to maintain the

Union, as Lincoln said repeatedly. The South seceded because the Northern majority in Congress passed a tariff that benefitted the North at the expense of the South. Lincoln guaranteed the South permanent protection of slavery if they would stay in the Union, but did not offer to repeal the tariff. Historians have studied the diaries and letters of soldiers on both sides, and can't find anyone who was fighting over slavery. Lincoln said that blacks were not sufficiently developed to live in society with whites. His plan was to send them back to Africa, which might have happened, as the North didn't want them, if Lincoln had not been assassinated.

Under the Reconstruction that the North imposed on the South, the South was divided into five military districts in which civil rights for whites were scant and their property was stolen by carpetbaggers and scalawags as whites lacked the protection of law and self-government. The vindictive Union simply reversed the roles of black and white to the extent that they were able.

As Lawrence Stratton and I show in our book, The New Color Line, despite the 1964 Civil Rights Act's prohibition of racial quotas, the Equal Employment Opportunity Commission established quotas as the EEOC's method of enforcement. A quota regime is a grant of privilege to those "preferred minorities" favored by the quota system, and privilege is a violation of the 14th Amendment's requirement of equality under the law.

Everything I have said in this short essay is factual and can be easily ascertained. But we have a black historian on NPR who thinks whites are racists but fought and died in order to bring human rights to imported blacks but not to native Indians, and who has no idea of the oppressiveness of Reconstruction (sometimes called Radical Reconstruction) or the violation of the 14th Amendment and the intent of Congress by the EEOC.

As I have emphasized over the years, Americans live in a matrix of misinformation in which facts, and history itself, are disappearing. Emotion, not reason, rules. We now have a mob, Antifa, that has introduced physical violence into politics. Those who control the explanations denounce Trump and Tucker Carlson, not Antifa's violence.

It is easy to see where this is going.

First published on November 9, 2018.

The Frustration of Ingrained Lies in Historical Explanations

From time to time readers ask what it is like trying to communicate with people in an era of mass disinformation. There are a few individual voices, as often as not censored and under attack, against which the TV and print media and the establishment's Internet sites are arrayed. It is frustrating, especially as so many people are content with a few minutes of managed news headlines. The insouciance in the population is massive.

Perhaps an even greater frustration is how ingrained falsehood is in people's consciousness, including that of conservatives. Consider, for example, Imprimis, a monthly newsletter usually featuring one article published by Hillsdale College, a conservative educational institution where it is still possible to acquire an education.

Imprimis claims 6,200,000 readers and usually presents a reasoned and informed article that encourages thought. But often even these articles sometimes contain historical lies.

For example, Harmeet Dhillon, CEO of the Center for American Liberty writes about "The Politicization of the Department of Justice" in the August 2022 issue of Imprimis. She makes her case and leaves us with the frightening fact that the US Department of Justice is a powerful force misusing law to destroy the civil liberty guaranteed by the US Constitution.

She makes the important point that 9/11 was used "to attack ourselves" with the Patriot Act that inaugurated an era of government spying, illegally and unconstitutionally, on citizens and weaponizing information against those Americans regarded as "political enemies. "

All well and good, but she accepts the official 9/11 story: "First the terrorists attacked us." Conservatives, who are more patriotic than liberals, who seem to prefer a Tower of Babel to a unified country, have a difficult time separating government from country. Consequently, if there is a claim of foreign attack, like the Gulf of Tonkin and 9/11, conservatives rush to the defense of the government. They wrap themselves in the flag and become dupes of the propaganda.

Another example of the perpetuation of a historical lie is Christopher Flannery's article in the December 2022 issue of Imprimis. In this curious article Flannery portrays Abraham Lincoln as a President who created a new birth of freedom for America with his Emancipation Proclamation.

This is absurd. The Emancipation Proclamation was a war measure intended to provoke a slave revolt that would cause Confederate soldiers to desert the front lines and rush home to protect their parents, wives, and children. Union officers were terrified that Lincoln would create the impression among Union soldiers that they were fighting and dying for the sake of blacks slaves. Lincoln's own Secretary of State criticized the proclamation for freeing the slaves only in the areas where we have no presence and leaving them in bondage where we rule. Lincoln's own words freed slaves only in Union unoccupied areas "in rebellion against the United States."

One can understand that Republicans, which essentially means conservatives, would try to court black votes by claiming to have fought a war to liberate them. But it hasn't worked.

It is a curiosity of our time that today blacks vote Democrat, the party that opposed Lincoln's war, and the conquered South vote for their Republican conquerors.

Another example of conservatives gone amiss is Glenn Loury. Writing in the Autumn 2022 City Journal, Loury says "Racial inequality is deep and abiding." But he is opposed to racial preferences for blacks as a method of their advancement. Loury believes, and I agree, that blacks are not helped by advancing them on a non-merit basis.

Racial inequality can have many other reasons than racism. There are many inequalities in the world. We see them in athletic performance, in the income distribution, in creative acts, and so on. These inequalities exist in all populations regardless of the presence or non-presence of blacks.

The racial inequality that we have today comes from treating white Americans as legally second class citizens. If you refuse to hire a black, the federal government will have you up on racial discrimination charges, but it is perfectly OK to refuse to hire a white. Affirmative action gives blacks rights to be hired and promoted before whites regardless of merit.

So what Loury should be analyzing is the second class citizenship of white Americans, especially heterosexual white males despite the prohibition against unequal treatment in the 14th Amendment. It is a paradox of history that the 1964 Civil Rights Act has been turned into discrimination against white Americans.

For my last example I take Matt Taibbi, one of the best journalists of our time. Taibbi has fallen for the disinformation that George Floyd was murdered. As the coroner's report made clear, as is reported on my website, George Floyd's blood showed the presence of fentanyl at 2.5 times the fatal dose. George Floyd complained of breathing problems prior to any restraint. The video taken at a distance by the teenage black girl, from which it seemed that officer Chauvin's knee was on Floyd's neck, is an example of perspective distortion as experts testified at the trial. The up close police videos show that Chauvin's knee was on Floyd's shoulder, an approved restraint measure. The reason for the restraint was to keep Floyd still, thus conserving his ability to use oxygen until the medics the police had called arrived.

Chauvin recognized that he had a fentanyl case and was trying to keep Floyd still until help arrived.

The media universally declared Chauvin a murderer, provoking burnings and lootings of many cities' business areas and making it impossible for any jurors to give Chauvin a fair trial. In the mid-20th century such irresponsible behavior by the media would have led the court to dismiss the case against Chauvin on the grounds that an impartial jury could not be found.

So how do we explain the ignorance of one of the few remaining journalists America has?

There is a limit to everyone's time and energy. None of us can focus on everything. Additionally, Taibbi, a former left-winger prior to being thrown out of the gang for telling the truth, might have grown up with the belief that white cops are racists who discriminate against blacks. If so, then for Taibbi the media's account of George Floyd was what he was prepared to believe.

So, dear readers, no, I do not enjoy writing. Yes, trying to communicate is frustrating. Why do I do it? Because when there is no truth there is tyranny. I do not claim to always be correct, but that is my goal. My agenda is truth. I find it very disturbing that it is truth tellers, not liars, who are censored.

First published on January 11, 2023.

The Lies About World War II

In the aftermath of a war, history cannot be written. The losing side has no one to speak for it. Historians on the winning side are constrained by years of war propaganda that demonized the enemy while obscuring the crimes of the righteous victors. People want to enjoy and feel good about their victory, not learn that their side was responsible for the war or that the war could have been avoided except for the hidden agendas of their own leaders. Historians are also constrained by the unavailability of information. To hide mistakes, corruption, and crimes, governments lock up documents for decades. Memoirs of participants are not yet written. Diaries are lost or withheld from fear of retribution. It is expensive and time consuming to locate witnesses, especially those on the losing side, and to convince them to answer questions. Any account that challenges the "happy account" requires a great deal of confirmation from official documents, interviews, letters, diaries, and memoirs, and even that won't be enough. For the history of World War II in Europe, these documents can be spread from New Zealand and Australia across Canada and the US through Great Britain and Europe and into Russia. A historian on the track of the truth faces long years of strenuous investigation and development of the acumen to judge and assimilate the evidence he uncovers into a truthful picture of what transpired. The truth is always immensely different from the victor's war propaganda.

As I reported recently, Harry Elmer Barnes was the first American historian to provide a history of the first world war that was based on primary sources. His truthful account differed so substantially from the war propaganda that he was called every name in the book.

Truth is seldom welcomed. David Irving, without any doubt the best historian of the European part of World War II, learned at his great expense that challenging myths does not go unpunished. Nevertheless, Irving persevered. If you want to escape from the lies about World War II that still direct our disastrous course, you only need to study two books by David Irving: Hitler's War and the first volume of his Churchill biography, Churchill's War: The Struggle for Power .

Irving is the historian who spent decades tracking down diaries, survivors, and demanding release of official documents. He is the historian who found the Rommel diary and Goebbels' diaries, the historian who gained entry into the Soviet archives, and so on. He is familiar with more actual facts about the second world war than the rest of the historians combined. The famous British military historian, Sir John Keegan, wrote in the Times Literary Supplement: "Two books stand out from the vast literature of the Second World War: Chester Wilmot's The Struggle for Europe, published in 1952, and David Irving's Hitler's War.

Despite many such accolades, today Irving is demonized and has to publish his own books.

I will avoid the story of how this came to be, but, yes, you guessed it, it was the Zionists. You simply cannot say anything that alters their propagandistic picture of history.

In what follows, I am going to present what is my impression from reading these two magisterial works. Irving himself is very scant on opinions. He only provides the facts from official documents, recorded intercepts, diaries, letters and interviews.

World War II was Churchill's War, not Hitler's war. Irving provides documented facts from which the reader cannot avoid this conclusion. Churchill got his war, for which he longed, because of the Versailles Treaty that stripped Germany of German territory and unjustly and irresponsibly imposed humiliation on Germany.

Hitler and Nationalist Socialist Germany (Nazi stands for National Socialist German Workers' Party) are the most demonized entities in history. Any person who finds any good in Hitler or Germany is instantly demonized. The person becomes an outcast regardless of the facts. Irving is very much aware of this. Every time his factual account of Hitler starts to display a person too much different from the demonized image, Irving throws in some negative language about Hitler.

Similarly for Winston Churchill. Every time Irving's factual account displays a person quite different from the worshiped icon, Irving throws in some appreciative language.

This is what a historian has to do to survive telling the truth.

To be clear, in what follows, I am merely reporting what seems to me to be the conclusion from the documented facts presented in these two works of scholarship. I am merely reporting what I understand Irving's research to have established. You read the books and arrive at your own conclusion.

World War II was initiated by the British and French declaration of war on Germany, not by a surprise blitzkrieg from Germany. The utter rout and collapse of the British and French armies was the result of Britain declaring a war for which Britain was unprepared to fight and of the foolish French trapped by a treaty with the British, who quickly deserted their French ally, leaving France at Germany's mercy.

Germany's mercy was substantial. Hitler left a large part of France and the French colonies unoccupied and secure from war under a semi-independent government under Petain. For his service in protecting a semblance of French independence, Petain was sentenced to death by Charles de Gaulle after the war for collaboration with Germany, an unjust charge.

In Britain, Churchill was out of power. He figured a war would put him back in power. No Britisher could match Churchill's rhetoric and orations. Or determination. Churchill desired power, and he wanted to reproduce the amazing military feats of his distinguished ancestor, the Duke of Marlborough, whose biography Churchill was writing and who defeated after years of military struggle France's powerful Sun King, Louis XIV, the ruler of Europe.

In contrast to the British aristocrat, Hitler was a man of the people. He acted for the German people. The Versailles Treaty had dismembered Germany. Parts of Germany were confiscated and given to France, Belgium, Denmark, Poland, and Czechoslovakia. As Germany had not actually lost the war, being the occupiers of foreign territory when Germany agreed to a deceptive armistice, the loss of approximately 7 million German people to Poland and Czechoslovakia, where Germans were abused, was not considered a fair outcome.

Hitler's program was to put Germany back together again. He succeeded without war until it came to Poland. Hitler's demands were fair and realistic, but Churchill, financed by the Focus Group with Jewish money, put such pressure on British prime minister Chamberlain that Chamberlain intervened in the Polish-German negotiations and issued a British guarantee to the Polish military dictatorship should Poland refuse to release German territory and populations.

The British had no way of making good on the guarantee, but the Polish military dictatorship lacked the intelligence to realize that. Consequently, the Polish Dictatorship refused Germany's request.

From this mistake of Chamberlain and the stupid Polish dictatorship, came the Ribbentrop/Molotov agreement that Germany and the Soviet Union would split Poland between themselves. When Hitler attacked Poland, Britain and the hapless French declared war on Germany because of the unenforceable British guarantee. But the British and French were careful not to declare war on the Soviet Union for occupying the eastern half of Poland.

Thus Britain was responsible for World War II, first by stupidly interfering in German/Polish negotiations, and second by declaring war on Germany.

Churchill was focused on war with Germany, which he intended for years preceding the war. But Hitler didn't want any war with Britain or with France, and never intended to invade Britain. The invasion threat was a chimera conjured up by Churchill to unite England behind him. Hitler expressed his view that the British Empire was essential for order in the world, and that in its absence Europeans would lose their world supremacy. After Germany's rout of the French and British armies, Hitler offered an extraordinarily generous peace to Britain. He said he wanted nothing from Britain but the return of Germany's colonies. He committed the German military to the defense of the British Empire, and said he would reconstitute both Polish and Czech states and leave them to their own discretion. He told his associates that defeat of the British Empire would do nothing for Germany and everything for Bolshevik Russia and Japan.

Winston Churchill kept Hitler's peace offers as secret as he could and succeeded in his efforts to block any peace. Churchill wanted war, largely it appears, for his own glory. Franklin Delano Roosevelt slyly encouraged Churchill in his war but without making any commitment in Britain's behalf. Roosevelt knew that the war would achieve his own aim of bankrupting Britain and destroying the British Empire, and that the US dollar would inherit the powerful position from the British pound of being the world's reserve currency. Once Churchill had trapped Britain in a war she could not win on her own, FDR began doling out bits of aid in exchange for extremely high prices—for example, 60 outdated and largely useless US destroyers for British naval bases in the Atlantic. FDR delayed Lend-Lease until desperate Britain had turned over $22,000 million of British gold plus $42 million in gold Britain had in South Africa. Then began the forced sell-off of British overseas investments. For example, the British-owned Viscose Company, which was worth $125 million in 1940 dollars, had no debts and held $40 million in government bonds, was sold to the House of Morgan for $37 million. It was such an act of thievery that the British eventually got about two-thirds of the company's value to hand over to Washington in payment for war munitions. American aid was also "conditional on Britain dismantling the system of Imperial preference anchored in the Ottawa agreement of 1932." For Cordell Hull, American aid was "a knife to open that oyster shell, the Empire." Churchill saw it coming, but he was too far in to do anything but plead with FDR: It would be wrong, Churchill wrote to Roosevelt, if "Great Britain were to be divested of all saleable assets so that after the victory was won with our blood, civilization saved, and the time gained for the United States to be fully armed against all eventualities, we should stand stripped to the bone."

A long essay could be written about how Roosevelt stripped Britain of her assets and world power. Irving writes that in an era of gangster statesmen, Churchill was not in Roosevelt's league. The survival of the British Empire was not a priority for FDR. He regarded Churchill as a pushover—unreliable and drunk most of the time. Irving reports that FDR's policy was to pay out just enough to give Churchill "the kind of support a rope gives a hanging man." Roosevelt pursued "his subversion of the Empire throughout the war." Eventually Churchill realized that Washington was at war with Britain more fiercely than was Hitler. The great irony was that Hitler had offered Churchill peace and the survival of the Empire. When it was too late, Churchill came to Hitler's conclusion that the conflict with Germany was a "most unnecessary" war. Pat Buchanan sees it that way also [1].

Hitler forbade the bombing of civilian areas of British cities. It was Churchill who initiated this war crime, later emulated by the Americans. Churchill kept the British bombing of German civilians secret from the British people and worked to prevent Red Cross monitoring of air raids so no one would learn he was bombing civilian residential areas, not war production. The purpose of Churchill's bombing—first incendiary bombs to set everything afire and then high explosives to prevent firefighters from controlling the blazes—was to provoke a German attack on London, which Churchill reckoned would bind the British people to him and create sympathy in the US for Britain that would help Churchill pull America into the war. One British raid murdered 50,000 people in Hamburg, and a subsequent attack on Hamburg netted 40,000 civilian deaths. Churchill also ordered that poison gas be added to the firebombing of German civilian residential areas and that Rome be bombed into ashes. The British Air Force refused both orders. At the very end of the war the British and Americans destroyed the beautiful baroque city of Dresden, burning and suffocating 100,000 people in the attack. After months of firebombing attacks on Germany, including Berlin, Hitler gave in to his generals and replied in kind. Churchill succeeded. The story became "the London Blitz," not the British blitz of Germany.

Like Hitler in Germany, Churchill took over the direction of the war. He functioned more as a dictator who ignored the armed services than as a prime minister advised by the country's military leaders. Both leaders might have been correct in their assessment of their commanding officers, but Hitler was a much better war strategist than Churchill, for whom nothing ever worked. To Churchill's WW I Gallipoli misadventure was now added the introduction of British troops into Norway, Greece, Crete, Syria—all ridiculous decisions and failures—and the Dakar fiasco. Churchill also turned on the French, destroying the French fleet and lives of 1,600 French sailors because of his personal fear, unfounded, that Hitler would violate his treaty with the French and seize the fleet. Any one of these Churchillian mishaps could have resulted in a no confidence vote, but with Chamberlain and Halifax out of the way there was no alternative leadership. Indeed, the lack of leadership is the reason neither the cabinet nor the military could stand up to Churchill, a person of iron determination.

Hitler also was a person of iron determination, and he wore out both himself and Germany with his determination. He never wanted war with England and France. This was Churchill's doing, not Hitler's.

262

Like Churchill, who had the British people behind him, Hitler had the German people behind him, because he stood for Germany and had reconstructed Germany from the rape and ruin of the Versailles Treaty. But Hitler, not an aristocrat like Churchill, but of low and ordinary origins, never had the loyalty of many of the aristocratic Prussian military officers, those with "von" before their name. He was afflicted with traitors in the Abwehr, his military intelligence, including its director, Adm. Canaris. On the Russian front in the final year, Hitler was betrayed by generals who opened avenues for the Russians into undefended Berlin.

Hitler's worst mistakes were his alliance with Italy and his decision to invade Russia. He was also mistaken to let the British go at Dunkirk. He let them go because he did not want to ruin the chance for ending the war by humiliating the British by the loss of their entire army. But with Churchill there was no chance for peace. By not destroying the British army, Hitler boosted Churchill who turned the evacuation into British heroics that sustained the willingness to fight on.

It is unclear why Hitler invaded Russia. One possible reason is poor or intentionally deceptive information from the Abwehr on Russian military capability. Hitler later said to his associates that he never would have invaded if he had known of the enormous size of the Russian army and the extraordinary capability of the Soviets to produce tanks and aircraft. Some historians have concluded that the reason Hitler invaded Russia was that he concluded that the British would not agree to end the war because they expected Russia to enter the war on Britain's side. Therefore, Hitler decided to foreclose that possibility by conquering Russia. A Russian, Victor Suvorov, has written that Hitler attacked because Stalin was preparing to attack Germany. Stalin did have considerable forces far forward, but It would make more sense for Stalin to wait until the West devoured itself in mutual bloodletting, step in afterwards and scoop it all up if he wanted. Or perhaps Stalin was positioning to occupy part of Eastern Europe in order to put more buffer between the Soviet Union and Germany.

[Since writing this, I have accepted Victor Suvorov's evidence that Stalin was about to launch an invasion of Germany and seize all of Europe. However, I don't accept that Hitler knew of an impending Soviet Attack. It seems to me that David Irving surely would have found evidence that Hitler's invasion of Russia was defensive and reported it. I think both Hitler and Stalin were preparing to invade one another and that by chance Hitler struck first, thereby saving Europe from Soviet Communism.]

Whatever the reason for the invasion, what defeated Hitler was the earliest Russian winter in 30 years. It stopped everything in its tracks before the well planned and succeeding encirclement could be completed. The harsh winter that immobilized the Germans gave Stalin time to recover.

Because of Hitler's alliance with Mussolini, who lacked an effective fighting force, resources needed on the Russian front were twice drained off in order to rescue Italy. Because of Mussolini's misadventures, Hitler had to drain troops, tanks, and air planes from the Russian invasion to rescue Italy in Greece and North Africa and to occupy Crete. Hitler made this mistake out of loyalty to Mussolini. Later in the war when Russian counterattacks were pushing the Germans out of Russia, Hitler had to divert precious military resources to rescue Mussolini from arrest and to occupy Italy to prevent her surrender. Germany simply lacked the manpower and military resources to fight on a 1,000 mile front in Russia, and also in Greece and North Africa, occupy part of France, and man defenses against a US/British invasion of Normandy and Italy.

The German Army was a magnificent fighting force, but it was overwhelmed by too many fronts, too little equipment, and careless communications. The Germans never caught on despite much evidence that the British could read their encryption. Thus, efforts to supply Rommel in North Africa were prevented by the British navy.

Irving never directly addresses in either book the Holocaust. He does document the massacre of many Jews, but the picture that emerges from the factual evidence is that the holocaust of Jewish people was different from the official Zionist story.

No German plans, or orders from Hitler, or from Himmler or anyone else have ever been found for an organized holocaust by gas and cremation of Jews. This is extraordinary as such a massive use of resources and transportation would have required massive organization, budgets and resources. What documents do show is Hitler's plan to relocate European Jews to Madagascar after the war's end. With the early success of the Russian invasion, this plan was changed to sending the European Jews to the Jewish Bolsheviks in the eastern part of Russia that Hitler was going to leave to Stalin. There are documented orders given by Hitler preventing massacres of Jews. Hitler said over and over that "the Jewish problem" would be settled after the war.

It seems that most of the massacres of Jews were committed by German political administrators of occupied territories in the east to whom Jews from Germany and France were sent for relocation. Instead of dealing with the inconvenience, some of the administrators lined them up and shot them into open trenches. Other Jews fell victim to the anger of Russian villagers who had long suffered under Jewish Bolshevik administrators.

The "death camps" were in fact work camps. Auschwitz, for example, today a Holocaust museum, was the site of Germany's essential artificial rubber factory. Germany was desperate for a work force. A significant percentage of German war production labor had been released to the Army to fill the holes in German lines on the Russian front. War production sites, such as Auschwitz, had as a work force refugees displaced from their homes by war, Jews to be deported after war's end, and anyone else who could be forced into work. Germany desperately needed whatever work force it could get.

Every camp had crematoriums. Their purpose was not to exterminate populations but to dispose of deaths from the scourge of typhus, natural deaths, and other diseases. Refugees were from all over, and they brought diseases and germs with them. The horrific photos of masses of skeleton-like dead bodies that are said to be evidence of organized extermination of Jews are in fact camp inmates who died from typhus and starvation in the last days of the war when Germany was disorganized and devoid of medicines and food for labor camps. The great noble Western victors themselves bombed the labor camps and contributed to the deaths of inmates.

The two books on which I have reported total 1,663 pages, and there are two more volumes of the Churchill biography. This massive, documented historical information seemed likely to pass into the Memory Hole as it is inconsistent with both the self-righteousness of the West and the human capital of court historians. The facts are too costly to be known. But historians have started adding to their own accounts the information uncovered by Irving. It takes a brave historian to praise him, but they can cite him and plagiarize him.

It is amazing how much power Zionists have gotten from the Holocaust. Norman Finkelstein calls it The Holocaust Industry. There is ample evidence that Jews along with many others suffered, but Zionists insist that it was an unique experience limited to Jews.

In his Introduction to Hitler's War Irving reports that despite the widespread sales of his book, the initial praise from accomplished historians and the fact that the book was required reading at military academies from Sandhurst to West Point, "I have had my home smashed into by thugs, my family terrorized, my name smeared, my printers [publishers] firebombed, and myself arrested and deported by tiny, democratic Austria—an illegal act, their courts decided, for which the ministerial culprits were punished; at the behest of disaffected academics and influential citizens [Zionists], in subsequent years, I was deported from Canada (in 1992), and refused entry to Australia, New Zealand, Italy, South Africa and other civilized countries around the world. Internationally affiliated groups circulated letters to librarians, pleading for this book to be taken off their shelves."

So much for free thought and truth in the Western world. Nothing is so little regarded in the West as free thought, free expression, and truth. In the West explanations are controlled in order to advance the agendas of the ruling interest groups. As David Irving has learned, woe to anyone who gets in the way.

First published on May 13, 2019.

[1]. "Churchill, Hitler, and 'The Unnecessary War': How Britain Lost Its Empire and the West Lost the World"
https://www.amazon.com/Churchill-Hitler-Unnecessary-War-Britain/dp/0307405168/ref=sr_1_3?keywords=Pat+Buchanan&qid=15 57709100&s=books&sr=1-3

The Truth About World War II Is Beginning To Emerge 74 Years Later

"The Lies About World War II" is my most popular column of the year. It is a book review of David Irving's Hitler's War and Churchill's War, the first volume of Irving's three volume biography of Winston Churchill. A person does not know anything about WW II until he has read these books.

Historians, and even book reviewers, who tell the truth pay a high price. For reasons I provide in my review, generally it is decades after a war before truth about the war can emerge. By then the court historians have fused lies with patriotism and created a pleasing myth about the war, and when emerging truth impinges on that myth, the truth-teller is denounced for making a case for the enemy.

Wars are fought with words as well as with bullets and bombs. The propaganda and demonization of the enemy are extreme. This is especially the case when it is the victors who start the war and have to cover up this fact as well as the war crimes for which they are responsible. When decades later the covered up crimes of the victors are brought to light, truth is up against the explanation that has been controlled for a half century. This makes the truth seem outlandish, and this makes it easy to demonize and even destroy the historian who brought the truth to the surface.

This makes a problem for a reviewer of revisionist history of World War II. If a reviewer gives an honest review, he faces the same demonization as the historian who brought the truth about the war to the surface.

This happened to me when I reviewed Irving's books, both of which were researched for decades and completely documented. I was supposed to denounce Irving, in which case my stock would have gone up, but giving him an honest review got me branded "a holocaust denier" by Wikipedia, in my opinion a CIA front created in order to protect the official stories by marginalizing truth-tellers.

I have never studied the holocaust or written anything about it. I simply reported Irving's assessment based entirely on documented evidence that many Jews were killed, but there was not the organized holocaust that is taught in the schools and which is a crime to dispute in many European countries.

So, this is how bad it is. I am, according to Wikipedia, a "holocaust denier" for the simple reason that I honestly reported Irving's findings instead of jumping on him with hob-nailed boots for giving evidence contrary to the protected official story. Anyone who does not protect official explanations is "suspect."

In my opinion what makes historians suspicious of the official holocaust story is the extreme resistance to any investigation of the event. One would think that investigation would support the story if it were true. It would seem that it is the Jews who raise questions about the holocaust by placing it off limits for open discussion. I personally am not very interested in the holocaust, because WW II itself was a holocaust. Tens of millions of people were killed. The Russians themselves lost 26 million, 20 million more than the holocaust figure of 6 million Jews. The Germans, after the war, lost considerably more than 6 million in the forced resettlements and General Eisenhower's murder of 1.5 million German POWs by starvation and exposure. (See John Wear, Germany's War, and James Bacque, Other Losses, for the massive evidence.)

Somehow World War II has become the Jewish holocaust, not everyone else's.

My interest is the predominance of propaganda and lies over truth. Ron Unz has the same interest. Four months after my column, "The Lies About World War II," appeared, Unz took the story further in his long report, "Understanding World War II" [1]. Unz's columns tend to be monographs or small books, well beyond the attention spans of most Americans. Unz has given me permission to republish his monograph in installments. This is the first installment.

I learned from Unz's article that getting rid of truth-tellers has been the practice of the West for a long time. Unz got interested in WW II when Pat Buchanan's book, The Unnecessary War, became an issue for The American Conservative, a magazine for which Unz was the major money man. Unz couldn't find that much difference between Buchanan's book and that of A.J.P. Taylor's The Origins of the Second World War. Yet The American Conservative, fearful of challenging WW II myths, was disassociating from its own founder, Pat Buchanan.

Disassociation from official truth cost Taylor his lectureship at Oxford University. Taylor's publication of The Origins of the Second World War, caused Oxford to decline to renew Taylor's appointment as a university lecturer in modern history. Taylor left Oxford for a lectureship at the University College London. Note that England's best historian at the time was a mere lecturer, not a professor of modern history. Truth-tellers don't advance very far in the world of information.

Harry Elmer Barnes explained that the origins of World War I were in France and Russia, not in Germany, which was the last to mobilize but was blamed for the war, resulting in the Treaty of Versailles, which led to WW II. Unz was stunned to find that Barnes, a historian of great stature, was unknown to him. Unz writes:

"Imagine my shock at later discovering that Barnes had actually been one of the most frequent early contributors to Foreign Affairs, serving as a primary book reviewer for that venerable publication from its 1922 founding onward, while his stature as one of America's premier liberal academics was indicated by his scores of appearances in The Nation and The New Republic throughout that decade. Indeed, he is credited with having played a central role in 'revising' the history of the First World War so as to remove the cartoonish picture of unspeakable German wickedness left behind as a legacy of the dishonest wartime propaganda produced by the opposing British and American governments. And his professional stature was demonstrated by his thirty-five or more books, many of them influential academic volumes, along with his numerous articles in The American Historical Review, Political Science Quarterly, and other leading journals.

"A few years ago I happened to mention Barnes to an eminent American academic scholar whose general focus in political science and foreign policy was quite similar, and yet the name meant nothing. By the end of the 1930s, Barnes had become a leading critic of America's proposed involvement in World War II, and was permanently 'disappeared' as a consequence, barred from all mainstream media outlets, while a major newspaper chain was heavily pressured into abruptly terminating his long-running syndicated national column in May 1940."

Unz next tells us how the establishment got rid of Charles A. Beard. Beard was an intellectual of high stature. But "once he turned against Franklin D. Roosevelt's warmongering foreign policy, publishers shut their doors to him, and only his personal friendship with the head of the Yale University Press allowed his critical 1948 volume, President Roosevelt and the Coming of the War, 1941, to even appear in print. Beard's stellar reputation seems to have begun a rapid decline from that point onward, so that by 1968 historian Richard Hofstadter could write: 'Today Beard's reputation stands like an imposing ruin in the landscape of American historiography. What was once the grandest house in the province is now a ravaged survival'. Indeed, Beard's once-dominant 'economic interpretation of history' might these days almost be dismissed as promoting 'dangerous conspiracy theories,' and I suspect few non-historians have even heard of him."

William Henry Chamberlin was one of America's leading foreign policy journalists, an author of 15 books whose writings appeared regularly in The Atlantic Monthly and Harpers. His career was terminated when his critical analysis of America's entry into WW II, America's Second Crusade, was published in 1950.

Unz gives other examples of highly credible authors being cast into darkness for telling the truth while the establishment provides lavish rewards to those who endorse the propaganda line. Unz concludes that "A climate of serious intellectual repression greatly complicates our ability to uncover the events of the past. Under normal circumstances, competing claims can be weighed in the give-and-take of public or scholarly debate, but this obviously becomes impossible if the subjects being discussed are forbidden ones."

The victors control the explanations and bury their own guilt and war crimes behind a humanitarian smokescreen of "saving democracy." It is the function of historians to penetrate the smokescreen and to dig up the buried facts.

One of the icons of the Anglo-American world is Winston Churchill. Unz summarizes some of the information historians have uncovered about Churchill:

"Until recently, my familiarity with Churchill had been rather cursory, and Irving's revelations were absolutely eye-opening. Perhaps the most striking single discovery was the remarkable venality and corruption of the man, with Churchill being a huge spendthrift who lived lavishly and often far beyond his financial means, employing an army of dozens of personal servants at his large country estate despite frequently lacking any regular and assured sources of income to maintain them. This predicament naturally put him at the mercy of those individuals willing to support his sumptuous lifestyle in exchange for determining his political activities. And somewhat similar pecuniary means were used to secure the backing of a network of other political figures from across all the British parties, who became Churchill's close political allies.

"To put things in plain language, during the years leading up to the Second World War, both Churchill and numerous other fellow British MPs were regularly receiving sizable financial stipends—cash bribes—from Jewish and Czech sources in exchange for promoting a policy of extreme hostility toward the German government and actually advocating war. The sums involved were quite considerable, with the Czech government alone probably making payments that amounted to tens of millions of dollars in present-day money to British elected officials, publishers, and journalists working to overturn the official peace policy of their existing government. A particularly notable instance occurred in early 1938 when Churchill suddenly lost all his accumulated wealth in a foolish gamble on the American stock-market, and was soon forced to put his beloved country estate up for sale to avoid personal bankruptcy, only to quickly be bailed out by a foreign Jewish millionaire intent upon promoting a war against Germany. Indeed, the early stages of Churchill's involvement in this sordid behavior are recounted in an Irving chapter aptly entitled 'The Hired Help.'

"Ironically enough, German Intelligence learned of this massive bribery of British parliamentarians, and passed the information along to Prime Minister Neville Chamberlain, who was horrified to discover the corrupt motives of his fierce political opponents, but apparently remained too much of a gentlemen to have them arrested and prosecuted. I'm no expert in the British laws of that era, but for elected officials to do the bidding of foreigners on matters of war and peace in exchange for huge secret payments seems almost a textbook example of treason to me, and I think that Churchill's timely execution would surely have saved tens of millions of lives.

"My impression is that individuals of low personal character are those most likely to sell out the interests of their own country in exchange for large sums of foreign money, and as such usually constitute the natural targets of nefarious plotters and foreign spies. Churchill certainly seems to fall into this category, with rumors of massive personal corruption swirling around him from early in his political career. Later, he supplemented his income by engaging in widespread art-forgery, a fact that Roosevelt later discovered and probably used as a point of personal leverage against him. Also quite serious was Churchill's constant state of drunkenness, with his inebriation being so widespread as to constitute clinical alcoholism. Indeed, Irving notes that in his private conversations FDR routinely referred to Churchill as 'a drunken bum.'

"During the late 1930s, Churchill and his clique of similarly bought-and-paid-for political allies had endlessly attacked and denounced Chamberlain's government for its peace policy, and he regularly made the wildest sort of unsubstantiated accusations, claiming the Germans were undertaking a huge military build-up aimed against Britain. These roiling charges were often widely echoed by a media heavily influenced by Jewish interests and did much to poison the state of German-British relations. Eventually, these accumulated pressures forced Chamberlain into the extremely unwise act of providing an unconditional guarantee of military backing to Poland's irresponsible dictatorship. As a result, the Poles then rather arrogantly refused any border negotiations with Germany, thereby lighting the fuse which eventually led to the German invasion six months later and the subsequent British declaration of war. The British media had widely promoted Churchill as the leading pro-war political figure, and once Chamberlain was forced to create a wartime government of national unity, his leading critic was brought into it and given the naval affairs portfolio.

"Following his lightening six-week defeat of Poland, Hitler unsuccessfully sought to make peace with the Allies, and the war went into abeyance. Then in early 1940, Churchill persuaded his government to try strategically outflanking the Germans by preparing a large seaborne invasion of neutral Norway; but Hitler discovered the plan and preempted the attack, with Churchill's severe operational mistakes leading to a surprising defeat for the vastly superior British forces. During World War I, Churchill's Gallipoli disaster had forced his resignation from the British Cabinet, but this time the friendly media helped ensure that all the blame for the somewhat similar debacle at Narvik was foisted upon Chamberlain, so it was the latter who was forced to resign, with Churchill then replacing him as prime minister. British naval officers were appalled that the primary architect of their humiliation had become its leading political beneficiary, but reality is what the media reports, and the British public never discovered this great irony.

"This incident was merely the first of the long series of Churchill's major military failures and outright betrayals that are persuasively recounted by Irving, nearly all of which were subsequently airbrushed out of our hagiographic histories of the conflict. We should recognize that wartime leaders who spend much of their time in a state of drunken stupor are far less likely to make optimal decisions, especially if they are as extremely prone to military micro-management as was the case with Churchill.

"In the spring of 1940, the Germans launched their sudden armored thrust into France via Belgium, and as the attack began to succeed, Churchill ordered the commanding British general to immediately flee with his forces to the coast and to do so without informing his French or Belgium counterparts of the huge gap he was thereby opening in the Allied front-lines, thus ensuring the encirclement and destruction of their armies. Following France's resulting defeat and occupation, the British prime minister then ordered a sudden, surprise attack on the disarmed French fleet, completely destroying it and killing some 2,000 of his erstwhile allies; the immediate cause was his mistranslation of a single French word, but this 'Pearl Harbor-type' incident continued to rankle French leaders for decades.

"Hitler had always wanted friendly relations with Britain and certainly had sought to avoid the war that had been forced upon him. With France now defeated and British forces driven from the Continent, he therefore offered very magnanimous peace terms and a new German alliance to Britain. The British government had been pressured into entering the war for no logical reason and against its own national interests, so Chamberlain and half the Cabinet naturally supported commencing peace negotiations, and the German proposal probably would have received overwhelming approval both from the British public and political elites if they had ever been informed of its terms.

"But despite some occasional wavering, Churchill remained absolutely adamant that the war must continue, and Irving plausibly argues that his motive was an intensely personal one. Across his long career, Churchill had had a remarkable record of repeated failure, and for him to have finally achieved his lifelong ambition of becoming prime minister only to lose a major war just weeks after reaching Number 10 Downing Street would have ensured that his permanent place in history was an extremely humiliating one. On the other hand, if he managed to continue the war, perhaps the situation might somehow later improve, especially if the Americans could be persuaded to eventually enter the conflict on the British side.

"Since ending the war with Germany was in his nation's interest but not his own, Churchill undertook ruthless means to prevent peace sentiments from growing so strong that they overwhelmed his opposition. Along with most other major countries, Britain and Germany had signed international conventions prohibiting the aerial bombardment of civilian urban targets, and although the British leader had very much hoped the Germans would attack his cities, Hitler scrupulously followed these provisions. In desperation, Churchill therefore ordered a series of large-scale bombing raids against the German capital of Berlin, doing considerable damage, and after numerous severe warnings, Hitler finally began to retaliate with similar attacks against British cities. The population saw the heavy destruction inflicted by these German bombing raids and was never informed of the British attacks that had preceded and provoked them, so public sentiment greatly hardened against making peace with the seemingly diabolical German adversary.

"In his memoirs published a half-century later, Prof. Revilo P. Oliver, who had held a senior wartime role in American Military Intelligence, described this sequence of events in very bitter terms:

Great Britain, in violation of all the ethics of civilized warfare that had theretofore been respected by our race, and in treacherous violation of solemnly assumed diplomatic covenants about "open cities", had secretly carried out intensive bombing of such open cities in Germany for the express purpose of killing enough unarmed and defenseless men and women to force the German government reluctantly to retaliate and bomb British cities and thus kill enough helpless British men, women, and children to generate among Englishmen enthusiasm for the insane war to which their government had committed them. It is impossible to imagine a governmental act more vile and more depraved than contriving death and suffering for its own people — for the very citizens whom it was exhorting to "loyalty" — and I suspect that an act of such infamous and savage treason would have nauseated even Genghis Khan or Hulagu or Tamerlane, Oriental barbarians universally reprobated for their insane blood-lust. History, so far as I recall, does not record that they ever butchered their own women and children to facilitate lying propaganda....In 1944 members of British Military Intelligence took it for granted that after the war Marshal Sir Arthur Harris would be hanged or shot for high treason against the British people...

"Churchill's ruthless violation of the laws of war regarding urban aerial bombardment directly led to the destruction of many of Europe's finest and most ancient cities. But perhaps influenced by his chronic drunkenness, he later sought to carry out even more horrifying war crimes and was only prevented from doing so by the dogged opposition of all his military and political subordinates.

"Along with the laws prohibiting the bombing of cities, all nations had similarly agreed to ban the first use of poison gas, while stockpiling quantities for necessary retaliation. Since Germany was the world-leader in chemistry, the Nazis had produced the most lethal forms of new nerve gases, such as Tabun and Sarin, whose use might have easily resulted in major military victories on both the Eastern and Western fronts, but Hitler had scrupulously obeyed the international protocols that his nation had signed. However, late in the war during 1944 the relentless Allied bombardment of German cities led to the devastating retaliatory attacks of the V-1 flying bombs against London, and an outraged Churchill became adamant that German cities should be attacked with poison gas in counter-retaliation. If Churchill had gotten his way, many millions of British might soon have perished from German nerve gas counter-strikes. Around the same time, Churchill was also blocked in his proposal to bombard Germany with hundreds of thousands of deadly anthrax bombs, an operation that might have rendered much of Central and Western Europe uninhabitable for generations."

Equally unsettling facts have emerged from their burial yards about Franklin D. Roosevelt and Dwight D. Eisenhower, but these revelations will await later installments of Unz's long report on WW II lies.

First published on November 19, 2019.

[1]. "American Pravda: Understanding World War II"
https://www.unz.com/runz/american-pravda-understanding-world-war-ii/

Germany Did Not Start World War II

This is the second installment of Ron Unz's long report on the emergent truth about World War II. Unz has a facility for summarizing vast works of scholarship into their essentials. Unz is also intellectually honest and has massive intellectual courage. He saves the rest of us a lot of work.

The aims of the National Socialist German Workers' Party, a mass movement that came to power legally in Germany, to correct the unemployment caused by unjust reparations forced on Germany by a starvation policy imposed by the British following World War I and to put Germany, dismembered by the unjust and demonic Versailles Treaty, back together, has been demonized and its intentions mischaracterized by most Western historians. There is no worse, or more uninformed, epitaph than to be called a Nazi.

World War II began when the Churchill government and the French, quickly betrayed and abandoned by the British, declared war on Germany [1]. The declaration of war on Germany resulted from an unenforceable "guarantee" given by Britain to the military dictatorship in Poland, a guarantee designed to provoke a German invasion of Poland. The German leader, Adolf Hitler, had re-acquired German territories given to Denmark, France, and Czechoslovakia by the humiliating Versailles Treaty and had united with German Austria without war. But three wanted war with Germany: Zionist Jews who saw war as a path to a Jewish state in Palestine, Winston Churchill, who dreamed of repeating the military conquests of his famous ancestor, and Franklin D. Roosevelt who intended to ruin Britain with war and take over the British pound's role as world reserve currency and destroy Britain's control of world trade. The British guarantee emboldened the Polish military dictatorship to refuse to negotiate the return of German territory and population.

World War II was a war started by private agendas. Jews understood these agendas and encouraged them. Roosevelt's lust for world hegemony and Churchill's lust to rival his famous ancestor's defeat of the Sun King of France with his defeat of Germany traveled roads paved for them by Jewish anti-German propaganda. All Hitler contributed was to force countries given German territory by the Versailles Treaty to release the lands and the Germans, who were heavily persecuted in Czechoslovakia and Poland. Hitler's restoration of Germany's national boundaries was misrepresented in the British and US press as "German aggression."

This fake news story of German aggression was used to build the case that Germany, which was merely recovering its national territory and rescuing German people from persecution in Czechoslovakia and Poland, was an aggressor with world conquest as its goal. The American people and in Britain the Chamberlain government resisted this false story for a long time, but as historians have revealed the British and American press was controlled by Zionist Jews, and these Jews had all the entrances they needed into Churchill and Roosevelt.

It is difficult to believe that a world war that killed 50, perhaps 60, million people and doomed the world to permanent war and misunderstandings was the product of a few personal interests. Hitler stated many times that he did not want, or intend, war with Britain and France and only intended to recover the lost German populations stolen from Germany by the unjust Versailles Treaty. No less an important Englishman than John Maynard Keynes, the father of modern economics, denounced the Versailles Treaty as certain to lead to a new war. Keynes was correct.

Never was a war as unnecessary, and only the US profited from it. Britain was ruined. Britain lost the reserve currency role and its control of world trade, which were Roosevelt's intentions, and Britain lost its empire, also Roosevelt's intention.

David Irving describes how Roosevelt played the drunken British Prime Minister into mortgaging the British Empire to America in support for his war against Germany. Roosevelt understood how war could rescue his administration from the Great Depression. He also understood how war, by bankrupting Britain, would leave the United States as the world hegemon.

Hitler had nothing to do with any of this. The war was forced on him. As established stories have an immunity to facts, Unz's report has a tough row to hoe.

Viktor Suvorov has produced documented books that Hitler had no choice but to invade Russia as Stalin had assembled on Germany's border the largest and most formidable invasion force in history. Hitler struck first before the Soviet invasion force was prepared. Consequently, the enormous early victories of German arms were a product of Soviet bases being overrun with enormous losses in men and equipment. John Wear's findings support Suvorov's conclusion [2].

The war forced on Germany was too much for Germany. Faced with having to occupy defeated Europe, with the threat of an American invasion, faced with a Russian front, and faced with having to rescue Italy in Greece and North Africa, German resources, despite the magnificence of the German Army, were too thin to prevail. Roosevelt, Churchill, and Stalin, each for his own reasons, had forced Germany into a war that Hitler did not want.

Unz reports that revisionist historians have "implicated FDR as a pivotal figure in orchestrating the world war by his constant pressure upon the British political leadership, a policy that he privately even admitted could mean his impeachment if revealed. Among other testimony, we have the statements of the Polish and British ambassadors to Washington and the American ambassador to London, who also passed along the concurring opinion of Prime Minister

Chamberlain himself. Indeed, the German capture and publication of secret Polish diplomatic documents in 1939 had already revealed much of this information, and William Henry Chamberlin confirmed their authenticity in his 1950 book. But since the mainstream media never reported any of this information, these facts remain little known even today."

With Churchill having set the stage for war with Germany, Franklin D. Roosevelt initiated the outbreak by exerting diplomatic pressure on the British and Polish governments to avoid any negotiated settlement with Germany. The Polish government's mistreatment of Germans in territories under Polish control forced Hitler's hand. The joint German and Soviet invasion of Poland, with the Soviet Union taking half of Poland resulted in England and France declaring war only on Germany. It was alright for the Soviets to invade Poland, but not for Germany.

Roosevelt orchestrated the Japanese "surprise" attack on Pearl Harbor to take the US into the war against Germany. The Polish ambassador to the United States, Count Jerzy Potocki, described the overwhelming Jewish hostility to Germany and its impact on American attitudes toward Germany in a secret report to the Polish Foreign Minister in Warsaw:

"There is a feeling now prevalent in the United States marked by growing hatred of Fascism, and above all of Chancellor Hitler and everything connected with National Socialism. Propaganda is mostly in the hands of the Jews who control almost 100% [of the] radio, film, daily and periodical press. Although this propaganda is extremely coarse and presents Germany as black as possible–above all religious persecution and concentration camps are exploited–this propaganda is nevertheless extremely effective since the public here is completely ignorant and knows nothing of the situation in Europe.

"At the present moment most Americans regard Chancellor Hitler and National Socialism as the greatest evil and greatest peril threatening the world. The situation here provides an excellent platform for public speakers of all kinds, for emigrants from Germany and Czechoslovakia who with a great many words and with most various calumnies incite the public. They praise American liberty which they contrast with the totalitarian states.

"It is interesting to note that in this extremely well-planned campaign which is conducted above all against National Socialism, Soviet Russia is almost completely eliminated. Soviet Russia, if mentioned at all, is mentioned in a friendly manner and things are presented in such a way that it would seem that the Soviet Union were cooperating with the bloc of democratic states. Thanks to the clever propaganda the sympathies of the American public are completely on the side of Red Spain.

"This propaganda, this war psychosis is being artificially created. The American people are told that peace in Europe is hanging only by a thread and that war is inevitable. At the same time the American people are unequivocally told that in case of a world war, America also must take an active part in order to defend the slogans of liberty and democracy in the world. President Roosevelt was the first one to express hatred against Fascism. In doing so he was serving a double purpose; first he wanted to divert the attention of the American people from difficult and intricate domestic problems, especially from the problem of the struggle between capital and labor. Second, by creating a war psychosis and by spreading rumors concerning dangers threatening Europe, he wanted to induce the American people to accept an enormous armament program which far exceeds United States defense requirements.

"Regarding the first point, it must be said that the internal situation on the labor market is growing worse constantly. The unemployed today already number 12 million. Federal and state expenditures are increasing daily. Only the huge sums, running into billions, which the treasury expends for emergency labor projects, are keeping a certain amount of peace in the country. Thus far only the usual strikes and local unrest have taken place. But how long this government aid can be kept up it is difficult to predict today. The excitement and indignation of public opinion, and the serious conflict between private enterprises and enormous trusts on the one hand, and with labor on the other, have made many enemies for Roosevelt and are causing him many sleepless nights.

"As to point two, I can only say that President Roosevelt, as a clever player of politics and a connoisseur of American mentality, speedily steered public attention away from the domestic situation in order to fasten it on foreign policy. The way to achieve this was simple. One needed, on the one hand, to enhance the war menace overhanging the world on account of Chancellor Hitler, and, on the other hand, to create a specter by talking about the attack of the totalitarian states on the United States. The Munich pact came to President Roosevelt as a godsend. He described it as the capitulation of France and England to bellicose German militarism. As was said here: Hitler compelled Chamberlain at pistol-point. Hence, France and England had no choice and had to conclude a shameful peace.

"The prevalent hatred against everything which is in any way connected with German National Socialism is further kindled by the brutal attitude against the Jews in Germany and by the émigré problem. In this action Jewish intellectuals participated; for instance, Bernard Baruch [financial adviser to Churchill]; the Governor of New York State, Lehman; the newly appointed judge of the Supreme Court, Felix Frankfurter; Secretary of the Treasury Morgenthau, and others who are personal friends of Roosevelt. They want the President to become the champion of human rights, freedom of religion and speech, and the man who in the future will punish trouble-mongers. These groups, people who want to pose as representatives of "Americanism" and "defenders of democracy" in the last analysis, are connected by unbreakable ties with international Jewry.

"For this Jewish international, which above all is concerned with the interests of its race, to put the President of the United States at this 'ideal' post of champion of human rights, was a clever move. In this manner they created a dangerous hotbed for hatred and hostility in this hemisphere and divided the world into two hostile camps. The entire issue is worked out in a mysterious manner. Roosevelt has been forcing the foundation for vitalizing American foreign policy, and simultaneously has been procuring enormous stocks for the coming war, for which the Jews are striving consciously. With regard to domestic policy, it is extremely convenient to divert public attention from anti-Semitism which is ever growing in the United States, by talking about the necessity of defending faith and individual liberty against the onslaught of Fascism."

Count Jerzy Potocki to Polish Foreign Minister in Warsaw, The German White Paper: Full Text of the Polish Documents Issued by the Berlin Foreign Office; with a foreword by C. Hartley Grattan, New York: Howell, Soskin & Company, 1940, pp. 29-31.

Unz summarizes the role of Jewish anti-German propaganda in launching World War II and the role of propaganda in general in distorting historical understanding:

"Given the heavy Jewish involvement in financing Churchill and his allies and also steering the American government and public in the direction of war against Germany, organized Jewish groups probably bore the central responsibility for provoking the world war, and this was surely recognized by most knowledgeable individuals at the time. Indeed, the Forrestal Diaries recorded the very telling statement by our ambassador in London: 'Chamberlain, he says, stated that America and the Jews had forced England into the war.'

"The ongoing struggle between Hitler and international Jewry had been receiving considerable public attention for years. During his political rise, Hitler had hardly concealed his intent to dislodge Germany's tiny Jewish population from the stranglehold they had gained over German media and finance, and instead run the country in the best interests of the 99% German majority, a proposal that provoked the bitter hostility of Jews everywhere. Indeed, immediately after he came into office, a major London newspaper had carried a memorable 1933 headline announcing that the Jews of the world had declared war on Germany, and were organizing an international boycott to starve the Germans into submission.

"In recent years, somewhat similar Jewish-organized efforts at international sanctions aimed at bringing recalcitrant nations to their knees have become a regular part of global politics. But these days the Jewish dominance of the U.S. political system has become so overwhelming that instead of private boycotts, such actions are directly enforced by the American government. To some extent, this had already been the case with Iraq during the 1990s, but became far more common after the turn of the new century.

"Although our official government investigation concluded that the total financial cost of the 9/11 terrorist attacks had been an absolutely trivial sum, the Neocon-dominated Bush Administration nonetheless used this as an excuse to establish an important new Treasury Department position, the Under Secretary for Terrorism and Financial Intelligence. That office soon began utilizing America's control of the global banking system and dollar-denominated international trade to enforce financial sanctions and wage economic warfare, with these measures typically being directed against individuals, organizations, and nations considered unfriendly towards Israel, notably Iran, Hezbollah, and Syria.

"Perhaps coincidentally, although Jews comprise merely 2% of the American population, all four individuals holding that very powerful

Treasury post over the last 15 years since its inception—Stuart A. Levey, David S. Cohen, Adam Szubin, Sigal Mandelker—have been Jewish, with the most recent of these being an Israeli citizen. Levey, the first Under Secretary, began his work under President Bush, then continued without a break for years under President Obama, underscoring the entirely bipartisan nature of these activities.

"Most foreign policy experts have certainly been aware that Jewish groups and activists played the central role in driving our country into its disastrous 2003 Iraq War, and that many of these same groups and individuals have spent the last dozen years or so working to foment a similar American attack on Iran, though as yet unsuccessfully. This seems quite reminiscent of the late 1930s political situation in Britain and America.

"Individuals outraged by the misleading media coverage surrounding the Iraq War but who have always casually accepted the conventional narrative of World War II should consider a thought-experiment I suggested last year:

'When we seek to understand the past, we must be careful to avoid drawing from a narrow selection of sources, especially if one side proved politically victorious in the end and completely dominated the later production of books and other commentary. Prior to the existence of the Internet, this was an especially difficult task, often requiring a considerable amount of scholarly effort, even if only to examine the bound volumes of once popular periodicals. Yet without such diligence, we can fall into very serious error.

'The Iraq War and its aftermath was certainly one of the central events in American history during the 2000s. Yet suppose some readers in the distant future had only the collected archives of The Weekly Standard, National Review, the WSJ op-ed page, and Fox News transcripts to furnish their understanding of the history of that period, perhaps along with the books written by the contributors to those outlets. I doubt that more than a small fraction of what they would read could be categorized as outright lies. But the massively skewed coverage, the distortions, exaggerations, and especially the breathtaking omissions would surely provide them with an exceptionally unrealistic view of what had actually happened during that important period.'

"Another striking historical parallel is the fierce demonization of Russian President Vladimir Putin, who provoked the great hostility of Jewish elements when he ousted the handful of Jewish Oligarchs who had seized control of Russian society under the drunken misrule of President Boris Yeltsin and totally impoverished the bulk of the population. This conflict intensified after Jewish investor William F. Browder arranged Congressional passage of the Magnitsky Act to punish Russian leaders for the legal actions they had taken against his huge financial empire in their country. Putin's harshest Neocon critics have often condemned him as "a new Hitler" while some neutral observers have agreed that no foreign leader since the German Chancellor of the 1930s has been so fiercely vilified in the American media. Seen from a different angle, there may indeed be a close correspondence between Putin and Hitler, but not in the way usually suggested. [Propaganda used to demonize both]

"Knowledgeable individuals have certainly been aware of the crucial Jewish role in orchestrating our military or financial attacks against Iraq, Iran, Syria, and Russia, but it has been exceptionally rare for any prominent public figures or reputable journalists to mention these facts lest they be denounced and vilified by zealous Jewish activists and the media they dominate. For example, a couple of years ago a single suggestive Tweet by famed CIA anti-proliferation operative Valerie Plame provoked such an enormous wave of vituperation that she was forced to resign her position at a prominent non-profit. A close parallel involving a far more famous figure had occurred three generations earlier [Lindbergh].

"These facts, now firmly established by decades of scholarship, provide some necessary context to Lindbergh's famously controversial speech at an America First rally in September 1941. At that event, he charged that three groups in particular were "pressing this country toward war: the British, the Jewish, and the Roosevelt Administration," and thereby unleashed an enormous firestorm of media attacks and denunciations, including widespread accusations of anti-Semitism and Nazi sympathies. Given the realities of the political situation, Lindbergh's statement constituted a perfect illustration of Michael Kinsley's famous quip that "a gaffe is when a politician tells the truth – some obvious truth he isn't supposed to say." But as a consequence, Lindbergh's once-heroic reputation suffered enormous and permanent damage, with the campaign of vilification echoing for the remaining three decades of his life, and even well beyond. Although he was not entirely purged from public life, his standing was certainly never even remotely the same.

"With such examples in mind, we should hardly be surprised that for decades this huge Jewish involvement in orchestrating World War II was carefully omitted from nearly all subsequent historical narratives, even those that sharply challenged the mythology of the official account. The index of A.J.P. Taylor's iconoclastic 1961 work contains absolutely no mention of Jews, and the same is true of the previous books by Chamberlin and Grenfell. In 1953, Harry Elmer Barnes, the dean of historical revisionists, edited his major volume aimed at demolishing the falsehoods of World War II, and once again any discussion of the Jewish role was almost entirely lacking, with only part of one single sentence and Chamberlain's dangling short quote appearing across more than 200,000 words of text. Both Barnes and many of his contributors had already been purged and their book was only released by a tiny publisher in Idaho, but they still sought to avoid certain unmentionables.

"Even the arch-revisionist David Hoggan seems to have carefully skirted the topic of Jewish influence. His 30 page index lacks any entry on Jews and his 700 pages of text contain only scattered references. Indeed, although he does quote the explicit private statements of both the Polish ambassador and the British Prime Minister emphasizing the enormous Jewish role in promoting the war, he then rather questionably asserts that these confidential statements of individuals with the best understanding of events should simply be disregarded.

"In the popular Harry Potter series, Lord Voldemort, the great nemesis of the young magicians, is often identified as 'He Who Must Not Be Named,' since the mere vocalization of those few particular syllables might bring doom upon the speaker. Jews have long enjoyed enormous power and influence over the media and political life, while fanatic Jewish activists demonstrate hair-trigger eagerness to denounce and vilify all those suspected of being insufficiently friendly towards their ethnic group. The combination of these two factors has therefore induced such a 'Lord Voldemort Effect' regarding Jewish activities in most writers and public figures. Once we recognize this reality, we should become very cautious in analyzing controversial historical issues that might possibly contain a Jewish dimension, and also be particularly wary of arguments from silence.

"Those writers willing to break this fearsome Jewish Taboo regarding World War II were quite rare, but one notable exception comes to mind. As I recently wrote:

'Some years ago, I came across a totally obscure 1951 book entitled The Iron Curtain Over America by John Beaty, a well-regarded university professor. Beaty had spent his wartime years in Military Intelligence, being tasked with preparing the daily briefing reports distributed to all top American officials summarizing available intelligence information acquired during the previous 24 hours, which was obviously a position of considerable responsibility.

'As a zealous anti-Communist, he regarded much of America's Jewish population as deeply implicated in subversive activity, therefore constituting a serious threat to traditional American freedoms. In particular, the growing Jewish stranglehold over publishing and the media was making it increasingly difficult for discordant views to reach the American people, with this regime of censorship constituting the 'Iron Curtain' described in his title. He blamed Jewish interests for the totally unnecessary war with Hitler's Germany, which had long sought good relations with America, but instead had suffered total destruction for its strong opposition to Europe's Jewish-backed Communist menace.

'Then as now, a book taking such controversial positions stood little chance of finding a mainstream New York publisher, but it was soon released by a small Dallas firm, and then became enormously successful, going through some seventeen printings over the next few years. According to Scott McConnell, founding editor of The American Conservative, Beaty's book became the second most popular conservative text of the 1950s, ranking only behind Russell Kirk's iconic classic, The Conservative Mind.

'Books by unknown authors that are released by tiny publishers rarely sell many copies, but the work came to the attention of George E. Stratemeyer, a retired general who had been one of Douglas MacArthur's commanders, and he wrote Beaty a letter of endorsement. Beaty began including that letter in his promotional materials, drawing the ire of the ADL [the Jewish Anti-defamation League], whose national chairman contacted Stratemeyer, demanding that he repudiate the book, which was described as a 'primer for lunatic fringe groups' all across America. Instead, Stratemeyer delivered a 'blistering reply to the ADL,' denouncing it for making 'veiled threats' against 'free expression and thoughts' and trying to establish Soviet-style repression in the United States. He declared that every 'loyal citizen' should read The Iron Curtain Over America, whose pages finally revealed the truth about our national predicament, and he began actively promoting the book around the country while attacking the Jewish attempt to silence him. Numerous other top American generals and admirals soon joined

Statemeyer in publicly endorsing the work, as did a couple of influential members of the U.S. Senate, leading to its enormous national sales.'

"In contrast to nearly all the other World War II narratives discussed above, whether orthodox or revisionist, the index of Beaty's volume is absolutely overflowing with references to Jews and Jewish activities, containing dozens of separate entries and with the topic mentioned on a substantial fraction of all the pages in his fairly short book. I therefore suspect that any casual modern reader who encountered Beaty's volume would be stunned and dismayed by such extremely pervasive material, and probably dismiss the author as being delusional and 'Jew-obsessed;' but I think that Beaty's treatment is probably the far more honest and realistic one. As I noted last year on a related matter: '…once the historical record has been sufficiently whitewashed or rewritten, any lingering strands of the original reality that survive are often perceived as bizarre delusions or denounced as "conspiracy theories.'

"Beaty's wartime role at the absolute nexus of American Intelligence certainly gave him a great deal of insight into the pattern of events, and the glowing endorsement of his account by many of our highest-ranking military commanders supports that conclusion. More recently, a decade of of archival research by Prof. Joseph Bendersky, a prominent mainstream historian, revealed that Beaty's views were privately shared by many of our Military Intelligence professionals and top generals of the era, being quite widespread in such circles."
"Who controls the past controls the future; who controls the present controls the past." The control over explanations means that the historical assumptions that govern the politics of today are entirely misleading.

It is the few revisionist historians and Ron Unz their explicator who possibly can save the world from destruction by deception.

First published on November 19, 2019.

[1]. "Britain and France declare war on Germany"
https://web.archive.org/web/20200406032202/https://www.history.co
m/this-day-in-history/britain-and-france-declare-war-on-germany
[2]. "Germans Cut Through Red Army in 1941 Because Soviets Were
Only Prepared to Attack" https://russia-
insider.com/en/history/germans-cut-through-red-army-1941-because-
soviets-were-only-prepared-attack/ri27845

CHAPTER 5
"THE BIG LIE"

Pearl Harbor: An Orchestrated Event?

In November, 1944, US Secretary of War, Henry Stimson snapped to the US Secretary of the Treasury that he was worn out "from working the last two weeks on the Pearl Harbor report to keep out anything that might hurt the President." – Churchill's War, Vol. II

December 7, 2020. Today is the 79th anniversary of the Japanese attack on Pearl Harbor, the event that brought the US into the war against Germany and Japan. Eight American battleships were sunk or put out of action, and about 3,600 American sailors were killed or wounded.

Washington needed scapegoats, and Admiral Husband Kimmel and General Walter Short were saddled with the blame for American unpreparedness for the Pearl Harbor attack. As time passed circumstantial evidence came to light that President Roosevelt knew of the attack and permitted the devastation in order that the American people would be so outraged by the attack as to give up their resistance to being dragged into another European war. The controversy continued for some years. I am unsure that it was ever resolved.

When I was a Wall Street Journal editor, the chief intelligence officer of the US Pacific Fleet at the time of the Japanese attack, Admiral Edwin T. Layton, published a book, And I Was There. Layton proved to my satisfaction that foreknowledge of the attack was known in Washington, perhaps not specifically that Japan would attack Pearl Harbor, but it was definitely known that Japan was about to attack in force. Layton attributed Pearl Harbor's vulnerability to the tendency of Washington to monopolize naval intelligence and not share it with operational commanders. Whether or not Layton believed this or simply could not say that the warning was withheld in order to clear the obstacle to war, I cannot say. Nevertheless, for Washington to know an attack was forthcoming and still take no action to put Pearl Harbor on high alert or send the fleet to sea is puzzling. Kimmel's predecessor had been fired because he would not agree with Washington's insistence on keeping the Pacific Fleet in such a vulnerable location as Pearl Harbor while the likelihood of war increased.

The publisher of Layton's book sent me a copy. As a Wall Street Journal editor with a column of my own, I assumed I could write a review of Admiral Layton's book, but I was prohibited.

I don't say this to embarrass my former colleagues. My point is that the Establishment is very protective of Establishment positions and institutions. The same protectiveness that can prevent the review of a book can prevent the correction of an obviously stolen presidential election.

Americans were brought up on the story of duplicitous Japanese who were fooling Washington with peace negotiations even as the Japanese fleet sailed to Pearl Harbor. Reading the second volume of David Irving's biography of Winston Churchill (published in 2001) makes it clear that it was Roosevelt and Churchill who were fooling the Japanese and manipulating them into war.

Irving himself seldom gives his opinion. He simply searches out all available documents and quotes from them, and he tells you where to find the documents so you can check up on him. The British and Americans had broken the Japanese codes and were reading the diplomatic and military secret messages and discussing them between themselves, sometimes withholding important information from one another. The documents indicate that Japan did not want war with the US and Britain and was trying to arrive at a peaceful settlement of the difficulty caused by Roosevelt's cutoff of Japan from oil. It was obvious to all that if Japan was denied oil, Japan would have to go for the oil in Dutch Indonesia, which meant that British and US bases in the region would come under Japanese attack. The documents show that both Roosevelt and Churchill agreed that the British and

Americans could not move first and that Japan had to be maneuvered into attacking Britain or the US.

Irving presents a large amount of official information, but he reports that many of the files remain under lock and key and that some files to which he gained access are empty. Some documents have been lost or misplaced or destroyed. Obviously, the facts are not convenient for the British and American governments and are still withheld many decades later.

There are two kinds of historians: court historians who make themselves popular by telling stories that please and revisionist historians who replace reassuring histories with factual ones that are upsetting. The latter have a rough time. This is especially the case for David Irving whose histories show that it was not only Hitler and Tojo who wore black hats but also Roosevelt and Churchill.

Once you escape controlled explanations, you can reasonably arrive at the conclusion that World War II was caused by Churchill and Roosevelt. Churchill rode to power as prime minister on his demonization of Germany and the gratuitous British guarantee to Poland that committed the British to war against Germany. Roosevelt caused war with Japan by a series of insults and cutting Japan off from oil. Roosevelt knew that this would force Japan into war with the US. Just as Hitler made it clear that he did not want war with Britain and France, the Japanese made it clear that Japan did not want war with the US and Britain. But they got war anyway. Roosevelt wanted Britain at war, because Roosevelt knew a bankrupt and exhausted Britain could be shorn of its empire, and American financial and economic leadership would replace British financial and economic leadership.

The American Empire was indeed the main outcome of World War II.

First published on December 7, 2020.

On 9/11 Doubts Were Immediate

On September 11, 2001, a neighbor telephoned and said, "turn on the TV." I assumed that a hurricane, possibly a bad one from the sound of the neighbor's voice, was headed our way, and turned on the TV to determine whether we needed to shutter the house and leave.

What I saw was black smoke from upper floors of one of the World Trade Center towers. It didn't seem to be much of a fire, and the reports were that the fire was under control. While I was trying to figure out why every TV network had its main news anchor covering an office fire, TV cameras showed an airplane hitting the other tower. It was then that I learned that both towers had been hit by airliners.

Cameras showed people standing at the hole in the side of the tower looking out. This didn't surprise me. The airliner was minute compared to the massive building. But what was going on? Two accidents, one on top of the other?

The towers – the three-fourths or four-fifths of the buildings beneath the plane strikes – were standing, apparently largely undamaged. There were no signs of fire except in the vicinity of where the airliners had hit. Suddenly, one of the towers blew up, disintegrated, and disappeared in fine dust. Before one could make any sense of this, the same thing happened to the second tower, and it too disappeared into fine dust.

The TV news anchors compared the disintegration of the towers to controlled demolition. There were numerous reports of explosions throughout the towers from the base or sub-basements to the top. (Once the government put out the story of terrorist attack, references to controlled demolition and explosions disappeared from the print and TV media.) This made sense to me. Someone had blown up the buildings. It was completely obvious that the towers had not fallen down from asymmetrical structural damage. They had blown up.

298

The images of the airliners hitting the towers and the towers blowing up were replayed time and again. Airliners hit the top portions of the towers, and not long afterward the towers blew up. I turned off the TV wondering how it was that cameras had been ready to catch such an unusual phenomenon as an airplane flying into a skyscraper.

I don't remember the time line, but it wasn't long before the story was in place that Osama bin Laden and his al Qaeda gang had attacked the US. A passport had been found in the rubble. Another airliner had flown into the Pentagon, and a fourth airliner had crashed or been shot down. Four airliners had been hijacked, meaning airport security had failed four times on the same morning. Terrorists had successfully assaulted America.

When I heard these reports, I wondered. How could a tiny undamaged passport be found in the rubble of two skyscrapers, each more than 100 stories tall, when bodies, office furniture and computers could not be found? How could airport security fail so totally that four airliners could be hijacked within the same hour? How could authorities know so conclusively and almost immediately the names of the perpetrators who pulled off such a successful attack on the world's only superpower, when the authorities had no idea that such an attack was planned or even possible?

These questions disturbed me, because as a former member of the congressional staff and as a presidential appointee to high office, I had high level security clearances. In addition to my duties as Assistant Secretary of the US Treasury, I had FEMA responsibilities in the event of nuclear attack. There was a mountain hideaway to which I was supposed to report in the event of a nuclear attack and from which I was supposed to take over the US government in the event no higher official survived the attack.

The more the story of 9/11 was presented in the media, the more wondrous it became. It is not credible that not only the CIA and FBI failed to detect the plot, but also all 16 US intelligence agencies, including the National Security Agency, which spies on everyone on the planet, and the Defense Intelligence Agency, Israel's Mossad, and the intelligence agencies of Washington's NATO allies. There are simply too many watchmen and too much infiltration of terrorist groups for such a complex attack to be prepared undetected and carried out undeterred.

Washington's explanation of the attack implied a security failure too massive to be credible. Such a catastrophic failure of national security would mean that the US and Western Europe were never safe for one second during the Cold War, that the Soviet Union could have destroyed the entire West in one undetected fell swoop.

As a person whose colleagues at the Center for Strategic and International Studies in Washington were former secretaries of state, former national security advisors, former CIA directors, former chairmen of the Joint Chiefs of Staff, I was troubled by the story that a collection of individuals unsupported by a competent intelligence service had pulled off the events of 9/11.

As a person with high level government service, I knew that any such successful operation as 9/11 would have resulted in immediate demands from the White House, Congress, and the media for accountability. There would have been an investigation of how every aspect of US security could totally fail simultaneously in one morning. Such a catastrophic and embarrassing failure of the national security state would not be left unexamined.

NORAD failed. The US Air Force could not get jet fighters in the air. Air Traffic Control lost sight of the hijacked airliners. Yet, instead of launching an investigation, the White House resisted for one year the demands of the 9/11 families for an investigation. Neither the public, the media, nor Congress seemed to think an investigation was necessary. The focus was on revenge, which the Bush neocon regime said meant invading Afghanistan which was alleged to be sheltering the perpetrator, Osama bin Laden.

Normally, terrorists are proud of their success and announce their responsibility. It is a way to build a movement. Often a number of terrorist groups will compete in claiming credit for a successful operation. But Osama bin Laden in the last video that is certified by independent experts said that he had no responsibility for 9/11, that he had nothing against the American people, that his opposition was limited to the US government's colonial policies and control over Muslim governments.

It makes no sense that the "mastermind" of the most humiliating blow in world history ever to have been delivered against a superpower would not claim credit for his accomplishment. By September 11, 2001, Osama bin Laden knew that he was deathly ill. According to news reports he underwent kidney dialysis the following month. The most reliable reports that we have are that he died in December 2001. It is simply not credible that bin Laden denied responsibility because he feared Washington.

But Osama bin Laden was too useful a bogeyman, and Washington and the presstitute media kept him alive for another decade until Obama needed to kill the dead man in order to boost his sinking standings in the polls so that Democrats would not back a challenger for the Democratic presidential nomination.

Numerous bin Laden videos, every one pronounced a fake by experts, were released whenever it was convenient for Washington. No one in the Western media or in the US Congress or European or UK parliaments was sufficiently intelligent to recognize that a bin Laden video always showed up on cue when Washington needed it. "Why would the 'mastermind' be so accommodating for Washington?" was the question that went through my mind every time one of the fake videos was released.

The 9/11 "investigation" that finally took place was a political one run from the White House. One member of the commission resigned, declaring the investigation to be a farce, and both co-chairman and the legal counsel of the 9/11 Commission distanced themselves from their report with statements that the 9/11 Commission was "set up to fail," that resources were withheld from the commission, that representatives of the US military lied to the commission and that the commission considered referring the false testimony for criminal prosecution. One would think that these revelations would cause a sensation, but the news media, Congress, the White House, and the public were silent.

All of this bothered me a great deal. The US had invaded two Muslim countries based on unsubstantiated allegations linking the two countries to 9/11, which itself remained uninvestigated. The neoconservatives who staffed the George W. Bush regime were advocating more invasions of more Muslim countries. Paul O'Neill, President Bush's first Treasury Secretary, stated publicly that the Bush regime was planning to invade Iraq prior to 9/11. O'Neill said that no one at a National Security Council meeting even asked the question, why invade Iraq? "It was all about finding a way to do it."

The leaked top secret Downing Street Memo written by the head of British intelligence (MI6) confirms Paul O'Neill's testimony. The memo, known as the "smoking gun memo" whose authenticity has been confirmed, states that "President George W. Bush wants to remove Saddam Hussein, through military action, justified by the conjunction of terrorism and WMD. But the intelligence and facts were being fixed around the policy." In other words, the US invasion of Iraq was based on nothing but a made up lie.

As an engineering student I had witnessed a controlled demolition. When films of the collapse of WTC building 7 emerged, it was obvious that building 7 had been brought down by controlled demolition. When physics instructor David Chandler measured the descent of the building and established that it took place at free fall acceleration, the case was closed. Buildings cannot enter free fall unless controlled demolition has removed all resistance to the collapsing floors.

If airliners brought down two skyscrapers, why was controlled demolition used to bring down a third building?

I assumed that structural architects, structural engineers, and physicists would blow the whistle on the obviously false story. If I could see that something was amiss, certainly more highly trained people would.

The first physicist to make an effective and compelling argument was Steven Jones at BYU. Jones said that explosives brought down the twin towers. He made a good case. For his efforts, he was pressured to resign his tenured position. I wondered whether the federal government had threatened BYU"s research grants or whether patriotic trustees and alumni were the driving force behind Jones" expulsion. Regardless, the message was clear to other university based experts: "Shut up or we'll get you."

Steven Jones was vindicated when chemist Niels Harrit of the University of Copenhagen In Denmark reported unequivocally that the scientific team in which he participated found nano-thermite in the residue of the twin towers. This sensational finding was not mentioned in the US print and TV media to my knowledge.

Several years after 9/11 architect Richard Gage formed Architects and Engineers for 9/11 truth, an organization that has grown to include 1,700 experts. The plans of the towers have been studied. They were formidable structures. They were constructed to withstand airliner hits and fires. There is no credible explanation of their failure except intentional demolition.

I also found disturbing the gullibility of the public, media, and Congress in the unquestioning acceptance of the official stories of the shoe-bomber, shampoo and bottled water bomber, and underwear bomber plots to blow up airliners in transit. These schemes are farcical. How can we believe that al Qaeda, capable of pulling off the most fantastic terrorist attack in history and capable of devising improvised explosive devices (IEDs) that kill and maim US troops and destroy US military vehicles would rely on something that had to be lighted with a match?

The shoe and underwear bombers would simply have pushed a button on their cell phones or laptops, and the liquid bomb would not have required extended time in a lavatory to be mixed (all to no effect).

None of this makes any sense. Moreover, experts disputed many of the government's claims, which were never backed by anything but the government's story line. There is no independent evidence that anything was involved other than firecracker powders.

The case of the underwear bomber is especially difficult to accept. According to witnesses, the underwear bomber was not allowed on the airliner, because he had no passport. So an official appears who walks him onto the airliner bound for Detroit on Christmas day. What kind of official has the authority to override established rules, and what did the official think would happen to the passenger when he presented himself to US Customs without a passport? Any official with the power to override standard operating practices would know that it was pointless to send a passenger to a country where his entry would be rejected.

The circumstantial evidence is that these were orchestrated events designed to keep fear alive, to create new intrusive powers for a new over-arching federal policy agency, to accustom US citizens to intrusive searches and a police force to conducting them, and to sell expensive porno-scanners and now more advanced devices to the

Transportation Safety Administration. Apparently, this expensive collection of high-tech gadgetry is insufficient to protect us from terrorists, and in August 2012 the Department of Homeland Security put in an order for 750 million rounds of ammunition, enough to shoot every person in the US 2.5 times.

Naive and gullible Americans claim that if some part of the US government had been involved in 9/11, "someone would have talked by now." A comforting thought, perhaps, but nothing more. Consider, for example, the cover-up by the US government of the 1967 Israeli attack on the USS Liberty that killed or wounded most of the crew but failed to sink the ship. As the survivors have testified, they were ordered in a threatening way not to speak about the event. It was twelve years later before one of the USS Liberty's officers, James Ennes, told the story of the attack in his book, Assault on the Liberty. I continue to wonder how the professionals at the National Institute of Standards and Technology feel about being maneuvered by the federal government into the unscientific position NIST took concerning the destruction of the WTC towers.

What will be the outcome of the doubts about the official story raised by experts? I worry that most Americans are too mentally and emotionally weak to be able to come to grips with the truth. They are far more comfortable with the story that enemies attacked America successfully despite the massive national security state in place. The American public has proved itself to be so cowardly that it willingly, without a peep, sacrificed its civil liberty and the protections of law guaranteed by the Constitution in order to be "safe."

Congress is not about to expose itself for having squandered trillions of dollars on pointless wars based on an orchestrated "new Pearl Harbor." When the neoconservatives said that a "new Pearl Harbor" was a requirement for their wars for American/Israeli hegemony, they set the stage for the 21st century wars that Washington has launched. If Syria falls, there is only Iran, and then Washington stands in direct confrontation with Russia and China.

Unless Russia and China can be overthrown with "color revolutions," these two nuclear powers are unlikely to submit to Washington's hegemony. The world as we know it might be drawing to a close.

If enough Americans or even other peoples in the world had the intelligence to realize that massive steel structures do not disintegrate into fine dust because a flimsy airliner hits them and limited short-lived fires burn on a few floors, Washington would be faced with the suspicion it deserves.

If 9/11 was actually the result of the failure of the national security state to deter an attack, the government's refusal to conduct a real investigation is an even greater failure. It has fallen to concerned and qualified individuals to perform the investigative role abandoned by government. The presentations at the Toronto Hearings, along with the evaluations of the Panel, are now available, as is the documentary film, "Explosive Evidence – Experts Speak Out," provided by Architects and Engineers for 9/11 Truth.

The government's agents and apologists try to deflect attention from disturbing facts by redefining factual evidence revealed by experts as the product of "a conspiracy culture." If people despite their brainwashing and lack of scientific education are able to absorb the information made available to them, perhaps both the US Constitution and peace could be restored. Only informed people can restrain Washington and avert the crazed hegemonic US government from destroying the world in war.

First published September 11, 2012.

Another Fake Bin Laden Story

RT, one of my favorite news sources, has fallen for a fake story put out by the Pentagon to support the fantasy story that a SEAL team killed Osama bin Laden, who died a second time in Abbottabad, Pakistan, a decade after his first death from illness and disease.

This fake story together with the fake movie and the fake book by an alleged SEAL team member is the way the fake story of bin Laden's murder is perpetrated. Bin Laden's alleged demise at the hands of a SEAL team was a propaganda orchestration, the purpose of which was to give Obama a hero's laurels and deep six Democratic talk of challenging his nomination for a second term.

Osama bin Laden died in December 2001 of renal failure and other health problems, having denied in his last recorded video any responsibility for 9/11, instead directing Americans to look inside their own government. The FBI itself has stated that there is no evidence that Osama bin Laden is responsible for 9/11. Bin Laden's obituary appeared in numerous foreign and Arabic press, and also on Fox News. No one can survive renal failure for a decade, and no dialysis machine was found in the alleged Abbottabad compound of bin Laden, who allegedly was murdered by SEALs a decade after his obituary notices.

Additionally, no one among the crew of the ship from which the White House reported bin Laden was buried at sea saw any such burial, and the sailors sent messages home to that effect. Somehow a burial was held onboard a ship on which there are constant watches and crew on alert at all hours, and no one witnessed it.

Additionally, the White House story of the alleged murder of bin Laden changed twice within the first 24 hours. The claim that Obama and his government watched the action transmitted live from cameras on the SEALs' helmets was quickly abandoned, despite the release of a photo of the Obama regime intently focused on a TV set and alleged to be watching the live action. No video of the deed was ever released. To date there is no evidence whatsoever in behalf of the Obama regime's claim. Not one tiny scrap. Just unsubstantiated self-serving claims.

Additionally, as I have made available on my website, witnesses interviewed by Pakistan TV reported that only one helicopter landed in Abbottabad and that when the occupants of the helicopter returned from the alleged bin Laden compound, the helicopter exploded on takeoff and there were no survivors. In other words, there was no bin Laden corpse to deliver to the ship that did not witness a burial and no SEAL hero to return who allegedly murdered an unarmed bin Laden. Moreover, the BBC interviewed residents in Abbottabad, including those next door to the alleged "bin Laden compound," and all say that they knew the person who lived there and it was not bin Laden.

Any SEAL who was so totally stupid as to kill the unarmed "Terror Mastermind" would probably have been court-martialed for incompetency. Look at the smiling face of the man Who Killed Bin Laden. He thinks that his claim that he murdered a man makes him a hero, a powerful comment on the moral degeneracy of Americans.

So what is this claim by Rob O'Neill about? He is presented as a "motivational speaker" in search of clients. What better ploy among gullible Americans than to claim "I am the one who shot bin Laden." Reminds me of the western movie: The Man Who Shot Liberty Valance. What better way to give Rob O'Neill's claim validity than for the Pentagon to denounce his revelation for breaking obligation to remain silent. The Pentagon claims that O'Neill by claiming credit has painted a big target sign on our door asking ISIS to come get us

What unbelievable nonsense. ISIS and anyone who believed Obama's claim to have done in bin Laden already knew, if they believed the lie, that the Obama regime claimed responsibility for murdering an unarmed bin Laden. The reason the SEAL team was prevented from talking is that no member of the team was on the alleged mission,

Just as the ship from which bin Laden was allegedly buried has no witnesses to the deed, the SEAL unit, whose members formed the team that allegedly dispatched an unarmed Terrorist Mastermind rather than to take him into custody for questioning, mysteriously died in a helicopter crash when they were loaded in violation of procedures in an unprotected 1960s vintage helicopter and sent into a combat zone in Afghanistan shortly after the alleged raid on "bin Laden's compound."

For a while there were news reports that the families of these dead SEALS do not believe one word of the government's account. Moreover, the families reported receiving messages from the SEALs that suddenly they felt threatened and did not know why. The SEALs had been asking one another: "Were you on the bin Laden mission?" Apparently, none were. And to keep this a secret, the SEALs were sent to their deaths.

Anyone who believes anything the US government says is gullible beyond the meaning of the word.

First published on November 7, 2014.

9/11 After 21 Years

Today is the 21st anniversary of the attack on the World Trade Center in New York City. There has never been an official US investigation of the attack. After much pressure from families of those who died in the collapse of the towers, the White House finally and most reluctantly assembled a 9/11 Commission consisting largely of politicians and a neoconservative staff director to sit and listen to the government's narrative and to write it down. This is what comprised the 9/11 Commission Report. Afterwards the Commission's co-chairmen and legal counsel wrote books in which they said the 9/11 Commission was set up to fail, that resources and information were withheld from the Commission, and that the Commission considered referring criminal charges to the Department of Justice against some of the government officials who falsely testified before the commission. These confessions were ignored by the presstitutes and had no effect on the government's highly implausible narrative.

NIST's account of the collapse is simply a computer simulation that delivered the results NIST programed into the simulation.

For 21 years I reported on the independent investigations and findings of scientists, scholars, engineers, and architects that concluded on the basis of hard evidence that the government's narrative was a false account. Initially, the distinguished scientists, architects, and engineers who rejected the official narrative were characterized by the presstitutes as "conspiracy theorists," following the line the CIA had employed against experts who disputed the official narrative of President John F. Kennedy's assassination. However, over time the efforts of Architects & Engineers for 9/11 Truth convinced more and more Americans that the official story was false. In recent years polls have shown that half of those polled no longer believe the official narrative.

It was obvious to me early that 9/11 was an inside job, a false flag event blamed on Muslims in order to justify two decades of a "war on terror" whose purpose was to destroy Israel's Middle Eastern opponents who were funding Hezbollah, the Lebanese militia that twice drove the vaunted Israeli Army out of Israel's attempted occupation of southern Lebanon. If Hezbollah's supporters – Iraq, Syria and Iran – could be eliminated, Israel could seize the water resource in southern Lebanon. This, and profits and power for the US military/security complex are all the "war on terror" was about.

The reason it was obvious to me that 9/11 was an inside job is that, as it was presented, it amounted to the worse humiliation a superpower had suffered in all of recorded history. A handful of young Saudi Arabians without support of any state or security agency had delivered a crushing blow to the image of the United States. The almighty National Security Apparatus was incapable of warding off a handful of foreigners who, magically, caused US airport security to fail four times on the same morning, hijack 4 airliners, cause the US military to conduct a simulation of the attack at the same time an actual attack was occurring, thus causing massive confusion that prevented the US Air Force from intercepting the hijacked airliners. The young men also prevented VP Dick Cheney, who was monitoring "the attack on America," from blocking the attack on the Pentagon.

When you look at this record of extraordinary failure of the multi-trillion dollar National Security State and hear no demand from the President of the United States, the Pentagon and Joint Chiefs of Staff, Congress, and the media for investigation and accountability for the government's total failure, hearing instead opposition to any inquiry, you know for an absolute fact that the highest levels of the US government were responsible for the attack in order to unleash war on the Middle East, just as Pearl Harbor was a Roosevelt orchestration to get the US into a war that Congress and the American people opposed.

If in fact the US government believed its narrative, the government, embarrassed to the hilt, would have been demanding explanation and accountability. There would have been endless investigation. Many heads would have rolled. I spent a quarter century in Washington, and I know for a fact that the government would not have been content to assemble a Commission and then read an implausible account to them and call that an investigation of America's and their own humiliation.

What the government did instead of an investigation was to quickly destroy all the evidence. The massive steel beams of the towers clearly cut at an angle by high temperature explosives were quickly collected over objections by fire marshals, shipped out of the country in order to get rid of the evidence, and sold as scrap metal in Asia. No explanation or even admission was given for the molten steel still under the ruble weeks after the event. The testimony of more than a hundred, firemen, police, and building maintenance workers that they experienced explosions all over the towers, including one in the basement before the alleged airliners even hit the towers, was ignored. That the three buildings collapsed into their own footprints as in controlled demolition was ignored. That the BBC reporter announced the collapse of the third building 30 minutes before it happened while she was standing in front of the still standing building was ignored.

But Americans were sitting ducks for their deception, as they always are. Americans, self-righteous, content in the goodness of their country with the belief reinforced by patriotism and flag-waving were pleased to believe that they were attacked, as President Bush said, because America is so good.

One wonders if today, after 21 years of Identity Politics, Aversive Racism, Critical Race Theory, transgender theory, the NY Times' 1619 Project, the demonization of our Founding Fathers, destruction of their reputations and removal of their statues, and the glorification of perversity, Americans would still have the confidence in their goodness to fall victim to another 9/11 deception?

Perhaps they would. Many of them seem to have fallen for "we have to save the liberty of Ukraine from Putin," by which is really meant is that "we must save the Biden family's and the Democrats' money laundering operation in Ukraine." The insouciant Americans sent over billions of dollars, and the money comes back, with a cut taken out for Zelensky and his henchmen, to the Democrats for advice, consulting fees, facilitators of wartime needs.

In recorded history there have been corrupt empires, but the American one takes the cake. It might yet take our lives.

First published on September 11, 2022.

An Orchestrated Fake "Covid Pandemic" Was Used to Destroy Health, Civil Liberty and the Doctor/Patient Relationship

Dear Readers, give the extraordinary coercive Covid vaccination program a moment of thought. What explains the emphasis, even the use of tyrannical methods in free societies, to force vaccination on populations when even Big Pharma and the corrupt medical establishment only claim a short-run and steeply declining protection from the vaccine? According to the medical establishment itself, double-vaxxed is no longer protection. Booster shots are needed every six months for the rest of your life.

This is especially puzzling when we consider the known facts that (1) The mortality of Covid is very low. It kills mainly those with co-morbidities and those who are untreated or wrongly treated. (2) The vaccine reduces our natural immunity. (3) The vaccine causes a large number of adverse reactions including deaths and lifelong disabilities. The CDC and WHO admit that the adverse reactions reporting system vastly underreports deaths and adverse reactions from the vaccine. No vaccine or medicine ever before in history has been kept in use that produced even a tiny fraction of the reported deaths and injuries. (4) The vaccine causes variants that are immune to the vaccine and to the weakened immune system of the vaccinated. New vaccines are needed to deal with the new variants, producing still more new variants. (5) The medical establishment has blocked to the extent of its ability the treatment of Covid with two known, safe, effective, and inexpensive medicines – Ivermectin and HCQ. Doctors who have saved lives with these medicines have been fired for using them. (6) Distinguished and renowned scientific and medical experts, including Nobel laureates, have been censored and deplatformed for warning about the dangerous vaccine and advocating effective treatment instead. (7) The media speaks with one lying voice that vaccination is our only hope. (8)

Evidence from a number of countries (I have reported it) demonstrates that Covid cases and deaths rise with vaccination and that the majority of cases and deaths for most age groups are the vaccinated. (9) The science is clear that the vaccinated spread the virus as easily, or more so, than the unvaccinated. (10) Indeed, the evidence is clear that the unvaccinated relying on natural immunity are better protected than the vaccinated.

With these known, established scientific facts, what is the justification for mass vaccination? Why the emphasis on vaccinating children when it is known that the spike protein attacks ovaries and testes unless the plan is to reduce fertility? Why can ignorant talking heads on TV who can barely spell their own name feel secure attacking renowned scientists who are telling us the truth?

There are certainly many sound reasons to conclude that the "Covid pandemic" is an orchestrated plot.

What are the obvious elements of the plot? (1) Profits forever for Big Pharma, the medical school recipients of Big Pharma grants, the profits of patents shared with NIH and NIH personnel, campaign contributions for Senators, Representatives and presidential candidates. (2) The use of fear to remove civil liberty protections and extend control over people. These two elements are obvious.

The third element of the plot is almost as obvious but much harder for many people to believe – population reduction. Before scoffing, ask yourself: (1) why vaccinate children, who are essentially unaffected by Covid, with a vaccine known to attack the reproductive system and to cause abortions. (2) Why vaccinate anyone when there are known, safe, and inexpensive cures? (3) Why attack these cures as dangerous and strive to prevent their use? How can the medical establishment claim safety and caution for blocking Ivermectin and HCQ when it has unleashed a dangerous experimental vaccine on the world's population? (4) Why suppress the warnings of renowned experts? If the vaccine was the only solution or even a solution, it could stand public discussion.

Consider that the World Economic Forum has had a half century to indoctrinate and brainwash business and other leaders. Founded January 24, 1971, the annual meeting in Davos has become a prestigious event. Leaders compete for invitations as attendance is a sign of prestige. The World Economic Forum is financed by 1,000 multi-billion dollar global corporations whose leaders have been sold on the "Great Reset" comprised of population reduction and the termination of national sovereignty and human autonomy. The "Great Reset" is a prescription for tyranny.

The orchestrated push for universal vaccination is so extreme that countries formerly considered part of the "free world" are now totalitarian states – witness Australia, New Zealand, Canada, Italy. The effort to extend the tyranny into France and Germany is meeting with strong public resistance. In America the main resistance comes from nurses and other medical-related personnel who have witnessed the devastating impact of the vaccine on those injected.

Every person needs to consider the implication of silencing independent experts who know the truth while ignorant talking heads dictate the official narrative.

When truth is murdered, so is all freedom, all morality, all justice. Are you just going to sit there and let it happen?

First published on November 1, 2021.

Covid: A Summary

Today in Florida the only places you need a mask are offices of medical conglomerates, such as Ascension (Sacred Heart), a hospital group that also has doctor's offices where the MD is hired and not in private practice, and Quest Diagnostics where medical tests are performed. In bureaucratic organizations, once a rule is introduced the enforcement bureaucracy tends to retain it.

As the news narrative shifted overnight from the "Covid crisis" to the "Ukrainian crisis," that is, from one deception to another, the "Russian threat" has replaced the "Covid threat" before people understand what was done to them.

Covid was a threat, not so much in itself as in the protocols enforced to combat it. Most of the people who died did so because they were denied effective treatment with Hydroxychloroquine and Ivermectin for the sole purpose of profit for pharmaceutical companies and profit for those, such as Tony Fauci, associated with them. The emergency use authorization of the untested mRNA "vaccines" could only happen because "medical authorities" declared that there were no known treatments or cures for Covid. To make this falsehood stick, scientists on Big Pharma's payroll wrote "studies" published in prestigious medical journals by gullible or corrupt editors falsely characterizing the known cures as dangerous and ineffective. To be clear, people died from lack of treatment.

The mRNA "vaccines" are not vaccines in the normal meaning of the word. As evidence conclusively shows, the "vaccines" turn the vaccinated person's immune system into a weapon against the person's health, producing in many severe adverse reactions and deaths, and makes the vaccinated more susceptible to Covid. A large amount of evidence, much of it posted on this website and available in thoroughly documented form in Robert F. Kennedy Jr.'s book, The Real Anthony

Fauci, indicates that the mRNA "vaccines" are more dangerous than Covid.

It is likely that the alleged "pandemic" was an orchestration. The falsehood that the virus originated in a bat to human transfer in a market in Wuhan China has been disproved. It is a manufactured virus. It is a fact revealed by NIH documents that Tony Fauci financed "gain-of-function" research first at the University of North Carolina and then at the Wuhan laboratory from which the virus allegedly escaped. There is circumstantial evidence that the research at Wuhan was financed as a cover-story for the intentional release of the virus for profit and control purposes. Simulations of the "pandemic" were conducted just prior to the appearance of the virus, and the protocols followed the procedures established by the simulation. This will never be investigated.

The only purposes served by the lockdowns and mask mandates, both ineffective in preventing Covid transmission, was to train and accustom populations to obey mandates that violate constitutionally protected civil liberty. The vaccine mandates are strictly medical crimes in violation of the Nuremberg Laws preventing coercive testing on human populations. There are legal efforts underway to hold those responsible for vaccine mandates accountable, but no government will indict itself or its own public health authorities.

In his book, Robert Kennedy describes the massive conflicts of interest between the NIH, CDC, FDA, and WHO and the pharmaceutical industry. In short, the so-called "public health agencies" are just shills for Big Pharma. The occasional fines are just window dressing to give the appearance of enforcement, but no pharmaceutical employee, whether executive or scientist, is ever indicted for inflicting death and injury. As Kennedy puts it: "By all accounts, Anthony Fauci has implemented a system of dysfunctional conflicts and a transactional culture that have made NIAID a seamless appendage of Big Pharma. There is simply no daylight between NIAID and the drug makers. It's impossible to say where Pharma ends and NIAID begins."

Several decades ago the University of Chicago economist George Stigler pointed out that the problem with regulation is that the regulatory agencies are sooner or later captured by the regulated industry and become servants of the industries they were created to regulate. This has happened in the United States, and the purest example is the pharmaceutical industry.

First published on April 26, 2022.

The Covid "vaccine" Is an Intentional Effort at World Genocide

Never before have there been massive excess deaths following vaccination.

Never before have there been children, young adults, athletes in their prime, entertainers, dropping dead "cause unknown" following vaccination.

Of course, the cause is known. The leading doctors and medical scientists of our time – which excludes health agency bureaucrats, such as Fauci, who serve as marketing agents for Big Pharma and corrupt, politicized state medical boards and HMOs – have explained why and how the mRNA "vaccines," which are not vaccines, kill, destroy the immune system, and cause health injuries. What is not known is why some die immediately after receiving the deadly substance, others a month later, and others remain, so far, alive. Some researchers think the content of the "vaccines" differed by lot, and some think some of the jabs were placebos for the purpose of producing an uninjured cadre to tout the safety of the jabs.

Professor Michel Chossudovsky has collected a number of videos documenting the widespread sufferings and deaths of the vaccinated [1]. It is not the unvaccinated who are "mysteriously" dropping dead all over the world. It is the vaccinated.

Yet the coverup continues. The western media – a collection of whores – are at work covering up for themselves as well as for Fauci, Biden, Bill Gates, Big Pharma, the FDA, NIH, CDC, and the utterly corrupt and irresponsible medical profession. Big Pharma and the FDA continue to push jabbing babies with the killer vaccine, and there are still parents so utterly stupid and insouciant that they participate in the murder of their own children.

With people all over the world so stupid and so blindly trusting of authority, we can see why the Satanic Bill Gates and Satanic Klaus Schwab are confident that they can succeed in reducing the world population and effecting their Great Reset.

What do I mean when I say Gates and Schwab are Satanic? Think about it this way. From time to time when discussing the subject, someone will say that people can be so awful they can understand why some would want to genocide them. I ask them if they would be willing to push the genocide button, and they say "no." They understand that they have no right to cause people's deaths in behalf of their opinion or a climate or ideological agenda. The difference between them and Bill Gates and Klaus Schwab is that Gates and Schwab are willing and eager to push the genocide button. What is so horrifying is that this willingness has acquired a high moral position. Exterminating people has become the way to save the planet.

The perpetrators of this mass murder are confident that their crime is too huge to be recognized as such. Naive populations simply won't believe that "their" governments would do this to them. No one wants to admit that they executed their own family members and their own children by blindly trusting "authorities" who had announced their genocide agenda in advance.

In the United States only a tiny percentage of the people have any idea what is happening. The time and energy of the population is used up in making ends meet and in entertaining themselves. They fall for one transparent crime after another. Whatever government announces they accept – President John Kennedy's assassination, Senator Robert Kennedy's assassination, the Gulf of Tonkin, 9/11, Saddam Hussein's weapons of mass destruction, Covid pandemic, "safe and effective" Covid vaccine. They never learn.

Now they face genocide, and they still haven't learned. The perpetrators of mass genocide are still in control. If it is not genocide, tell me what it is when distinguished medical scientists warm in advance about the mRNA "vaccine" and are censored and punished, when the inventor of the PCR "Covid test" states that the test does not indicate the presence of the virus and is ignored, when the evidence of the harmful effects of the "vaccine" are kept secret by Pfizer and the FDA, when medical doctors are prevented from treating Covid with known cures Ivermectin and HCQ, when pharmacies refuse to fill doctors' prescriptions for the cures, when illegal and unconstitutional mandates are used to force citizens under threat of loss of job to submit to being injected, when no official attention is paid to the massive increase in excess deaths among the vaccinated, when the media carries on a deceptive campaign of lies and propaganda?

Americans – indeed the world – are faced with a monstrous criminal enterprise. Do they have the strength and intelligence to recognize it? Are they going to do anything about it?

First published on January 8, 2023.

[1]. "The Covid "Killer Vaccine". People Are Dying All Over the World. It's A Criminal Undertaking"
https://www.globalresearch.ca/the-covid-killer-vaccine-people-are-dying-all-over-the-world-its-a-criminal-undertaking/5800358

The Proof Is In: The Election Was Stolen

I have read enough of the fraud reports, affidavits, and statements from election security and forensic experts to be comfortable in my conclusion that the election was stolen. But I am not confident that anything will be done about the fraudulent election. The American elite no longer believe in democracy. Consider, for example, the World Economic Forum's Great Reset. It is anti-democratic, as is globalism. Democracy is in the way of elite agendas. Indeed, the reasson the elite despise Trump is that he bases himself in the people.

For those of you who find it too technical and voluminous to read through the massive evidence of election fraud, here is a brief summary:

Electoral fraud was organized in all of the states. The purpose was not to try to steal the red states, but to make the vote look closer than the expected pattern in order to provide cover for extensive fraud in the critical swing states.

The voting machines were programmed to allocate votes with a bias toward Biden. The result was to cut back Trump's margin of victory in red states. In swing states more extensive measures were used. The Biden bias programmed in the voting machines was raised. As a backup, large numbers of fraudulent mail-in ballots were accumulated in the Democrat-controlled cities in the swing states – Milwaukee, Detroit, and Philadelphia. Although Georgia is a red state, the same occurred in Democrat-controlled Atlanta. The reason voting was stopped in the middle of the night in these cities was to prepare the mail-in ballots necessary to overtake Trump's sizeable lead and enter them into the count. This is a time when poll watchers were told to go home, and it is a period when both Democrat and Republican watchers observed numerous acts of fraud of every description. You can review the types of fraud in the references at the end of this article.

There are proven votes from the grave, from unregistered people, from out-of-state people. There are back-dated mail-in ballots. There are mail-in ballots without a crease, that is, ballots never folded and placed in an envelope, and so on and on. There are places where the vote exceeds the number of registered voters.

A number of independent unbiased experts have reported that the Biden vote spikes in the early hours of the morning are either impossible or so improbable as to have a very low probability of occurring. For them to occur simultaneously in different states falls outside the range of believability.

It is clear that the voting procedures imposed by Democrats in Pennsylvania are in violation of the Pennsylvania state constitution. A Pennsylvania state judge has permitted that suit to go forward and gave her opinion that it would succeed. I am confident that the corrupt Pennsylvania state Supreme Court will overturn her ruling.

If following all of this is too demanding for your time and energy, fall back on common sense:

Consider that Joe Biden's Twitter account has 20 million followers. Trump's Twitter account has 88.8 million followers.

Consider that Joe Biden's Facebook account has 7.78 million followers. Trump's Facebook account has 34.72 million followers.

How likely is it that a person with four to five times the following of his rival lost the election?

Consider that Joe Biden, declared by the biased presstitutes to be president by landslide, gave a Thanksgiving Day message and only 1,000 people watched his live statement. Where is the enthusiasm?

Consider that Trump's campaign appearances were heavily attended and that Biden's were avoided. Somehow a candidate who could not draw supporters to his campaign appearances won the presidency.

Consider that despite Biden's total failure to animate voters during the presidential campaign, he received 15 million more votes than Barack Obama did in his 2012 re-election.

Consider that Biden won despite underperforming Hillary Clinton's 2016 vote in every urban US county, but outperformed Clinton in Democrat-controlled Detroit, Milwaukee, Atlanta, and Philadelphia, the precise cities where the most obvious and most blatant electoral fraud was committed.

Consider that Biden won despite receiving a record low share of the Democrat primary vote compared to Trump's share of the Republican primary vote.

Consider that Biden won despite Trump bettering his 2016 vote by ten million votes and Trump's record support from minority voters.

Consider that Biden won despite losing the bellwether counties that have always predicted the election outcome and the bellwether states of Ohio and Florida.

Consider that Biden won in Georgia, a completely red state with a red governor and legislature both House and Senate. Somehow a red state voted for a blue president.

Consider that Biden won despite the Democrats losing representation in the House.

Consider that in Pennsylvania 47 memory cards containing more than 50,000 votes are missing.

Consider that in Pennsylvania 1.8 million ballots were mailed out to voters, but 2.5 million mail-in ballots were counted.

Consider that the presstitutes have zero interest in this massive list of improbables.

Consider that the pressititues, the Democrats, the social media and tech executives, and universities have far more loyalty to getting Trump out of office regardless of the means than they have to democratic outcomes and fair elections. The massive fraud of the 2020 election was only possible because the liberal part of America has divorced American values and has no respect for them. The American liberal is no longer liberal. He has morphed into a fascist who suppresses speech and denies legitimacy to other opinions. Indeed, liberals are so hostile to electoral integrity that they want those who bring evidence of electoral fraud to be imprisoned.

It is educated Americans brainwashed by Critical Race Theory and Identity Politics who are liberals, not the working class who are the real Americans. Red state people are Americans. Blue state people are not. Blue state people demonize real Americans and have branded them racists and misogynists. Real Americans – the majority of the population – are "the Trump deplorables."

The Real Americans have just had their democracy stolen from them by people who have no integrity and no honor.

If the stolen election stands, America falls.

But more than an election has been stolen. The deep state, Democratic National Committee, and media whores did not steal the election because they don't like Trump's hair, or because he is a racist, a misogynist, a Russian agent or caused Covid, or for any of the other false accusations raised against him for four years. Trump is hated because he is anti-establishment. Trump opposes the elite's sacrifice of Americans' jobs and hopes to globalism and the elites' own bulging pocketbooks. Trump opposes the elite's erasure of American monuments and history, such as the New York Times 1619 Project that paints all white Americans racist. Trump objects to the elite's

326

demonization of white Americans and the discrimination that elites enforce against heterosexual white males in schools and employment. Trump stands against Identity Politics, the hate-filled ideology of liberal America. When liberals call Trump a racist, they mean he doesn't share their demonization of white people. If you don't demonize white Americans, you are a racist.

Trump is a populist, a president of ordinary people. Trump is hated, because he was intent on rescuing ordinary Americans from subservience to the agendas of the elite. Unfortunately, being a populist is not enough to overthrow an entrenched elite. Only a revolutionary can do that, and Trump is not a revolutionary leader.

The elite are getting rid of Trump in a way that makes it clear to all presidential candidates in the future that their only choice is to represent the elite. If somehow an anti-establishment person slips in, he will experience the same fate as Trump's four years. The Dominion machines and corrupt Democrat big city regimes will steal his reelection even if enough voters have escaped their intended brainwashing to defend their champion in the voting booths.

Trump's Department of Justice has failed him. So has the FBI, CIA, NSA, and Homeland Security. This is easy to understand. These are establishment institutions. They protect the establishment, not law and justice. Will the judiciary be the next to fail the president and American democracy?

If the stolen election, which is a coup, stands, after Trump no presidential candidate will dare to attempt to represent the American people.

If this stolen election stands, there is no hope that government can be returned to the people.

First published November 30, 2020.

[1]. https://nonperele.com/nolte-rachel-maddow-says-people-who-contest-elections-should-go-to-jail

[2]. "What you've been asking for: A (fairly) complete list of (some of) the most significant claims of 2020 election miscounts, errors or fraud" https://sharylattkisson.com/2020/12/what-youve-been-asking-for-a-fairly-complete-list-of-some-of-the-most-significant-claims-of-2020-election-miscounts-errors-or-fraud/

[3]. "Joe Biden Gets Only 1,000 Viewers to Watch His Thanksgiving Address Live" https://www.thegatewaypundit.com/2020/11/joe-biden-gets-1000-viewers-watch-thanksgiving-address-live-got-80-million-votes-hah-complete-joke/

[4]. "Election Bombshell! the US Constitution Goes to Court" https://www.unz.com/article/election-bomb-shell-the-us-constitution-goes-to-court-or/

[5]. "5 More Ways Joe Biden Magically Outperformed Election Norms" https://thefederalist.com/2020/11/23/5-more-ways-joe-biden-magically-outperformed-election-norms/

[6]. "Trump won record minority support — yet the left is calling it 'racism'" https://nypost.com/2020/11/06/trump-won-record-minority-support-yet-the-left-is-calling-it-racism/

[7]. "PA Data Scientist: I Saw USB Cards Being Uploaded To Voting Machines" https://publicintegrityforum.com/pa-data-scientist-i-saw-usb-cards-being-uploaded-to-voting-machines/?utm_source=Email_marketing&utm_campaign=Content_11.28.20&cmp=1&utm_medium=HTMLEmail

[8]. "DATA: Michigan Analysis Suggests Absentee Votes 'Manipulated By Computer', Flags Hundreds Of Thousands Of Ballots" https://thenationalpulse.com/2020/11/27/michigan-election-fraud-analysis/

[9]. "Republican Arizona State Legislature to Hold 'Urgent' Election Integrity Hearing With Trump's Lawyers" https://www.theepochtimes.com/arizona-state-legislature-to-hold-urgent-election-integrity-hearing-with-trumps-lawyers_3594607.html?utm_source=morningbrief&utm_medium=email&utm_campaign=mb-2020-11-28

[10]. "Data Scientist: 'Weird' Spike in Incomplete Nevada Voter Registrations, Use of 'Casinos' as Home Addresses" https://www.theepochtimes.com/data-scientist-weird-spike-in-incomplete-nevada-voter-registrations-some-using-casinos-as-home-address_3595924.html?utm_source=morningbrief&utm_medium=email&utm_campaign=mb-2020-11-28

[11]. "Anomalies in Vote Counts and Their Effects on Election 2020"
https://votepatternanalysis.substack.com/p/voting-anomalies-2020
[12]. "Thousands in Georgia Registered at Postal, Commercial
Addresses, Portraying Them as Residences, Researcher Says"
https://www.theepochtimes.com/thousands-in-georgia-registered-at-
postal-commercial-addresses-portraying-them-as-residences-
researcher-
says_3592165.html?utm_source=morningbrief&utm_medium=email&
utm_campaign=mb-2020-11-25
[13]. "Google Shifted a 'Minimum' of 6 Million Votes in 2020
Election: Dr. Robert Epstein" https://www.theepochtimes.com/google-
shifted-a-minimum-of-6-million-votes-in-2020-election-dr-robert-
epstein_3592527.html?utm_source=morningbrief&utm_medium=emai
l&utm_campaign=mb-2020-11-25
[14]. "Sidney Powell's Allegations in Georgia Serious Enough to Alter
the Election Results: Expert" https://www.theepochtimes.com/sidney-
powells-allegations-in-georgia-so-serious-any-class-may-alter-the-
election-results-
expert_3596412.html?utm_source=news&utm_medium=email&utm_c
ampaign=breaking-2020-11-28-2
[15].

The "Trump Insurrection" — a Fantasy that Did Not Happen

On October 11, FBI Special Agent Justin Eller testified at the seditious conspiracy trial of four Oath Keepers in federal court. An attorney for the defense asked Eller if in the Oath Keepers' communications that he reviewed there was any indication that the Oath Keepers intended to storm the Capitol or stop the certification of the stolen presidential election. He answered "no" to both questions.

In other words, the FBI and the federal prosecutor had no evidence in support of the charges against the Oath Keepers who were on trial.

Today this is commonplace in America.

Before we go further, let us establish the identity of Oath Keepers. According to the whore media they are far rightwing white supremacists who are a threat to American democracy. But in actual fact they seem to be for the most part military veterans who swore the oath to uphold the Constitution of the United States. As the Oath Keepers were formed for that purpose, why, if they are Oath Keepers, would they violate their oath by conspiring against the United States?

The Democrats know, as does the whore media, that the Democrats stole the last presidential election. The presstitute mantra that "there is no evidence of a stolen election" is demonstrably false from the hard evidence and its presentation by many independent experts. But as the presstitutes say it is not so, it is not so.

People do not know because the whore media have not told them that prior to the vote certification that was to be held on January 6, dissenting Republicans had an opportunity to present evidence that the vote was fraudulent. The Democrats used the "insurrection" that they orchestrated with federal agents to prevent the presentation of the evidence of electoral fraud.

This suited Rino Republicans such as Republican Senate leader Mitch McConnell, who, himself being a member of the Washington Establishment, was both threatened and outraged by Trump's assault on the Washington Establishment. Rino McConnell was instrumental in using the orchestrated "insurrection" to break up the vote certification before the evidence of fraud could be presented.

If Oath Keepers are aligned with Trump against the Establishment, which is the case, why would they act to prevent the presentation of the evidence that the election was stolen? It makes no sense. In other words, the Oath Keepers had no motive for the behavior for which they are on trial.

As the joint party Establishment and its media whores control the explanations, few Americans are aware that the allegedly vote certification session that Oath Keepers are accused of disrupting was also a certification to determine whether the election was fraudulent. It was the presentation of evidence of electoral fraud that was blocked by using the cover of a "Trump Insurrection."

An insurrection needs insurrectionists. The Democrats had none to put on trial except the federal agents at the Capitol who tried to incite incidents while President Trump addressed the rally at the Washington Monument a mile or more away. How could there be an insurrection at the Capitol when the Trump supporters were attending a rally at the Washington Monument?

The whore media, of course, never asked this question. And neither did federal prosecutors prosecuting innocent people.

Where did the Democrats get the needed "insurrectionists"?

They got them from social media, cell phone, and email providers who turned over to the FBI social media messages and emails that indicated who attended the Trump rally. Americans who attended the rally were designated "potential insurrectionists." Those who filtered down to the Capitol became the "insurrectionists." The "Trump Insurrection" was the first unarmed insurrection in history.

According to media reports there are 600 "Trump insurrectionists" serving prison sentences. The worse offense seems to have been to take your photo sitting in Nancy Pelosi's chair and posting it on social media, clearly a non-intelligent thing to do, but hardly an indication of insurrection.

Some of the imprisoned insurrectionists copped a plea, so the Democrats use these "confessions" as proof that there was a Trump insurrection. But in America today all sorts of people cop a plea, both the innocent and the guilty. The reason is that defending oneself is extremely expensive and fraught with high risk. Few defendants have the financial means or toleration of risk to face a jury trial. In times past juries were protective of defendants; today juries are wrapped around the prosecutor's finger.

Those without resources are dependent on government subsidized public defenders. Public defenders who defend their clients are not assigned clients by the system as they waste prosecutors and judges' time in jury trials when the system wants cases quickly disposed of with plea bargains. The incentive of public defendants is to encourage their clients to cop a plea.

Defense attorneys' convincing argument to their clients is that if you demand a jury trial, you face these problems that your attorney can do nothing about. First, you make problems for the prosecutor, whose career and political aspirations depend on his conviction rate. Trials take time, during which the prosecutor could have achieved numerous plea bargain convictions, thus boosting his all-important conviction tally. The prosecutor can respond to your refusal to cop a plea by enlarging the criminal accusations against you. Prosecutors have the ability to hire people to testify falsely against you. If the prosecutor wants you as an addition to his conviction rate, I cannot help you. Let me make a plea for you that will get you off lightly compared to the sentence you will get if you go to trial. Your innocence aside, you are going to jail regardless. The only question is for how long. I can shorten your imprisonment if you cooperate with me.

This is the way American "justice" works. It works the same way for rich and poor. The same thing happened to billionaire Michael Milken, to billionaire Leona Helmsley, and to centimillionaire Martha Stewart. They were all falsely accused, they all had the best and most prestigious attorneys, and they were all convicted and went to prison, Milken with a plea bargain and Helmsley with a trial. And their prosecutor, Rudy Giuliani, used their high profile convictions to become Mayor of New York.

Second, protesting your innocence you make problems for the judge whose docket is already full and crowded. You are making the judge's life stressful by making him have a trial that might take a week or longer while his docket builds.

Third, you have close to zero chance with a jury. Juries composed of brainwashed Americans who see themselves threatened by crime are predisposed, unless black, to believe the prosecutor, and if the defendant is white, the blacks on the jury are all predisposed to convicting him for being a racist. It would be interesting to know how many white defendants have been found innocent by black jurors.

In short, a jury trial angers prosecutor, judge, and your defense counsel who wants to collect his fee and move on to his next fee by having you cooperate with the system. Plea bargains are so prevalent that according to the US Department of Justice, 96% of felony cases are resolved by plea bargains.

The plea bargain that the defendant has to make does not have to have anything whatsoever to do with the charges that are the basis for his indictment. He can be accused of A and confess to B. All the prosecutor and judge need in order to avoid a time-consuming trial is an admission to something. Some years ago I read that most people in prison are there on charges that are not in their original indictment. They were in prison on plea bargains that provided shorter sentences in exchange for admitting to offenses that were not even charged in the original indictments.

In the Unites States "justice" is a weapon to discipline and to punish people who are out of step with official narratives. The Oath Keepers are out of step, because they point to the erosion of the US Constitution, still a governing, though much weakened, document.

In the United States, the British Isles, and Europe the presstitutes can destroy anyone – even a President of the United States – by printing lies about him. Look at what has happened to Trump. Look at what has happened to Julian Assange. Look at what has happened to the medical scientists and doctors who were on the side of the people instead of on the side of Big Pharma and its marketing agents such as Fauci, Biden, NIH, CDC, FDA.

In the Western world today nothing is based on truth. Facts are inconvenient for the ruling elites and are discarded in George Orwell's 1984 Memory Hole.

The failure of the American people to correct the situation on November 8 and the success the Democrats have had in stealing another election tells us that the only future Americans and the entire Western world face is tyranny.

In America it is only patriots who are persecuted. Voters in Pennsylvania, if the election was not stolen, actually elected a US Senator who wants to release the criminals from prison. It is not the innocents wrongly convicted that he wants to release, it is the real criminals who rob, rape, and murder.

Before America lost its way, who would ever have thought that Americans would elect a US Senator who believes that it is robbers, rapists, and murderers who are abused and not their victims.

Sodom and Gomorrah was once regarded as the epitome of evil, but not today. Sodom and Gomorrah pales in comparison to the evil that rules the West today.

And the Russians still place hopes in "negotiations" with the Evil Empire. How can such a self-deceived people as Russians survive?

First published on November 14, 2022.

The Disastrous Events of the year 2022 Will Plague Us for as Long as We Exist

2022 planted the seeds for tyranny and death. My analysis today will focus on only four of the many terrible events of 2022.

One is the FBI raid on President Trump's home.
One is the second stolen national election.
One is the war against Russia that is leading to Armageddon.
One is the deception about the effectiveness and safety of the Covid mRNA "vaccine."

The unprecedented raid on President Trump's home revealed the Gestapo State that has replaced American Democracy. Few comprehend the threat that the raid reveals. First there is the disrespect shown a recent President of the United States who clearly has far more public support than any president since Ronald Reagan. If a President of the United States can be treated in such a high-handed way, what prospect do the rest of us have?

The raid was not only beyond the pale, it was gratuitous in its justification. The FBI had access to the documents and had gone through them previously. The documents were not being withheld from inspection. The story planted in the presstitute media that Trump left the documents lying around in Mar-a-Largo for Russian spies on his staff to photo is absurd. Trump has Secret Service protection, and the agents would certainly notice any top secret documents lying around on the furniture. If Russian agents had penetrated Trump's household staff, the CIA would have warned him. That media actually discussed this fabrication as if it were real reveals the incompetence and dishonesty of the media.

Normally, presidents and high government officials do not concern themselves with documents unless they are writing memoirs. They don't have time for documents. Most of what is signed off on is from advice not from reading. Presidential appointees and I assume presidents are entitled to copies of all documents that moved through their offices. I would have needed a moving and storage service to deal with documents to which I was entitled during my time at the Treasury. I very much doubt Trump knows what documents are in the boxes. I would have advised him not to take documents packed by others as anything could be planted on him. All documents should have gone to a presidential library, which once set up was probably where the documents were headed.

The "raid" by a FBI SWAT team was an orchestrated political event. In a political system where there is accountable government, the FBI director and the attorney general would have been fired for political use of a police agency. The fact that they got away with it shows that the days of accountable government in the United States are past.

The purpose of the raid was to create the image of Trump in the public mind as a criminal, so that the pubic already saw him that way and it would be old hat when the criminal referral from the Democrats in the House and subsequent Department of Justice indictment materialized. Any jurors involved would be accustomed to Trump as criminal and have the same view as the prosecutor. This is what happened to Derick Chauvin.

Not many understood what was happening in front of their eyes. Democrats and Trump haters were simply thrilled that the orange man was being had. Trump supporters simply saw biased Democrats and biased media. This was the way the public saw the transformation of a federal police force subject to the rule of law into an unaccountable Gestapo political operation dedicated to the Democrats' seizure of power by eliminating the opponent. This is how the police were transformed in the Third Reich. A question before us is whether the audacious raid on an American president's home could have happened if the Deep State had been held accountable in the past for its crimes. But having got away with so much despite overwhelming evidence of

Deep State guilt – for example, the murders of President Kennedy, Senator Kennedy and Martin Luther King, the Bay of Tonkin, 9/11, Saddam Hussein's weapons of mass destruction, and two stolen national elections – to set up a president for indictment on false charges is not a big step.

Trump's reelection was stolen after four years of vilification of President Trump while in office accused as a Russian agent elected by the Kremlin's interference in the election, a charge exploited by the presstitutes and Democrats for years during the Russiagate investigation. Russiagate was followed by two attempted impeachments, and by an orchestrated "Jan. 6 insurrection," a fabrication still ongoing with the House's criminal referral of Trump to the Department of Justice (sic). Trump's reelection meant 4 more years of the same, and people were tired of it. Therefore, despite overwhelming evidence that the Democrats stole the election, the public acquiesced in the theft. The 2022 national election did not involve the president, so the public was less moved by its theft. Moreover, the Republicans, despite the theft, recaptured the House. But the inattention to the theft paves the road for more thefts.

The theft of the Arizona governorship from Kari Lake is completely obvious. In Maricopa County, Arizona's most populous, voting machines failed to function in the precincts known to be Republican. Voting lines were hours long. The Republicans who suffered them were given paper ballots dropped into a box that the Democrat election officials said would be counted later. When later arrived, it turned out that the uncounted ballots were "accidentally" mixed in with the counted ballots and could not be separated.

Even this was not enough to elect Kari Lake's opponent, who was serving as Election Commissioner and controlling every step of the voting and counting. So for three days running the vote count stopped for 19 hours, 15 hours, 17 hours while Democrats forged Democrat votes.

When presented with the evidence, the Republican judge said that whereas all these failures occurred, there was no proof that they were intentional.

To be clear, a Republican judge ruled that as long as Democrats steal elections accidentally, it is OK.

So expect more accidentally stolen elections.

What two stolen national elections in a row means is that the electorate is powerless. It is unable to put into office politicians who represent the voters and the country's interest. The electorate is powerless against the organized private interests, the ideologues who are erasing America, and the Deep State. Elections have become a democratic cover for a stolen route to a one-party state.

So what is the Deep State? We have some idea but we don't know precisely. We don't know because political science in the universities and in high school civics classes if they still exist, teaches about what might once have existed years ago – democratically elected leaders who represent the people and the national interest.

Today there is no such process. The President, House, and Senate are elected by the campaign contributions of powerful interests. It is the interests of these interests, not those of voters, to which politicians respond.

Together with these private interests, permanent government networks between some of these interests, social media and the remnants of print and TV media, and established government bureaucracies such as the CIA and FBI control the explanations that the public receives.

When the media is in service to government and is not watching government and holding government accountable, there can be no accountable government.

The fact that Democrats, with little public opposition, have succeeded in stealing two national elections proves the point.

Whether any of this matters depends on how determined are the neoconservatives who control US foreign policy to pursue Washington's hegemony over the world in the face of Russian and Chinese opposition, and how long Putin will continue to drag out his "limited military operation in Ukraine," thus enabling Washington to become too involved to let go. Putin does not realize it, but he has empowered Washington to turn his ill-considered, indeed mindless, limited operation into a general war that leads to nuclear Armageddon.

Trump and Putin share gullibility in common. Both have been slow to understand the Satanic forces confronting them. The consequences will be horrendous.

The fourth disastrous event is the Covid deception. 2022 is the year when it became completely clear that the Western medical establishment, media, and politicians lied through their teeth about the dangers of Covid and the safety and effectiveness of the mRNA "vaccines." Thanks to independent medical scientists, who stood their ground despite being censored, discredited, and punished, we know for certain that the Covid "vaccines" are neither safe nor effective. Moreover, the Pfizer internal documents forced into release by federal court order show conclusively that Pfizer knew the "vaccine" was deadly. As Pfizer shared the documents with its marketing agent, the US Food and Drug administration, the FDA also knew, yet gave approval to the Emergency Use Authorization of the mRNA "vaccines." As Professor Michel Chossudovsky has pointed out, the failure by Pfizer and the FDA to recall the "vaccines" based on Pfizer's own internal study is mass murder. At this point, very little is being done to hold Pfizer and the FDA accountable for murdering millions of people.

Almost all who died from Covid died from lack of treatment. The medical protocols imposed prevented doctors from treating the virus with two known cures – HCQ and Ivermectin. Some doctors in independent practice refused to follow the imposed protocols and saved thousands of lives. In other parts of the world – Brazil, India, Africa – use of Ivermectin both as cure and preventative essentially eliminated Covid as a health threat. But in the "scientific" Western world, the cures were obstructed by official medical authorities. The Lancet, formerly a respected British medical journal, today a marketing shill for Big Pharma, denounced Brazil's use of HCQ and Ivermectin as "an anti-scientific decision" and accused "a populist government" of "undermining science" [1].

There is no longer any doubt. Following the vaccination campaign, excess deaths rose dramatically, and the excess deaths are among the vaccinated. Still nothing is being done to help the millions of people whose health has been adversely impacted by the mRNA "vaccines."

The orchestrated "pandemic" is a massive crime against humanity. There has been no accountability and no help for the injured, which leaves the "pandemic" with the smell of organized genocide. If so, we have reached the point where crimes against humanity is the official policy of the West.

How does a civilization recover when morality has been stripped of authority? What has happened to us that Pfizer's profits are elevated above life and public health, that executive branch mandates can override the US Constitution and the judgments of doctors and patients, that official narratives can be enforced by censorship? Clearly, the foundation of our society is rotten and our civilization is collapsing.

In our society truth is dismissed as misinformation, normality is demonized as oppression, and perversity is normalized as liberation. Transgender propagandizing of children is now common fare in public schools and public libraries. This child abuse, ignored by Child Protective Services, is possible because laws require equal access to all organizations, depraved or normal. The drag queen lobby has mastered the ability to manipulate the system. The pretense is that it is just a matter of inclusion, but in fact it is revolution. Sexual relations between a heterosexual man and a heterosexual woman is "heterosexual capitalist oppression," but sex between adults and children is "the sexual liberation of children." The drag queen agenda is to undermine traditional notions of sexuality, to replace the biological family, and to arouse transgressive sexual desires in young children, and it is being financed with taxpayers' money. You can read about this in Christopher Rufo's article in the Autumn 2022 City Journal.

So, just as prominent doctors and medical scientists who cured Covid patients with Ivermectin and HCQ are punished for saving lives by having their licenses and certifications stolen by bureaucrats whose protocols resulted in mass murder, parents who protest against public schools indoctrinating their children into sexual perversity are thrown out of school board meetings. This is what I mean when I said morality has been stripped of authority.

Authority rests with those who are normalizing perversity. Authority rests with the Satanists. It is going to be very difficult to get it away from them.

First published on January 2, 2023.

[1]. "Brazil's COVID-19 guidelines: political hijack of public health" https://www.thelancet.com/journals/lancet/article/PIIS0140-6736(22)00338-5/fulltext

Index of Names

The Gifts They Leave Behind

By April L. Rohde

I dedicate this book to Tom with love and gratitude in my heart. Thank you for the many gifts you gave me to show me that life does go on and we are connected even more in spirit than we were before. My life has been forever changed.

To our boys, I hope you always remember how much you are loved. Keep those happy memories we shared close to your heart because that love is what we take with us. I love you both very much.

Table of Contents

Introduction

You might be wondering what possible gifts could there be in losing someone you love. I would have thought the same thing, as a matter of fact; I never wanted to discuss loss in any way at all. It was a subject that I didn't like to think about or talk about.

I remember once as a young girl about the age of nine hearing that somebody had died. I had never really given death much thought. At first I felt shocked, so many questions popped into my head and I wondered why we had to lose those we love. I could never imagine love being gone, but something within my heart knew differently, but my mind had questions. A gentle voice came into my head and said, "Don't worry, you'll get the answers you seek someday" I was able to leave behind the many questions I had that day and continued on with my life. I had a gut feeling that what we perceived as death wasn't the final conclusion. There was a lot more to the story than that!

Tumor Discovered

Little did I know that my first loss would be the loss of my best friend and the love of my life. Tom and I had been married for seventeen years and had two boys when he was diagnosed with a brain tumor. Tom had been really sick for almost six months. He was always getting bad headaches, often feeling very tired and nauseated. We had no idea what it was. Several doctor visits came up with nothing; and at one point we were even told he had Lyme disease.

It was in December of 2004, when Tom's brother offered us tickets to see the Green Bay Packers in Lambeau field. I asked Tom, "Are you sure you want to go; you have been so sick?" but Tom had always wanted to see the Packers play in Green Bay, so I knew there was no talking him out of it. The drive up was hard and I could see how bad Tom was feeling, but Tom had a way of keeping upbeat despite the pain he was in. We had to stop several times at rest areas because his headaches were making him very nauseated.

The whole trip was just a blur for me. I just could not stop worrying about what was making him sick. I remember thinking as we sat in the

living room at his brother's house, "Should I tell someone?" It was hard keeping this concern all to myself, but Tom never liked to talk about being sick. I looked over at Tom across the room, and as if he had read my mind, he gave me a smile to assure me that everything was fine. I smiled back weakly, forcing my worries aside for the time being.

The night of the game was bitter cold, but we had seats behind the glass, so we were all nice and warm. The Packer game was great. I watched Tom as he looked out at the football field, his eyes soaking in the whole scene. He looked so happy, but my heart was aching. What was wrong with him? I just felt so helpless. I just wanted him well again. I admired his strength more than anything because I knew he was in pain.

After the game was over, we went to the souvenir shop and we all bought something. Tom insisted I get these Packer earrings that I doubted I would ever wear, but he wanted each of us to get something to remember this trip. The boys got baseball caps and some posters. Although I had my doubts about taking this trip, I was so glad we went. Tom had such a good time. It was to be his last visit home before he passed and he got to see his whole family one last time.

The trip back was again, stop after stop. Tom's headaches were getting worse. When we got back home I told him to call the doctor and get another appointment. The next day while I was at work, he called me

and told me that he was passing out and that his head hurt really bad. He asked me to come home. By the time I got home our son had called 911 and we went to the emergency room. They did a series of tests and took some x-rays to finally find out that the mystery illness that had plagued him for months was a large brain tumor.

When we heard the news, I felt my heart stop. I saw Tom close his eyes and saw tears fall to the side. I didn't know what to do or say, I squeezed Tom's hand and told him that everything would be okay, then I quickly left the emergency room and went outside. I needed to breathe. My stomach hurt and so did my heart. I told myself to be strong for Tom, but I could not stop crying. It was just a few days before Christmas that we found out and our entire lives changed.

Tom had a seven-hour surgery in January to remove the tumor and was kept in ICU for about a week. I remember going to visit every time I could during visiting hours. Tom was pretty scared when he realized he could not swallow after the surgery. It broke my heart to see what he was going through. I couldn't stay the night with him in ICU, so I would call up before I went to bed and talk to the nurses to check on him every night. I prayed every night that Tom would be okay and still be able to do all the things he loved to do. Tom had a feeding tube because he could not swallow; he had slight paralysis on the right side, and could not hear out of his right ear. He also spoke in a whisper. The doctors assured us that most of this would go away, but somehow we

could not feel this to be the case, but we remained hopeful.

"Unusual Day"

After Tom's surgery and him finally getting out of ICU and back into a regular room, I decided to take a break and go have lunch with my mom. The weatherman called for snow, but only a slight dusting, so I was not worried at all about not getting back. Tom's mom who had come down from Wisconsin to help us with the boys was on her way to see Tom at the hospital. Just like with all pieces of a puzzle, things were coming together to make for an unusual day, a day that was written about in the newspapers; that wreaked havoc on the traffic that virtually froze an entire city.

After lunch we came out to find it had snowed and the roads were very slick. What was supposed to be a dusting was mixed with sleet and snow and made the roads almost impossible to drive on. Schools were letting out due to the dangerous road conditions, but it was a little too late. As everyone was leaving work and school early the conditions were proving to be quite treacherous. People were sliding off the roads and the traffic was gridlocked in many places.

I remember driving very slowly home and so relieved to make it. The boys were home safe too, so with Tom's mom en-route to the hospital, I knew there was no traveling back there for me. Tom kept calling me,

insisting that I stay home. I assured him that I was home to stay, but he kept saying, "I mean it April, I don't want you to try to drive back here, it's dangerous!" I laughed and assured him again, "Tom, I promise I won't."

Tom's mom finally made it to the hospital, but as she parked, she noticed that she had a flat tire. We called to get the car towed, to have the tire fixed, but of course with the snow and the traffic, the tow truck never made it. So, it seemed that Tom's mom and me had switched places for the night.

Tom's mom got to spend some quality time with him. She stayed that night in the waiting room of the hospital. With all the traffic problems, cars on the side of the road, people spending hours in traffic trying to get home, not one person died that day. It was such a freaky little snow storm that snarled up the whole city, but a mother got to spend quality time with her son alone at the hospital. A place I know she didn't like to be, but as fate would have it, it was meant to be.

The next day, things were back to normal, the sun quickly melted the ice and snow. The freak storm was on the front page of the local newspaper and they commented on how the storm and the timing of the cancellations literally brought the city to a halt. I still have that newspaper to this day.

"Circle of Light"

Tom was a very active guy. He loved playing basketball, football, and softball. I knew this was so hard on him. He didn't even want the kids to see him this way. Tom was a fighter though, he wanted to get better so fast, but better would not come. Things only seemed to get worse. Tom was talking about being dizzy and on Friday night he had a seizure. The staff at the hospital didn't want to call it that for some reason, but Tom was literally snoring for like 5 seconds, then he came back to. I even asked several nurses what could possibly cause this and I asked for some additional testing. The nurse had to get the doctors permission first then they ran a few tests and said he was fine.

The rest of the weekend went by without another incident. Tom and I spent time just talking and he was so happy when he was told he could suck on some lollipops. Since he had a feeding tube since surgery, I know it must have been a real treat for him. A few friends came by to visit and a nurse came in that we had not seen before. She looked at Tom and me and said, "I bet you were a football player and you a cheerleader," Tom and I just laughed. I was not a cheerleader and he didn't play much football. She said, "How does such a beautiful couple like you find each other?" We only saw her once and I felt that maybe she wasn't a nurse, but a special messenger sent to be with us during this difficult time. We also had a cleaning lady that we just loved. She seemed to resonate such peace and love. We just adored her.

Everyone was so kind and was really trying to assure us that everything would be okay.

We spent our last night together watching a movie that Tom had said on several occasions he wanted to see. After the movie was over Tom said he wasn't even tired. He seemed to have something on his mind, but I was really tired and told him I was going to bed. Now more than ever I wish I had stayed up that night and talked to him more. Little did I know it would be our last night together.

The next day, was our son's Sixteenth birthday. We got up pretty early and I called to see if Bryan was out of bed yet. Tom's mom said that Bryan was taking a shower, so I said we would call back in a few minutes. Tom had gotten up and went to the restroom and as he was coming back I asked him if he was okay, and he said, "I am fine." This was a question that I asked Tom many times before; his answer was always the same.

As I lay on the cot next to Tom's bed, I was suddenly drawn to a bright circle of light on the ceiling of the room. The circle was slightly larger than a frisbee and inside of it was all these sparkles, shimmering like a million diamonds. I looked out the window to see if something was shining in or if a cup of water was projecting the light, but nothing was around. The sun hadn't even come up just yet. I then asked Tom, "Tom, what is that?" no reply, so I asked once again, "Tom, what is

that?" still, no reply.

I turned around and I see Tom laying down facing the window. He was very still and his gaze was towards the window, but as I looked deeper into his eyes, I sensed he was not completely there. His eyes were empty, I pushed on him, he did not move. Knowing that something was extremely wrong, I ran out to get someone to help. As the nurse entered the room she grabbed Tom's arm and said his name, but he pulled his arm away from her quite strongly. I got the impression that he was experiencing something and she was disturbing him. Was he seeing what I saw on the ceiling? I left the room as I felt myself start to panic. Suddenly other nurses ran in as the code blue siren was activated. The sound was deafening. I remember thinking, "this can't be happening," I started praying and pacing the hall floor, I heard one of the nurses tell someone to call the chaplain, I thought, "Why are they calling the chaplain, what does this mean?"

My greatest fear was happening, the one thing I feared all my life; losing someone I love. I always felt in control, like I kept them safe and protected. I found myself absolutely helpless. I was sitting at a nearby desk when the chaplain showed up. I really didn't want to speak to her, I was upset and her presence reminded me of the possibility that I didn't want to think about.

I called my mom at work and told her to come up quickly that

something was wrong with Tom. As I sat there, the sweet cleaning lady that Tom and I really liked came up to me and told me that Tom wanted to see me. I was rather surprised since the code blue was still going off, but I thought maybe he was better. Looking back I thought it was strange that she told me Tom wanted to see me, even though the room was full of nurses who could have easily came to get me. Plus, even stranger was the fact that Tom still had a breathing tube in his mouth; there was no way he could speak!

As I entered the room, the room was filled with this soft white light. I could not see anything, but I found Tom's hand. He squeezed my hand softly as if to tell me "I'm okay, it's going to be alright." I could not even see Tom's face, even though I was so close to him. As I looked on the other side of Tom's bed I was aware of nurses standing over there, but I could only see their feet because of the light that engulfed everything. The warm light in the room covered everything like a soft blanket. Then I heard the doctor tell Tom to be still. His voice sounded far away and had an echo effect to it. I felt like I was in the way or causing Tom to get upset, so I quickly let go of Tom's hand and left the room.

As I went back out into the hall I noticed there was no white light in the hall or anywhere else; it was just in Tom's room. The chaplain came over to me and guided me into this room that had a large table with chairs, then moments later a doctor came into the room. She looked at

me and said, "I am very sorry, but he didn't make it." "What had she just said?" My heart felt so heavy and my mind could not believe what she had just said.

The words just didn't make sense. I had been with Tom for 20 years, how can it be he is gone? Everything felt wrong; my mind was not able to make sense out of what I just heard. My heart was aching in my chest. I kept hearing a voice saying, "Everything is going to be okay." But everything wasn't okay; Tom was not here.

"Word Soon Traveled"

My son kept calling from school within minutes of Tom's passing. I could not answer. Then I got a call from a friend of mine who called to see if everything was okay because my son was calling her from school and I told her what happened. Word soon traveled and the next time I looked out into the hall I saw many of our friends standing out there, looking down, hearts broken.

Then I thought back to the boys, how could I tell them that Tom was gone? Bryan had continued to call but no one wanted to tell him what happened and neither did I. Finally able to answer the phone Bryan said, "Mom, what is going on, is Dad okay?" and I said, "Bryan, we will come by and pick you up" he persisted, "I know something is wrong, I can feel it," still I said, "We will be there to pick you up soon" I

couldn't even utter the words that Tom was gone. Telling the boys was the worst thing I ever had to do in my life.

I am not sure if I did it in the best way possible, but I did the best I could when I did it. There is no right or wrong when something like this happens, you just do the best you can. How do you tell your kids something like that? They saw their dad as bigger than life; he was so alive and active his whole life. I can't imagine what they must have been feeling and thinking because I could not stand the pain I was feeling.

Later that day I asked Bryan why that particular morning he had constantly called the hospital from school. He said that he was in the band room and saw a ball of light of the wall, he quickly thought of his dad and just felt something was wrong. Could it have been the same ball of light I saw on the ceiling of the hospital?

"The Service"

The house was full of family and friends when we got back home. I was in a state of shock, my mind still trying to figure out what happened, and my biggest question was, "Why Tom?" Over the next few days I had to prepare the service. It was such an odd experience to prepare for something like this when I hadn't even wrapped my head and heart around the fact that Tom was gone. I wanted to be anywhere

but here making these decisions.

A man that worked so hard, loved to laugh, a wonderful dad, husband and friend. I still couldn't believe he was gone. I barely remember what I wore that day. I felt I was outside of my body watching somebody else experiencing this. I remember driving to the service and looking up at the sky and seeing this beautiful rainbow in the clouds. It felt like it was a reminder or a message somehow, but I could not find any meaning to it at the time.

At the service we had so many pictures of Tom everywhere. We played country music because that was his favorite. Of course, there were many Green Bay Packer wreaths sent by family and friends. You could not think of Tom and not think of the Packers. I remember hugging family and friends as they arrived, and yet I can't tell you who was there, or what was said. I was just going through the motions. I do remember that the boys and I didn't cry. It felt as if we were being held up by some loving energy that surrounded us. After the service a few people said I had a glow to me.

I found that during the service and while everyone was around I was doing okay. We all came together out of love for Tom and supported each other. The hardest part, when the real grieving began, was when everyone went back to their lives and mine was still shattered. That is when it really starts to sink in that they are gone. Picking up the pieces

17

of our lives after a loss can be the toughest experience we ever go through, but nothing prepared me for what I was about to learn as a result of all of this.

The Gifts Begin

If you have lost someone that you love, you know that the messages you often get are quite simple and yet so profound. You feel such a strong connection and a "knowing" that they are from your loved one. Often times we wish to share this joy with others, but our joy is short lived when they fail to believe that what you are receiving is communication. Many of my friends thought it was "wishful" thinking, but I knew it was more. No one was going to convince me the things I was seeing and feeling were mere coincidence. I knew that life could respond to our grief and love could find a way. I knew that our loved ones could let us know they are still with us.

Hold onto your messages and believe. They are for you, they are sent to you from one heart to another. How could anyone else possibly understand, unless they themselves have received these types of messages? When you know, you know.

A new world was unfolding and I was beginning to discover that there is no death, just a change of condition. I started to see Tom in a new way as well. I could feel him in spirit. It was like getting to know the essence of Tom without a physical body. Below are some special

communications I received. I can't even explain in words just what they meant to me and how I was feeling at the time. Words just can't describe the child-like joy I felt at times. Nature and simple things were now enhanced and my perception of everything was changing. Each sign, each universal truth was changing my life forever.

Every message I received from Tom was wrapped with a gift, a gift of love, awareness and expansion of the mind. I had to let go of some limited beliefs to believe in something more. Is there life after-death? I used to wonder, but now I know. Yes, there is!

"You love the Moon Remember"

The night after the service the house was so full of people. I felt like I was walking in a daze, half there, half not. The outpouring of love for Tom, the boys and I, was what was keeping us from breaking down completely. Suddenly, a friend called us outside, she said, "April, now tell me Tom isn't sending you a sign" then she pointed up to the sky. It was a clear night and there was an amazing full moon. The clouds that were passing near the moon had the most magnificent array of colors, like a rainbow. Every cloud that got near the moon; lit up in a kaleidoscope of colors. I had never seen anything like it. I just stood there in awe. It was beautiful, but my heart still not convinced it was from Tom.

As I went to bed that night I was writing in my journal and out of the blue I heard a voice say, "You love the moon, remember?" I couldn't believe it; it just popped into my mind out of nowhere! I started shaking then crying because I knew it was Tom saying, "Yes, that was a sign for you!" I quickly called my aunt and mom into the room and told them what I heard. It was the first glimmer of hope that Tom was making contact. I felt so happy, that I finally drifted off into a deep sleep.

I had always gone outside to look at the moon. The year before Tom passed was the time I looked at it the most. I felt changes were coming and although I didn't know what, I found myself outside at night looking into the night sky. I would tell Tom, "I am going outside to look at the moon and think." I felt like I was going to lose someone, but I would never allow my heart to believe it would be Tom. Even when he got sick, I still could not even allow the thought to enter my mind or heart. I had told mom several times during the year that I felt I was going to lose someone, and that someone I loved would be faraway. It was weird, the feelings were so strong and yet, I didn't have any mental details.

The following weeks were just passing by. The kids and I were in the same house, but did not talk much. I tried to speak to them about the loss of their dad, but the tears flowed every time I did. It was so hard for each of us to express to the other how we were feeling. I heard the

boys cry themselves to sleep many nights; it broke my heart. Meanwhile I began searching for answers and the biggest one I had was, "Is Tom okay, is he still around?" The one thing that I felt, that shocked me the most was that although I knew Tom was not here physically, I could still feel Tom in my heart.

I had always wondered what it was like to lose someone. I had friends who had lost parents and I tried to imagine what it was like, but I could only imagine what I thought it would feel like; the emptiness that must be felt in the heart, but I didn't feel emptiness in my heart, I felt Tom. I knew he was still with us, just in a different way.

"Sounds and Orbs"

Many people have reported lots of popping sounds after the loss of a loved one. These sounds were all in my room and it felt like an expansion of energy. I sensed it for years after Tom's passing. After having my experience and realizing that their world is all around us, but just at a higher vibration, these pops made more sense. Their energy cuts through the densest of materials and if we listen carefully we can feel their energy as they enter a room.

Each night these popping sounds were in my room. I remember having the thought, "Has my house always made this much noise?" I was actually lying in bed, my house full of people when I heard it. I was

crying and wasn't even thinking about anything at all and the noise in my room literally made me turn around. I knew I had never heard that sound before because it would have literally kept me up at night. This would continue for years after Tom's passing, but not to the degree it did that night. I felt like my room was packed full of spirit. I knew Tom was around.

On the nightstand right beside my bed I had a heart case that I kept our wedding rings in. Every night just after turning off my light to go to bed, I would hear a loud tap on that case. I knew it was Tom saying, "Goodnight"

Orbs are something else that people often report seeing. They show up in pictures especially ones taken with family. Orbs are something that I was always "iffy" about. I had seen them in photos and wondered if they were dust. I knew many people believed in them, but for me I felt neutral about it. I was always taking pictures and I never had any appear until after Tom passed.

On my birthday about 6 weeks after Tom passed, I was still in a daze. Family and friends came over. They brought tons of food and they even had brought over a karaoke machine. I remember feeling so much love and that was holding me together. My aunt had taken a picture of me eating in Tom's favorite spot, the recliner. After the film was developed she came over and brought me the pictures. Right

behind my head was a really big orb. I was shocked. I even looked through other photo albums before Tom passed to see if I could see any orbs, but I could not find a single one. But now here one was.

Later on I took a picture of my living room and there were orbs everywhere. In fact so many of them, that I knew spirits were all around me, and not just Tom; I had lots of company!

That following Christmas I took a picture of the boys in front of the Christmas tree and what did I see in the picture? Right between their heads was an orb. I could imagine seeing Tom standing there saying, "cheese!"

"If anything happens to you"

For some reason, I always worried about Tom. I had told him for years that if something happened to him I would go nuts. He used to tell me, "No you won't, you'll be fine." I don't know if it was an inner-knowing that I would lose him early or not, but I could never shake my worry for him. He told me about a year after we started dating that he always felt that he would not live past the age his dad died. I actually felt angry when he told me this. I said, "Great, after I fell in love with you, you tell me this." He just laughed. Of course I would do it all over again, even if I had advance knowledge of his early departure. Years passed and we never had that conversation again. Of course

24

Tom did not live past the age his dad died. I had always hoped he was wrong. The one thing that always stood out to me was that he always said it without fear, just very matter-of-factly.

A few weeks after Tom's passing I was suddenly awakened with what felt like someone hitting my bed. The first time I just woke up and looked around and went back to bed. It did remind me of something Tom would do; slap the bed to get my attention. The next night I felt it again. This time it was harder and actually startled me a little bit, so I got up and looked under the bed. Then I sat on the edge of the bed and I actually laughed because I remembered what I had told Tom for years, "If anything ever happens to you, you haunt me until I know you're okay" He must have remembered. It was weird that although I couldn't see Tom, I felt so connected to him, almost as if I could hear what he would say. Even in my mind's eye I could see him laughing, while trying to get my attention.

"The Feathers"

The Feathers came to be "my thing". Some people see dimes, pennies, birds and many things that cause them to think of their loved ones. I specifically asked for a feather one day and within 2 hours saw one fall to the ground outside my window. I had no idea what I had started and that it would literally rain feathers at times. I remember talking on the phone sharing some of my experiences with friends and family and

while doing so I would look outside and see many feathers blowing around in the wind. Several friends joked that they sure felt sorry for the birds!

As my mind was starting to take in these signs and I began to trust what I was feeling, I took a bold step in actually asking Tom for a sign, a specific sign. My first thought was to make it something light and easy. So I stood in my room and I said, "Tom, please send me a feather."

I walked off and went about cleaning the house. Tom's sister called me a few hours later and I was standing in the kitchen looking out the window while we talked and then suddenly something caught my eye. It was so white it seemed to glow. It looked like a white rose petal falling to the ground. I told Tom's sister to hold on for a minute; I had to go outside to see what it was. As I got outside I began to look around, then there right beside my foot was a single white feather!

I had almost forgotten about my earlier request for a feather and as I stood there looking at that feather my heart started racing with excitement! I could not believe I had asked for a feather; then almost 2 hours later I was standing there with one at my feet. The timing was perfect and I could not believe what I was seeing. Of course I went in and shared the story with Tom's sister!

Little did I know, this was just beginning of all the feathers that I would receive from Tom. Many of my days were spent outside reading on the deck. I was being drawn to so many spiritual books. These books had great messages of love, the stories resonated with me and what I was experiencing. While reading I would stop and look up to see a single feather falling right down in front of me. I could literally catch it in my hands.

Whenever I needed assurance, magically a feather would appear. Just like the day my son flew for the first time. Him and his friend were flying to San Antonio. Naturally I was worried and as he backed out of the driveway and I waved goodbye, a feather floated right down in front of me and landed in the bush. I knew that was Tom telling me "He will be fine."

With every message I felt myself changing, as if my whole being was reaching up towards the sky and my heart was filling up with so much love and eternal truths. I could feel this divine plan for each of us. Each of us was so special, so loved. We were all being looked after more than we could ever know, now that I could touch on that, I would often cry from the sheer joy of that knowing. I began to feel a connection to everything and everyone. I felt my vibration rising higher and higher. I have heard this described as a "Quickening of Spirit."

Many afternoons were spent walking and it didn't even feel as if my

feet were hitting the ground. I would look up at the sky, trees, and the birds as if I were seeing it all for the very first time. I knew I was seeing it all from a whole new perspective. Some people may have thought I was out of mind. I think I literally was, at least out of the lower mind where stress and worry dominate. It was the most peace I had ever experienced in my whole life.

"The firework"

This communication shows what faith and believing can do. I could have easily not have believed and therefore missed the most amazing sign.

I am so happy that Tom came through to my mom and that she was actually brave enough to share the messages she believed she was getting. Although we had our doubts, having never dealt with anything like this before, this sign proved she was getting messages from Tom.

During the few weeks after Tom passed my mom called. I could tell she was quite upset and nervous about telling me what she wanted to say. She started out by saying, "April, I am not sure about this, but I feel with all my heart I am supposed to give you this message." She said she was seeing Tom at night, and she could hear his voice too. The message she got from Tom was "Tell April to look for my face." That was it.

At first I wasn't sure mom was really getting a message, but I knew her heart was in the right place. I then began to wonder if I was somehow blocking Tom from my mind and heart. I could not see his face or remember the sound of his voice. Maybe it was my way of coping for the time being. Whatever the message was meant to be, I had no clue.

Then approximately two weeks later mom called and said, "April I got another message, I know this is going to sound strange, but I heard Tom say, "Look to the sky, Fourth of July" She said she was not going to tell me because it just seemed like something she might have made up, but then she heard Tom say, "Just tell her." Mom was having a hard time convincing herself she was even getting these messages.

Of course in my mind I was thinking about what she had said. I thought that maybe I would have to wait until the fourth of July. Would I see his face in the sky that night? Since the fourth of July was a few months away, I put it to the back of my mind for the time being. Meanwhile I had sent in a roll of film to be developed from our last family vacation together before Tom passed. We had gone to Niagara Falls. I thought back about the long drive, and how we always had a great time driving and talking. Tom would make us laugh so hard and of course I was always keeping an eye on him to make sure he wasn't falling asleep while driving. Often I caught him with one eye open and the other shut. He said he was just resting one eye at a time. That was when I knew it was time for him to pullover and let me drive.

The pictures came back in the mail. I took a deep breath as I opened the envelope. I was part excited, but part sad, knowing the memories would send me back to a happy time when we were all together. As I slowly started looking through the photos, I found myself smiling and crying at the same time. I came to a firework picture I had taken over Niagara Falls one night. I didn't waste much time on it since none of us were in the picture, but as I sat it off to the side, I kept feeling pulled to look at it again.

As I looked at the picture more closely, I could suddenly see Tom's face in the smoke of the firework! It was definitely the outline of his face, his features, eyes, nose and mouth. I then remembered the message from Tom to "Look to the sky, Fourth of July" and "Tell April to look for my face!"

I could not believe it! I called my mom immediately at work and asked her if I could meet her for lunch. As I pulled up to her in the parking lot, I handed her the picture and I asked her, "What do you see?" She saw Tom's face right away; she got tears in her eyes and she was so shocked. She said, "We need to tell someone about this!" Of course we did, we shared it with many friends and family. Most everyone that knew Tom could see his face clearly in the firework. Tom's mom even walked by one day and looked at it and said, "That is Tom." I still have this photo and whenever I start to have doubts creep in, I just pull that picture out and remember the sequence of events that lead to this

amazing message from Tom.

Mom continued to get many messages from Tom. Most were messages that he was happy, but it was hard for him to be happy when we were all so sad. Often times he wanted to assure me that we would see each other again and that he would be standing there saying, "See, I told you so!" I have no doubts I will see him again when it is my time to crossover.

"The Owls"

This message almost seemed universal in nature. I felt Tom was working with many in spirit to get this message across, for which I am so very grateful. This message had so much magic and meaning contained in it. The air that night felt different. Everything seemed to glow and I had just seen a rainbow around the moon. A light hue surrounded the trees reminding me that everything here has a counterpart made of light.

I missed Tom dearly and I wanted more and more of what his world was like, more assurance that he was okay. Mom's confidence in the messages she was receiving was allowing her to get more. She could actually see Tom at times, though it was of a lighter substance. She could even make out what he was wearing. He always had a smile on his face.

One day she came over and told me that I would receive a message on May 5. I was so excited; I could hardly wait. I am not a patient person by nature so waiting for this day was hard for me to do! As the day got closer I felt my excitement increase. I wondered what kind of sign I would get. My mind and heart ran wild with the possibilities. I was hoping for a dream visit, but that isn't what I got, but what I got was amazing.

The night before May 5, I was sitting outside looking up at the night sky. I wasn't out there long before I started hearing these owls hooting back and forth in the backyard. It was so loud, it seemed to echo and it was obvious they were talking to each other. One would hoot, then the other.

I just sat there listening in such amazement. I have lived in this house for 13 years and I had never heard owls before. Suddenly, I could hear the sound of wings flying toward me. One owl landed in the tree right in front of me. I ran inside to get the boys; I wanted them to hear this. Bryan came out quickly, but Brandon was lost in a game. Bryan and I listened, as the owls continue to hoot back and forth. The communication between the owls was beautiful beyond words. They spoke of love and departure. Suddenly, the owl in the tree in front of us took flight again. You could hear the direction of where it was heading and as we looked, all we saw was this big ball of light traveling across the trees. I looked back to see if something could have made the

light, but there was nothing anywhere, no cars, nothing.

Suddenly the scene before me was filled with a beautiful and meaningful message. A message so significant; it was as if the universe had orchestrated this whole scene for me to understand that Tom and I were together, but that he had to go home, back to the light. Tom was now a being of light. Bryan and I just stood there in silence. I knew this scene contained a message of love and transformation.

The more messages I received the more I came from the heart and not the mind. I felt like I could feel the joy and love of where Tom now resided. That he could be with me anytime, there was no light to go towards that separated him from me. He was there to help me; we helped each other.

"The Stereo"

This sign still baffles to me to this day. I still smile when I think of this one. It rarely happens anymore, nor did it ever happen before Tom's passing. What I loved the most about this sign was knowing that Tom was right there with me as I looked through our family photos. He could feel my sadness and wanted to assure me he was nearby.

This communication happened when I was in my room. I was lying on my bed and I had the radio playing. I was going through some old family photos. As I looked back at the pictures of Tom and the boys

33

being goofy, I felt the tears welling up in my eyes. I could feel the sadness in my chest. The grief was almost unbearable as I looked through the photos, longing to have all those precious moments back. Although it hurt to look at the pictures, I wanted to remember a time when we were all together.

Suddenly I realized that I could not hear the radio at all. I thought maybe something was wrong with the station, so I got up and looked at it. The numbers on the volume showed it was turned down, so I turned it back up. At this point I didn't think much of it and continued to look at the photos, after a few minutes I realized once again I could not hear my radio.

Again, I got up and see it is turned down again! I am starting to think, "this is really weird," but I was focused on getting back to the pictures. I got back on the bed to look at the photos once more. Soon I noticed I could not hear the radio at all. I got up and looked at the stereo again; which was now totally turned off. Finally I realized it had to be Tom. I am sure he was thinking, "It is about time!" I was so excited! I turned it back on and a song was playing that I felt Tom had sent especially for me; a song that I heard often after he passed. Just imagine, Tom was standing right there in our room, it's just I couldn't see him! But he made his presence known.

On many occasions when I have really needed a sign, Tom always

came through in the most amazing ways. Sometimes I just simply asked and the messages would come quickly. I was standing on the deck one day and I asked Tom to please send me a sign and when I went back into the house my cd player had started playing all by itself. This happened a lot during the first few years of his passing. Tom had bought me that cd player one Christmas years ago. Nothing like this had ever happened before his passing, therefore convincing me beyond all doubt it was Tom.

"Butterflies and Nature"

The year after Tom's passing I felt I was experiencing everything from a different vibration. It was as if I didn't note any change in weather, it seemed to be perfect out all the time. I would sit outside and butterflies just seemed to flit all around me, as if they were attracted to my energy or maybe someone was directing them towards me. I would be outside reading one of my books and as if to say, "Yes, keep going" butterflies would draw near. Nature has an amazing way of healing. I always knew this from my childhood, but never realized just how much until now. I noticed I needed to go outside to feel the expansiveness of my spirit. I could just sit outside for hours watching the sky, the birds and feeling the soft breeze on my face. I felt like I was mesmerized with it, seeing it for the first time from a completely different point of view. Everything exuded love, I felt so much gratitude.

One afternoon the boys and I had plans to go to a friend's house for dinner. We noticed a beautiful butterfly stayed near our side porch as we went in and out of the house that day. When the door opened it would fly off but would always come right back. The kids got into the car and waited for me while I stopped on the porch to play with the butterfly. It kept circling around me playfully when suddenly I could not find it. I thought it landed on me somewhere and I didn't want to hurt it. I asked the kids, "Do you see the butterfly?" They both started laughing because the butterfly had landed on my backside!! That was so like Tom. Tom had a wonderful sense of humor, one that always brought me back to reality when I was upset. He taught me that life is to be enjoyed, not to be taken so seriously. Even on the other side it was good to see he maintained his sense of humor.

For about six months after Tom passed I would awaken in the night to the sounds of birds, but it sounded like they were in my head and not outside. I would wake up around 3 a.m. and hear it, so I would open the window to see if the sounds were coming from outside, but it clearly wasn't. You know how you go to a concert and the music is so loud you can still hear it when you leave? That is what it felt like to me. It seemed at night I was going somewhere in my sleep that was beautiful and full of birds singing and I was bringing the sound back with me as I was waking up.

One particular night I remember having a dream, this dream was so

vivid. I was on this beautiful green mountaintop. All around me were rolling hills of green and down in this valley was big grey castle. I was walking barefooted atop the hill looking around at the beautiful scenery. I could feel the coolness of the lush green grass beneath my feet. I was surrounded by the sweet sounds of birds and there were rabbits everywhere. I sat down on the plush grass and a rabbit came over and plopped right down across my lap, just like a cat would. End of dream. Maybe that is where I was going every night and was bringing back the sounds. It was so peaceful.

Another strange experience I was having was seeing lights. I would go outside and see a flash of light as if someone had just taken a picture. I would see a light around the trees, something like an aura I suppose. I could even see this light around the trees during the day. It was even around the furniture in my house. Again, this confirmed what I was feeling about everything having a spiritual counterpart. I was sitting outside one night when I saw this bright light in a tree next to our house. I kept looking at it wondering what it could be. I even went into the house to see if there was light coming out of my skylight and reflecting onto the tree, but that was not the case. It did not move, but just stayed in that spot. As I stood there looking at the light I heard an older man's voice say with a chuckle, "My child, patience" I had heard this voice before, it reminded me of a wise old man. Maybe this is one of my spirit guides, maybe it was the source of the light on the tree, but

I was not certain. Telling me to be patient was definitely what I needed to hear. I wanted to experience so much more of the world that was opening up within me that I simply could not get enough.

I have actually had dreams of this spirit. I had a dream of large, white clouds in the sky, a moon and several other planets. The dream almost seemed like a cartoon. There in a cloud was the face of the sweet man; he had a white beard and the warmest sweetest eyes you have ever seen. He seemed to be connected to me somehow. He was definitely watching over me.

Never had I felt such a strong connection to nature. I felt and knew nature was part of us and we are part of nature. We should watch and observe the pace of nature as it is truly magnificent and can teach us much about life. It accepts the rain when it falls; it takes on the summer heat, and can handle the bitter cold. There is no resistance to that which is. It even knows when to shed the old leaves; lie dormant until spring arrives to summon a new beginning, new growth. In a way, a tree dies to its old self each fall; it is then re-born in the spring when new branches and new leaves spring forth. This was what I felt like I was going through, an old me was fading away and something new was emerging.

This is very much like our own lives. We are given opportunities to grow, to shed old thought patterns. We have changes and challenges in

our lives to show us just how strong we can be. If we are brave enough to let go, we can start to see something new emerging.

"The Visitor"

This experience was very strange for me. It happened only a few times, but each time I felt so much love. I realized that we don't only have these physical bodies, but we have another body made of light. This was definitely something that made me re-think what I thought I once knew.

One night as I lay sleeping I was awakened by voices. As I opened my eyes a part of me was sitting up and talking to someone in the room. This part of me was exactly as I am, but seemed more of a lighter substance. It was so odd to think of there being more than one of me. As I looked over in the direction of where the sound was coming from, I saw a man's silhouette in the doorway of my bathroom. As if he was aware that I was now waking up, he stepped into the darkness of the bathroom. I was not afraid at all, but the information that I got, I knew was important. I remembered I was given a date and thought to myself, "Okay I will remember this" This date seemed important to me but I wasn't sure why, but deep within I felt a peace about it. Was Tom telling me when I would see him again, when I would be crossing over? I am not sure, but the date seemed to bring my spirit comfort. Feeling

content with what I heard, I fell back into a deep sleep.

In the morning as I opened my eyes, I immediately remembered what happened, then I tried to recall the information, but it was gone! I felt frustrated, as I knew this date was important, but all I could remember was the number five. I could not believe I didn't take the time to write down the date when it happened. Finally I had to let go and realize that the date was in my subconscious and when I needed to know I would.

People that I shared this story with asked me if I was afraid, but I wasn't. It actually seemed like a very loving and natural thing, like I was connected to something much more than I knew. This spirit was watching over me. Was it Tom? I think it was. Although I had no physical features to tell me it was Tom, I could feel the love. Love was consuming me and wrapping itself around me. I never felt so safe and loved.

The date was not meant for me to focus on or to live in anticipation of something in the future, but to focus on the here and now. It was important to continue to grow and trust in life, each day, one moment at a time.

On another night I awoke to that same male presence. Again, the spirit looked more like a shadow, no color at all, but I felt so much love. Then the spirit embraced me. My mind didn't question, I knew this

spirit, this love. I believe it was Tom, but had I of seen Tom like he was when he was with us, it would have been like losing him all over again. It would have set me back emotionally. Getting to know him in spirit was forming a new relationship between us.

I realized that even though at times we might feel lonely and isolated, that we are never alone. That world of spirit isn't far off, it is right here among us, but just at a higher vibration. If we could raise our vibration, it would and does change the way we view the world. We have to let go of things that limit us. We have to let go of things like fear, worry and stress. These things block our view and we can't expand and grow. These fears are like weights that keep our vibration low. If we can free ourselves of these lower thoughts then we will soar higher and higher into a new world. We have to let go and trust.

This was all new to me. I had never felt what I was feeling now. The trick was trusting what I was seeing and feeling. It was all new territory and I had to come from the heart and not the mind in order to really stay in the flow. Trust and faith were taking the place of fear and doubts.

Trusting what we feel can be tricky. The mind will try to bring doubt to what we are feeling, especially when it is something new. Not only had all my old friends fallen away, I was increasingly finding myself alone on most of this journey. It wasn't due to anything anyone had

41

said or done, it was just that I was changing. Although it may have appeared that nothing was changing in my outer world, much was changing within me.

One thing I knew for sure was that Tom's loss answered many questions I had in my life. What was this life about, why are we here, and do we continue on? I felt the answers to all these unraveling like a mystery novel, each revelation bringing me much happiness and joy.

I was starting to feel whole again, but not like the old me at all. My world was expanding and I was changing so fast. In a way it was very hard, as I tend to be a very stubborn person, especially when it comes to change. At times I wanted what I had in my life; I wanted my old life back. A life I knew and in many ways was more comfortable with, but the new kept pulling me forward, forward onto a wondrous path.

"Just One Feather"

The first summer after Tom passed, the boys really wanted to go somewhere. I just couldn't imagine a vacation without Tom. My mom and sister said they would be willing to go too. Somehow I managed to book a cabin in the mountains of Tennessee. We had never been there before and I wanted to go somewhere new.

Before we left I remember saying out loud to Tom, "I am not trying to be a pest, but if you would just send me ONE feather, I will know you

are there with us," I really thought Tom must be sick of me asking for signs, but I just really needed to know he was there. Another feather seemed like a reasonable enough request since I had already received so many.

We packed up the van, loaded up the dogs and headed for the mountains of Tennessee. I know the boys were glad to get out of the house and I was glad too. As we got to the mountain cabin, I remembered looking discreetly around the front door as we entered the cabin. I went upstairs and looked around the balcony, nothing. No feather anywhere. I decided that I was looking too hard and it would happen when it happened.

We spent the evening unloading the van and making dinner. I looked at the dogs running around and the kids talking and laughing. It was good to be away and with family, but my heart still ached for Tom. When you have spent so much of your time with someone and they are suddenly not there, it feels as if a part of you is missing. Sometimes you even feel guilty for having fun without them there. I knew that I had to make this trip fun for the kids, but the big void of Tom not being there, was hard to fill.

Finally we all went to sleep and the next morning I was sitting on the couch looking out over the beautiful mountain scenery with coffee in hand. I thought how much Tom would have loved it here and I quietly

whispered "Tom, where are you?"

Bryan walked over in front of me and started talking about something. To this day, I can't remember what he said. As I looked at him, something behind his head caught my attention. I tried focusing in on it, but still could not make it out. It blended with the wood knots in the cabin walls. It was right over the front door of the cabin. I interrupted Bryan by saying, "What is that over the door?" He looked over and very nonchalantly said "It is a feather in the door" I was like, "What?"

I was so excited, I jumped off the couch and got closer to the door and sure enough there was one large feather stuck in the doorframe. I could not believe it! I had asked Tom for one feather, and just so happened to make a reservation to a cabin that I had never been to before, and there was one large feather sticking in the door! I had not seen it the night before, had it been there the whole time? I will never know, but it was there now.

The whole trip was more enjoyable, I knew in my heart and soul Tom was there. I could feel this world of light and love each time I got a sign. My imagination could see and match what I was feeling. I once read that the mind doesn't know the difference between what it is real and what is imagined, other than the fact that we believe or we don't believe what we imagine. I was really starting to believe in this new world. It was like opening a door that had been closed for a long time,

but upon opening my heart remembered this magical place does exist. It is there that we find our loved ones who have passed over and where, when it is our time to make the journey, we will be able to stay forever, rather than temporarily visiting in dreams or perceiving them in signs.

As we started to pack and head home my mom suggested I take the feather. I didn't feel right taking it because no matter how it got there, one thing is for sure it was a sequence of wonderful events that led to me seeing that feather. I did not know if the owner of the cabin put that feather there or not. I really wanted to take it, but thought it was not the best thing to do.

As fate would have it, I was meant to have that feather. When I got back from vacation, my neighbor who had just been on vacation with her family at the beach; came over to visit and what did she happen to bring me back from her trip? A feather! A feather almost identical to the one we saw in the cabin!! I still have that feather to this day. I also have a picture of the feather over the cabin door, plus not to mention "three" baggies full of feathers I have received over the years.

"Happy 34th B-day Mom"

It was seven months before I started to consider removing some of Tom's clothes. I remember thinking I could not believe this was

45

actually happening. Even with the messages I was getting, it was mixed with the normal heavy grief in between. The knowing he was around and happy was wonderful, but the absence of him physically was so hard.

I had decided that I would just consider this spring-cleaning and that I would also get rid of some of my clothes. I had already packed a bag full of clothes I wanted to get rid of. I took a deep breath as I opened up Tom's drawer. His clothes still smelled like him, as I started going through his clothes I felt heaviness in my chest.

I had gathered a few items that I felt Tom didn't like anyway and as I picked up an old pair of sweat pants that Tom had made into shorts, I finally broke down. I remembered the kids saying, "If Dad wears those we are not going" it made me laugh a little through the tears and as I stood there with the shorts I brought them up to my face to wipe away the tears and just as I did, I heard, "Happy 34th Birthday mom, you're old." I just stood there for a second wondering what had just happened. A talking picture frame that the boys had recorded on my birthday three years earlier came on all by itself. It went off at just the right time, just when I needed it the most, conveying the message, "I am right here, I am not gone."

I stood looking at that picture frame for a long time. Of course, the doubtful mind wants to know for sure, so I picked up the picture box,

I shook it. I tapped it. Nothing. I had been in Tom's dresser many times looking at stuff in the top drawer. I even kept some of my stuff in the bottom drawer, so it wasn't as if the movement had done it. Completely satisfying my mind that this was from Tom, the old doubting mind, never doubted again. I was learning to trust my heart and what I was feeling and experiencing. I knew these things were not just a coincidence. By the way, I no longer believe in coincidences!

Finally having gotten rid of some of Tom's clothes, I felt forward movement. For me, I had to see myself as April now, not Tom and April. I even wondered when I should start to take off my wedding ring. I noticed when I would go out with friends some would look to see if I was still wearing it. I am sure it was just a curiosity thing. I wondered too, when I should take it off, or if I ever would. I decided that I would do what felt best to me.

This period of time proved to be both very hard and yet very enlightening for me. When you are used to having someone with you all the time that you love so much and have started a family together; it is so strange not to have them there anymore. My world revolved around Tom and the boys. It just felt like my whole world had shattered. I knew I had to find a way to want to live life again.

Grief is one of the hardest things we will ever go through. We must do things in our own time. Everybody is different. At times we might

47

look at others and think they should be at this point or that point, but we must allow each person as much time as it takes. Listening is the best thing we can do for someone who is experiencing a loss. I also found that I wanted to talk about Tom a lot, but others found it hard to do. I felt at times like he never even existed, even though I understood their reason for not bringing it up. I wanted to always see Tom's life as a celebration because that is how he lived life.

Letting go does not mean you block their memory, or you don't think about your loved one. It simply means you stop resisting what has happened. We can resist it by not accepting it, refusing to see our life as it is now. This causes us to feel stuck with no forward movement. After a while you start to let go and start to accept, that is why time is the greatest healer after a loss. It takes time to heal and each one of us is different.

Never worry because our loved ones in spirit will continue to be a part of our lives, but what is more important is that we continue to live our lives. It is great to look back at the memories we have shared, but never allow them to become a crutch. I now often look back and my heart overflows with love. I am so grateful that Tom was a part of my journey and that the boys had such a wonderful dad. I know he continues to be a part of our journey and he still does what he needs to do there on the other side.

A Place to Share

As the communication with Tom was becoming more frequent I started reading many books on the subject. I had found a book that shared many of the same types of communications I was receiving. The book was called, "Hello From Heaven."

On the back of the book was a website. I found that the site had a message board. For a few days I just read what others were experiencing. The people were so kind there and no one doubted what other people were sharing. It felt like a safe and loving place to share what I was feeling and the communications I was receiving. It was so nice not to have anyone cast doubt on my communications with Tom.

I was able to talk about my fears of what I needed to do and when to do it. I found many answers to the questions I was having from others on the board. They all expressed that there was no right or wrong way to handle grief, you just stay in the moment and try to do the best you can. This board had come to be my place of comfort. Some of us had lost our spouse, others children and of course parents and

grandparents. All of us received beautiful communications and the love contained within each story was reflected in each and every post.

We all became really good friends. We could really share our deepest fears, our days of heavy grief and our days of happiness. As anyone knows who has lost a loved one, there are times you feel like you are on a roller coaster. As time goes on, you are just so excited to have one good day then you might have five bad days. But the good days get longer and longer.

I had never lost anyone close to me before. Tom was the only loss I had ever experienced. At times I wondered if I would survive. Would I ever feel like I wanted to really live life again, engage in the world?

While the world I had known felt like a million miles away, a new world was opening up to me, a world of spirit. A beautiful new world that was full of light that illuminated everything it touched. It was beyond the limits of the mind. You could feel so much from the soul. I felt like my spirit was taking charge and so much of what I was learning was setting my soul on fire. I was like a sponge and I could not stop absorbing everything I could about this new world. It was a mix of emotion to say the least. Part of me was dying and part of me was being re-born.

This place on the board was a saving grace for me because sometimes

it is so hard to believe in something when no one else believes it. It is almost like we need others to validate it for our hearts and minds to finally believe, or at least not have someone cast doubt on what you're experiencing. It is like seeing something amazing in the woods while you're all alone, but no one else is there to see it. You start to question, "Did it really happen, or did I just imagine it?" But you know it happened.

We have a shared reality that most of us believe in. Why? Because everyone else does too, but when something comes along which isn't what we are taught or what we might have believed in, it can be hard to hold onto. If we come from the heart and trust, it can cause an awakening for sure. Hold on and don't let the mind cast doubts. Trust your heart. Connect with others who are having the same experiences as you are.

A More Expansive View

My heart was overflowing with this new knowledge and a strong desire to know more kept pulling me toward different books. I would sit outside for hours on end just absorbing the life giving energy. I would go for walks and I would literally feel as if I was floating. What was happening to me I had no clue, but I felt more alive than I had ever felt in my whole life. It was as if I could feel Tom's joy too, joy in his new surroundings.

I realized that thoughts are things, it was important to observe your thoughts. What was I focusing on every day? I found that what you focus on grows. I also knew it wasn't so much what happens to you in life, but how you choose to see it.

I had to stop resisting what was, let go and stay in the moment. This moment is where everything is happening. I never realized just how much the mind could chatter on, until I was completely out of my mind! It felt like heaven to just allow and trust. Trusting in something new, taking a new path in life is sometimes hard to do. As human beings we are hard wired towards security, even if this involves trying

to live an old life in which the characters and scenery have changed and yet trying to kid ourselves nothing has changed. Consequently we don't take chances, and live our lives more fully. It is fear that is the real ruler for most of us. The walls we build by believing we can't do this or that. We believe we are not good enough when, in fact, we are part of all that exists.

We are part of life itself, an ever-flowing source of love that connects us all. Anything is possible if we just believe. If we can let go of all thoughts that limit us, that block our view of something better; then our lives could be spent seeing the beauty of the world, one where we can experience fully the love and joy of each other.

I refused to see Tom's passing as a random act of neglect from the hospital, or just an unfair loss of someone passing too young. I knew Tom's passing meant more, more to him, more to me and everyone that knew him. Our communications were more than I could have ever imagined and yet I always believed that with love all things were possible.

This whole experience had expanded my awareness to encompass far more of life than what I had previously known. I wasn't about to miss anything and my desire to know if Tom was okay was sure bringing me the answers. If it was destined that Tom had to pass, then I was determined to learn all I could from this experience and open each and

every gift. I was amazed and continue to live in awe and inspiration of the experiences that have transpired since Tom's passing. In all our experiences and struggles a more meaningful message can be found.

Miracles became part of my life, everyday, in the most amazing ways. I had always believed that everything happens for a reason and I was always able to see a reason but a few years before Tom passed, life got confusing, I started to forget this and life seemed so random and I felt joy slipping away from me. I didn't feel connected to source anymore. Tom's passing brought me back to this deep knowing. St. Augustine reminds us of this, "Miracles are not contrary to nature, but only contrary to what we know about nature."

Many of us can look at the same scene, witness a certain event and most surely we will all take away a different meaning. Some might say it was just a random act, or some might find a deeper more precious meaning. It is surely in the eyes and heart of the beholder. What lies in our hearts is what we will see and take away from the situation. Don't take anything personal and realize all our experiences in life are here to teach and allow us to grow.

It is also our choice as to how we react throughout our day. Do we decide to get angry over waiting in line at the grocery store, or do we choose to let go of the resistance of our circumstances and find patience? It is always our choice. Many people don't even think about

this being a choice, they just respond with emotion. The mind is like a computer, we are the one filling it with the thoughts and we must control what goes in it and how we react.

I discovered how my thoughts throughout the day, and what I chose to focus on determined how I felt. I found myself becoming so keenly aware of them that I suddenly found it hard to have those days when I felt like, "I hate this weather, I hate this shirt" as I knew the source of my unhappiness was because I was choosing to focus on the negative. I rejected those "hates," and instead chose to focus on things I "loved."

When the weather was nice I would go for a long walk. I started calling them "Gratitude" walks. I started thinking about how grateful I was for the many things in my life. When I first started it began with the obvious, the boys, family and friends. Then, as I started feeling the gratitude swell within me, I found myself feeling grateful for the moon, stars, butterflies, and everything else I could think of. It shifted my attitude for the whole day. Instead of coming from a place of lack, I was coming from a place of abundance. I had a full heart. Joy was mine for the day.

I found this shift in perception amazing and I realized that life was really meant to be joyful, joyful beyond words. Don't we all want to thrive, really express ourselves to our fullest potential? What holds us back from doing this? It is easy, fear. It was fear for me and I still

struggle with that from time to time. It is insecurity. We will sit in utter despair and discontentment just for security. We feel safe, unwilling to step outside of what we know to experience something new, which is really what we are here for; to experience, learn and grow.

Unfortunately many of us are stuck, like in a cocoon, afraid to poke our heads out to explore a new area in our lives. I realized I could not do that anymore. No longer was I going to just sit there, waiting for something to happen. I was going to start doing more, taking more chances on me. I didn't want to just survive; I wanted to thrive.

Susan Jones, Ph.D. writes, "To live fully means living passionately, peacefully, joyfully, and healthfully while celebrating and play at this game of life. In order to do this, look at your life from a higher perspective rather than getting caught up in the day-to-day inconsequential matters. Love all aspects of your life. Be grateful for your challenges for they make you grow and become stronger."

Intuition

As the months following Tom's passing went by, I found myself trusting in my intuition like never before. I had always followed it, but now with the mind out of the way I was able to discern with increasing clarity my intuitive thoughts. For example, one morning before going out for the day, I felt an overwhelming urge to put on my xoxo's bracelet Tom had gotten for me for Valentine's Day. For some reason I knew without any doubt that I was going to hear that song "xoxo's" from Trisha Yearwood sometime that day.

Ever since getting up that morning I experienced this happy "knowing" that I would hear it. I got in my car and drove to the store and as I put my car in park something playing in the background caught my attention. I turned up the radio and guess what song was playing? Yes, that song from Trisha Yearwood. I could barely believe it. I know my mouth must have dropped open! Part of me knew it would happen, but part of me was shocked that it did. My heart knew, but my mind was always casting doubt. I would say this was one reason why my intuition expanded so much.

This inner knowing often comes fast and with the conviction of utmost certainty. When we feel that knowing, it is sometimes easy to let the mind disturb the clarity of intuitive thought with fears and doubts of the mind. How many times have you had an intuitive feeling over a choice to be made, but then having thought about it chose another option; only to later find out that your intuitive first choice would have been correct!

It is my belief that intuition comes from our higher self, which exists both here in the physical world and in the spirit world where our loved ones reside. Our higher-self acting as the conduit between the physical and spiritual realms places the intuitive thought into your conscious mind. It is easy though for doubts of the reasoning mind to stifle or stop this intuitive flow. Therefore we must just get in the flow and know!

There were also times when I just "knew" there was a feather near my car and sure enough I would walk outside to see one sitting right beside my car. I was amazed at how I could trust this "Knowing" and how I was seeing exactly what I knew would happen. It is this "Knowing" beyond any doubt that seemed to allow me to tap into this area of my life and it seemed as if I was in perfect harmony with everything around me.

Slowly I was breaking free from the person I once was. I barely

recognized at times the new me that was emerging, but it was a wondrous new me. Sometimes out of fear, uncertainty or wanting some false security I would try to go back to the "old" me. This was uncomfortable, as resisting the "new" caused me to feel physical, mental and spiritual resistance within my body. The tension this created was powerful and tiresome. My dreams would often reflect this conflict. Consequently I would be coaxed once more to move forward, even when it felt really uncomfortable at times.

I could feel the resistance of my mind versus my spirit. My spirit was strong, it kept pushing me forward, but my mind was full of fears it would sometimes cling frantically to what it once knew. But little by little it let go and the new took hold. My intuition now enhanced more than ever, I knew it was a part of me that I could trust. It came from my heart and soul. It put my busy mind to rest.

Key points to remember are that this all takes time. Coming to certain realizations don't come over night, it can sometimes take months, years and even a lifetime. But that is what life is about, growing and evolving. In this process we come to realize that we are much more. We are more than our minds, our thoughts, our physical bodies; we are eternal beings with no beginning or endings.

Love doesn't end, nor do we ever cease being us. So the next time you feel your loved one close by, just close your eyes and imagine them

there, because most likely they are. Trusting our intuition takes time, it is beyond our five senses that we are so used to using, but the more you trust it, the clearer it becomes. It will become so natural to you.

A New Chapter Opens

My time on the message board was life changing. Little did I know that I would meet someone that would be part of the next chapter in my life. It was about a year after Tom passed and I had not even considered dating, nor was I looking. I had said many times that I would never marry again. I was not thinking about any of that, but as fate would have it I began speaking to a gentleman on the board from the UK, who had also lost his wife. The way he spoke of her, the way he shared his pain and communications he had received, touched my heart.

I found that I was starting to look for his posts daily. If days passed by without seeing any from him on the board, I would send him an email to see how he was doing. We then started talking by email. He helped me so much during the anniversary of Tom's first year passing. It was so hard on me. I could remember everything that happened the year before when Tom got sick and the days leading up to his passing. The memories were so vivid and it was a tough time.

Paul would send me the most compassionate emails that were filled

with much wisdom and understanding. It helped me so much to have Paul to talk to because I didn't share the pain with many people. I only shared some of the wonderful things I was getting. It seemed important for me to tell most friends and family about the good that happened. I wanted to change the way we saw death, to allow people to see it from another point of view and get caught up in the magic and love I was feeling. Although the pain was there, I only shared that with Paul.

Paul knew what I was going through, he supported me and understood the emotions that I was feeling. Coming to terms with the loss of a loved one is like a roller coaster ride, full of highs and lows. I would have days when I felt I would never be sad again, because I knew Tom was happy and that when it was my time I would see Tom again. The knowing was so strong and there were times I had absolutely no doubts at all, but on other days my heart was broken and I just missed him so much.

After 6 months of writing back and forth and having spoken to him several times over the phone, Paul flew over. At first I was reluctant, my heart still saying I was not ready to meet anyone, nor would I let anyone in. While my mind was rejecting the whole idea, my spirit pushed forward. When I first saw Paul, I was still holding onto much resistance, but once we started talking I felt like I had known him before. I recognized his spirit.

I felt like I had connected with someone that truly knew me, all of me. He always listened so patiently when I would talk about Tom and our boys. He was never threatened by my love for Tom, ever. He also was experiencing his own grief, dealing with his own sense of loss of an old life, reluctant to start a new. Still both of us carried on because it felt like the universe was indeed conspiring to get us together.

Before he even flew out and doubts were entering both our minds, I kept seeing the name Paul everywhere. I remember sitting down at a restaurant and I was facing a wall with a picture on it. There on the picture was not only his first name, but his last name as well!! I thought, "What are the odds of that?" Paul also said during one of his many moments of doubt that as he was watching TV he heard the name, "April" which he has seldom ever heard. He said that convinced him that "Yes, I must go"

Paul and I connected on a really deep level of mutual love and respect for each other's journey. We have both grown so much. We have been seeing each other for almost 7 years now. I can still remember the first time we met; we both actually saw colors in our vision like blue and greens. Time seemed to stand still. It was even hard to recognize who we were at times. It was as if our spirits knew each other, but the physical was unfamiliar. As we have grown, our paths have become clearer.

Although we are separated by the Atlantic Ocean, we are still so close at heart. Paul flies over every 6 months to visit. We spend some quality time together and each time it has gotten harder and harder to say goodbye. I know we were meant to meet and the distance was necessary for the growth that we both wanted to experience after our losses. We both found we needed a lot of space afterwards. We both had many communications from our loved ones and a spiritual awakening.

As stubborn as I can be, I never really saw myself getting married again. Paul stood by patiently and lovingly while I went through more growth, more grief. The changes at home were coming fast. The boys had moved out and I found myself living on my own for the first time in my life. I actually looked forward to the challenge, but missed my little family. The house was now quieter and I slowed down to a slower pace. It took time to adjust to the silence and of course adjust to the kids being gone. It was a hard transition to say the least, but Paul knew my journey; he never doubted or lost faith in what could be for us both.

Change is something we often resist. We find that these changes don't break us, but often reveal eternal truths and strengths. If we can let life unfold as it is meant to, without resistance, we see a perfect plan designed just for us. By the way, I resisted a lot and became quite familiar to what it held in store for me physically vs. when I would let

go and just allow. Letting go and trusting sure brought peace of mind.

Loss can change many things in our lives. We can find that the same friends we once had are no longer the same. It isn't anything anyone did or said; it is just the whole dynamic of the life you once had has changed. This doesn't happen in all cases, but many times it does. It is important to know that this is okay, sometimes you just feel you need a whole new start. The person you once were is gone in a sense. The roles you once played have now just shifted and changed forever.

So many of our beliefs can change due to loss. Are you brave enough to let go of who you were and let a new you begin? It is a hard thing to do. Change is very hard, it might mean breaking old ties, starting a new job, spending more time alone. But what a wonderful opportunity to get to know who you are and seek a more meaningful life.

I believe that everything in life happens for a reason. And if you believe that too, then you have to ask yourself even in the toughest experiences of your life, "What can I learn and gain from this situation?" Since we can't change the event itself, isn't it better to gain a broader view of life? That is how I chose to honor Tom's passing and his amazing life.

How We Receive Communication

Have you ever heard that saying that "I will believe it when I see it?" Well, I found that maybe you need to believe it to see it. I guess for me, I always believed that love could find a way. If a message needed to be received from one heart to another, even from across the veil, then it could happen. I believe in what I feel in my heart and not just my five senses.

We are spirit, and spirit animates these bodies. Spirit animates everything. Once these bodies are finished, the spirit simply retreats and rises to its own vibration. The body is the vessel in which we come to experience this realm, to allow us to reach a higher vibration, to break free of the limits of the lower mind and realize that with love anything is possible.

Communication can come in various ways. It can be subtle like a butterfly flying around you, trying to get your attention. It can be a song on the radio, a flicker of your light at night while you're reading. It is that "feeling" you get as it happens. Often times our minds try to talk us out of that feeling by thinking it was just a coincidence, but the more it seems we can trust what we are feeling, the more frequent the

communications.

After Tom passed, the Green Bay Packers were playing on TV. They had made it to the Super Bowl and as you know Tom was a huge Packer fan. As me and the boys were watching the game the light in our hallway kept flickering. I kept looking over there at it and wondered if the light bulb was about to blow, but it would stop each time I walked into the hallway. I started to think that "somebody" wanted us to know that he was watching the game with us.

It is even more amazing now to think back about that day because that light never flickered anymore after that. I continued to use that same bulb for about a year. Tom was really trying to show us that he was there watching the game with us. Tom always had such a great attitude in life. Everyone that knew him could feel his warm nature. It still touches my heart now to think of him trying his hardest to assure us that he was okay.

Many times our loved ones can and do come to us in our dreams. We awake feeling so happy and you "just know" they came to let you know they are still there and watching over you. Sometimes our dreams of loved ones can be distorted and make little sense, or even sometimes make us sad. What we must remember is that the way we are feeling can sometimes influence our dreams as well. Even our dreams are filtered through our minds, so what is on our minds can be reflected in

our dreams. Even our perception of the dream might be influenced based on our thoughts.

If we feel bad about something we did or said before they passed, or things we felt were left unsaid, then these can sometimes show up in our dreams confirming our fears. But anytime you feel your loved one in a dream, they are trying to come through to let you know they are safe and still watch over you.

Since we are made of energy, it is easy for them to work through electrical items. Lights flickering, phone ringing, doorbell going off and no one is there. Many have even reported computer communications. Tom was not good with the computer, so no surprise I didn't receive any of my communications in this way! But I did get a phone message.

This happened to me one day while I lay in bed. I was having a really bad day. I was exhausted but funny enough it was as if I could hear Tom telling me to get up. I said, "Tom, I am not getting up unless you send me a sign!" and right then my phone that was lying on my bed rang one time and one time only. The caller ID read, "No Data," Well needless to say that was enough to convince me to get up and do something. On many nights around 9pm the phone would ring just once, the caller ID read, "No Data." I felt it was Tom telling us, "Goodnight."

Smells are another common communication we may get. We might suddenly smell the cologne or perfume they used to wear. Many have reported smelling cigar or cigarette smoke that reminded them of their loved one. It will just seemingly come from nowhere. It is your loved one saying, "Hello, I am here."

Animals are tuned into spirit and can see our loved ones. I remember my cat sitting in my bedroom on several occasions following something around my room. I followed her eyes and she went from the end of my bed to my nightstand. It was as if someone was walking back and forth and she was following the whole time with her eyes.

Another time was on my first birthday without Tom. It had been just a little over a month since Tom had passed and friends and family came over to cheer me up. We had gotten a new puppy a few weeks before and we heard her barking in the boy's room. As we entered the room we see her barking at something in the corner and just wagging her tail so happily. Of course nothing was there that we could see. I knew it was Tom playing with her and getting her to bark so I would know he was there. Message received!! That was also the same birthday I mentioned earlier with the orb behind my head. Tom sure was making his presence known.

There may be times when you are driving and your loved one suddenly pops into your mind and that special song comes on the radio. Trust

that is them letting you know they have just popped in to say "Hello." Don't over analyze it, just smile and accept they are near.

The more we tune in and trust, the more we will see. During the day the mind can stay so busy and everyday life can distract us from messages they send. It can be as simple as driving to work in the morning and the car in front of you has a license plate that has a number or letters that has special meaning for you and your loved one or possibly their name or date of birth can be seen.

I remember the first time I went to meet Paul. I was so nervous and as I was turning into the restaurant to meet him for the very first time, a car cut right in front of me and the license plate read, "1963" the year Tom was born. I knew meeting Paul was part of the plan and that Tom was happy about it.

Not everyone will get the same kind of communication. It really depends on the things that mean something to you and your loved one. What connected you when they were here physically? It might be a special number or song that connected you with your loved one. Your loved one knows this is the link to your heart. Your souls merge together and you find you're suddenly drawn to all these special messages. You could even set up a special sign early on like I did with my feathers, just by asking! Then be prepared to see it!

After Tom passed I came from the place of "Where is Tom, is he okay" that was all I really wanted to know. My focus was so intent on him. My heart needed to know he was okay more than anything else in the world. I knew I would eventually be okay, knowing that he was okay. I got my answers and you will too. If you really feel from your heart and desire to know that your loved ones are okay, answers will come. Seek and seek some more and you will find that your loved ones are not far away at all.

Many of us are given signs from our loved ones, but most of them are taken as just a "coincidence" and are overlooked. Even when it does cause one to think of their loved one, it still might not be in their realm of possibilities that this could truly be a sign.

Some people can't imagine something as simple as a feather or a butterfly being sent from those we love, but it is that simple. Love is speaking to the subtle aspects of our spirit.

Some people also try to dictate with the mind what signs they will believe in and which ones they won't. I had a friend that once told me that he would believe it was a sign only if he saw his dad with his own eyes. This of course is what the mind wants and considers "proof," but sometimes love is trying to teach us to trust our hearts over our minds.

There is an eternal knowing beyond this physical body, a connection

that is felt and not necessarily seen. Once we allow the mind to dictate what we will believe, we have already limited our point of view. We have shut the door to the communication that we could receive. If only we could believe what our hearts were telling us, and not let doubt get in the way.

If we don't believe communication is possible or it conflicts with certain beliefs, then they will gladly step aside and allow your journey to move in the way it was meant to be. They do not want to confuse or alter your journey. Everyone's journey is respected and cherished.

For some, it might be easier not to have that communication because it might stop you from moving forward in life. As I got the messages that confirmed to me of Tom's continued existence, I felt an opening that allowed me to move forward because I knew in my heart he was alive and well. So, even though these messages are meant to show us of their continued existence, they are not meant to stop us from growing. Please know that they do send signs and messages of love, but don't stop living to wait for the next sign. They will come and hopefully fill you with joy and the motivation to keep moving forward.

Just like there are many ways for them to communicate with us, there are many things we can do for our loved ones. On Father's Day, the boys and I wrote notes to Tom and put them in a balloon, then blew the balloon up and sent it off. We silently watched as it floated off into

the sky. Often times, I will light a candle and just send Tom much love. This brings a smile to my face and draws Tom near.

We can send our loved ones in spirit love every day. I like to remember things that we all did together. I never wanted to be in a place where it was too painful to remember our journey together. It was the best part of my life; a very happy part and I didn't want to block it due to sadness. I wanted to be able to recall all of it and the love that we shared.

I have often read that if we want to give our loved ones a gift, then just imagine it. For example, if you want to give your loved one some flowers, just imagine the flowers and they will see it too. Imagine giving them a hug, and they will feel it. Thoughts are very powerful.

I always imagine Tom over there laughing and smiling. He was a great people person. I know he is loved and has adapted quite well to his new environment. Tom was always good with change. He seemed to be getting through quite well to let us know he was okay, even at the time of his departure. Then again, I think he had a little help!

Live life, celebrate their life and the time you spent together, this is a never- ending journey. We are eternal, so we have forever.

So, light a candle, write them a note, or even speak to them. They are always listening.

What our loved ones want us to know

One of the most important things that Tom wanted to get through was that "We will be together again" This life is just one aspect of who we are. Part of us resides on the other side where they are, we can sometimes access it when we are at peace and are feeling really happy.

Our loved ones want us to know that they can still see us and that they still share events that mean something to us. Their heaven is where we are; heaven is where love is. They don't want us to ever feel like we are holding them down, because we are not. They understand that grief is a hard process. They want us to continue to grow and live this life to the fullest.

The greatest gift we can give them is to live our lives. Sure, they know we will grieve, they know we will miss them. It takes time to get used to their absence in our lives, but just remember that love continues and that special place in your heart will always be for them. No one else can ever take their place in our hearts. Remember that you have a huge heart, and it can love again; it can find joy again. Love is never limited. It is the most powerful force in the Universe. We can love so much

more.

Our loved ones want us to live a life of joy. They do not want us to feel alone or isolate ourselves in our grief. They don't want us to walk around life with a huge weight on our shoulders, as a result of their passing. They want us to love again, be happy. They feel our joy and our sorrows. If we can open up to a broader view of life, what a wonderful gift this is for both us and for them. Our happiness makes them happy, our joys bring them joy.

They also want us to know that if there was something we feel we didn't say, or an argument we might have had with them before their passing, they understand. They know we are all here sharing this earthly experience and doing the best we can at the time we are doing it. Don't be so hard on yourself. Forgive yourself of any guilt you may be feeling, set yourself free. We are here to learn and grow.

They love you; they know life can sometimes be hard here. Don't allow those emotions to weigh you down your whole life.

Death is an Illusion

Another thing that Tom said was, "Death is an illusion" When he gave mom this statement, she said he was sitting down at the end of the bed looking kind of sad. It was as if I could feel what he was feeling. I could imagine the whole scene. Our loved ones know that death is no more than going from one room to another more expansive room. Knowing this it must be sad for them to see their loved ones struggle with their loss, but they know that someday we will all come to know the truth. There is nothing that can separate us from love.

They can see us, they see the bigger picture, but they know we are not aware of much of this. In many ways we are even closer to them now than we were before. They can feel what we feel; they know our journey. They know that there is a plan for us all, something to be learned from all our struggles and experiences on this realm.

Imagine their joy when they depart from the body to feel so much love and freedom. To know that they didn't go far away from those they love. We will all come to know this as we continue to grow and trust that love never dies or ceases to exist. It is just a change of condition.

We find our paths have parted for now, but we will meet up once again.

I knew that our beliefs could sometimes be the thing that holds us back from seeing the bigger picture. Sometimes we have to let go of deeply held beliefs to allow love to flow. Every time we put love first, over our beliefs, we are truly living our life's purpose.

We have heard it said many times that God won't give us more than we can handle and. I never thought I would survive losing my sweet Tom, but I found I didn't lose him at all. He is here just at a higher vibration that I can't see right now, but I can feel him. It isn't from the lower mind that we will know of their continued existence, but by our inner awareness and intuition which is a special gift given to each of us. If we can tune in, then we can connect more closely to our loved ones and to ourselves.

Knowing that death is not an ending, but a new beginning has changed my life forever. The questions I had for many years about life and death were all answered. Tom was showing me he was there in my room, in my car, and in my heart. I was not going to let any of those signs pass me by without being noticed. The more I felt I needed in my heart and soul, the more I got. As I started picking up the pieces of my life and started moving forward, my signs came less often. I knew this was because I was taking in the information and the seeds that had

been planted and were growing. The doubts of the lower mind subsided and the new was taking hold.

I believe as we change the way we see death, the veil that separates us will grow thinner and thinner. Communications between the two worlds will get easier and easier. We will come to understand that this is just a shifting from one dense reality to one of more light, but it is still there. Maybe as our faith and knowing in this grows, we will see these higher vibrations, as we ourselves will vibrate higher. As Einstein once said, "Energy cannot be created or destroyed, it can only be changed from one form to another." Since we are made of energy, we don't just end.

One of my favorite books called, "Spiritual Unfoldment," sums it up well, "The so-called dead have never died! You will know beyond all doubt that your own dead are with you, but your conviction will be based not on proof or evidence of the outer mind, but on an inward awareness from which nothing can shake you" This means to really trust what you feel when you see something that reminds you of your loved one, trust it is a "Hello" from heaven.

You might say, "Well death feels very real to me," and it does because we have just had our lives change completely. The space that our loved ones filled in our daily lives is gone and can leave a big void. It is up to us to fill it back up again with something new, more love. It isn't that

we replace the love we had, we can never do that, but we make room for more. Just knowing our loved ones are alive and well means we can go through life knowing that we will see them again.

Again, if we can change the way we see death, much can change. Do you think there is really ever anything that can separate us from that which we love? Sometimes we have to re-think what we thought we once knew. I am glad I was open to this experience in my life. I could have easily disregarded what I felt, and just considered the many synchronicities nothing more than mere coincidence. The more I trusted, the more I got!

None of us like the idea of death, but what our loved ones have come to realize is that there is no fear in death. It is just a change of condition, like going to another country to visit. You are still you, but you have new surroundings. Another passage from a book again confirms this to be true. The book is called, "The Other Side of Death" by Jan Price. "I say again that there is nothing to fear about death. Most fear centers around the loss of the body, but I can tell you that the only body we lose is the one made for earth, not the real one, with which we cross over. When vital signs cease, we simply move up and out of the fleshly vehicle, and we're on our way. I didn't have to think about how to get out-the soul takes care of that in a perfectly normal and natural process."

The Greatest Gift

The Greatest gift Tom gave me was eternity. The once limited world I thought we lived in suddenly became limitless, expansive and full of possibilities. I realized there is a plan that weaves in and through all of our lives, a plan so perfect and created by us to help us remember who we are. We come to realize with every gift we are loved and we are connected to everything.

Each of us comes here with a purpose, to give a message to the world, to try to expand our consciousness to its full potential. There is a higher and lower aspect of the mind. The higher mind is more expansive and it touches only the deepest truths, the thoughts are more positive, a higher frequency. The lower aspects of the mind are ones of limitation, negativity and fear. They are the lowest frequencies.

To reach the higher mind we really have to let go of the many thoughts that limit us; along with the inner walls we build which we believe serve to protect us. In reality those things have only ever served to limit us. Thoughts of "I can't do that" or "I am not good enough" keeps us vibrating at the lowest frequency and we can't begin to shift out of that

if we don't start believing that we can live a more vibrant and colorful life; a life where anything is possible.

Tom's passing, I can gladly say, opened up an entire new world. That is how powerful love is and I was not going to allow his passing to swallow me up, to cause me to shut down and not reap every gift that his passing could bring. His love went to great lengths to show me he was still here, that death was just an illusion. Maybe once we truly realize that they are not gone to some far off distant place, the two worlds will come together.

Tom's passing was very hard on me and yet at the same time I was opening up more spiritually. Questions I had always had about life and who we are were being revealed in every message. I could see love in everything and everyone. It was the most peace I had ever experienced and at the same time the most pain I had ever experienced. I knew beyond a shadow of doubt that even in our toughest struggles there was something we could gain and how we choose to see it is up to us.

I realized that I never had to say "Goodbye." I knew that our loved ones would always be with us because we are connected by that love always. That love has no boundaries or limits. Our happiness is truly their happiness. When I am feeling really happy and I raise my vibration, I feel Tom even more. By us knowing of their continued

existence and that they are happy, makes them happier than we could ever know.

Sometimes it is very easy to forget that there is a rhyme and a reason for everything. We get lost in our doubts and fears and it is hard to recognize the gifts, but when we can come from a place of love and trust, the signs are easy to see.

Our love was stronger than time, stronger than death. Even today when I think of the great lengths Tom went through to stay in contact with me it brings me to tears. Tom knew I would see the messages, he knew I would believe. He also knew this experience would take me to places I had never been. It forever changed the way I see things. I had to trust what I was seeing and most importantly, feeling. I had to trust the messages mom was getting from Tom.

It doesn't matter how much time has passed, that love is just as strong as the day you fell in love with that person. Love never dies. So don't worry as you start to move forward in your life and new things enter in that you will ever forget. It is impossible to forget a love like that. It will always be reunited again. Love always finds a way.

If you believe that with love anything is possible, then believe our loved ones can let us know they are okay. If we can get past the doubts of our minds and others, we can receive the most amazing messages of

love. Always take time to look up at the stars and fall in love with the beauty of this world. We are eternal beings on an amazing journey of discovery.

Until that time we meet again, I will remember Tom with so much love in my heart. I will always think of him whenever I find a feather. To some a feather might just be a feather, a butterfly just a butterfly, but to me they are so much more. They will always remind me of Tom and the love that connects us all.

The End....

Made in the USA
Coppell, TX
24 November 2023

24655450R00049

Printed in the USA
CPSIA information can be obtained
at www.ICGtesting.com
LVHW040936050823
754287LV00001B/108